AF600344

THE CATHOLIC UNIVERSITY OF AMERICA
CANON LAW STUDIES
No. 121

A COMMENTARY ON CANON 1125

TOGETHER WITH A HISTORY OF THE LEGISLATION CONTAINED IN THE CANON

A DISSERTATION

Submitted to the Faculty of Canon Law of the Catholic University of America in Partial Fulfillment of the Requirements for the Degree of Doctor of Canon Law

BY

FRANCIS JAMES BURTON, C.S.C., A.B., J.C.L.
Priest of the Congregation of Holy Cross

THE CATHOLIC UNIVERSITY OF AMERICA PRESS
WASHINGTON, D. C.
1940

Imprimi Potest:

THOMAS A. STEINER, C.S.C.,

Superior Provincialis.

Nostrae Dominae, Ind., die XIII Maii, 1940.

Nihil Obstat:

LUDOVICUS MOTRY, S.T.D., J.C.D.,

Censor Deputatus.

Washingtonii, D. C., die III Iunii, 1940.

Imprimatur:

✠ MICHAEL J. CURLEY, D.D.,

Archiepiscopus Baltimorensis et Washingtonensis.

Baltimorae, Md., die IV Iunii, 1940.

COPYRIGHT, 1940

THE CATHOLIC UNIVERSITY OF AMERICA PRESS

Printed by

THE PAULIST PRESS

New York, N. Y.

Nostrae Dominae
Dedicatum

TABLE OF CONTENTS

CHAPTER VI

PART TWO—CANONICAL COMMENTARY

CHAPTER VII

CHAPTER VIII

INTRODUCTION

No one can successfully question the Church's uniform and unflinching championship of the sacred character of the marriage bond. The Church remained true to its God-given duty as guardian of morals when the refusal to permit a deviation from the divinely established marriage discipline cost it the allegiance of a nation. The possibility of bringing millions of pagans into its fold by relaxing that discipline has not caused it, nor will ever cause it, to make any change not sanctioned by God's law.

With the supreme benefit of man, the attainment of salvation through acceptance and perseverance in the true Faith, as an object, the law of God permits certain exceptions to the indissoluble character of marriage. If God had not permitted these exceptions, embracing the Faith would often include the burden of living a celibate life. For thousands upon thousands of men and women this would be an invincible obstacle to conversion. As occasion and the needs of mankind required, the Church has explored the nature of these exceptions, these privileges, and put them into effect.

From Apostolic days the Pauline privilege has been in force. When the conditions of the times and the salvation of souls required it, the power of the Church in regard to other exceptions was invoked. Canon 1125 has extended to the whole world certain of these exceptions the use of which was originally restricted by the Church to particular territories. The early commentaries on the matrimonial legislation of the Code of Canon Law did not go into a very detailed consideration of canon 1125. Within the past twelve or fifteen years, however, a fair amount of discussion on this important legislation has appeared.

As an aid in arriving at the mind of the legislator on the points of doubtful interpretation an inquiry is made, in the present dissertation, into the circumstances of the places and times for which the constitutions mentioned in canon 1125 were originally given. An effort has been made in the commentary proper to anticipate questions that may arise in the use of the constitutions and, as far as possible, to give a definite answer to them.

The writer wishes to express his gratitude for the untiring assistance and helpful direction given him by the Faculty of the School of Canon Law, and his sincere thanks to the Catholic University Library staff and to his confrères in the Congregation of Holy Cross for the generous assistance they freely gave in the mechanical details of preparation.

Part One

Historical Synopsis

CHAPTER I

PRELIMINARY DISCUSSION

Up to the end of the Middle Ages there had not arisen any urgent need for the use of the Papal power in regard to the dissolution of legitimate marriages.[1] The sixteenth century saw a change. The unprecedented missionary activity among the pagans that marked the century brought with it new problems in regard to the sacrament of matrimony. The study of the problems led to a more complete knowledge of the powers of the Vicar of Christ.

In the history of theology this development was not at all a singular phenomenon. Theologians are familiar with the similar development or progress of Catholic dogma. All know that the basis of dogma is Revelation, and that Revelation as contained in Tradition and Holy Scripture is complete and full. With the passage of time and the birth of controversy and errors concerning the meaning of certain parts of Revelation, it became necessary for the Church to clarify obscure meanings through the use of exact formulae. The successive promulgation by the Church of these exact statements of the true teaching of Our Lord constitutes the development of dogma. Such progress has been only the exercise of the Church's right and the fulfillment of its duty, as the infallible magisterium established by Christ, to maintain the integrity of the deposit of faith. The progress in the understanding and use of the power of the Roman Pontiff to dissolve legitimate marriage *in favorem fidei* when there is question of the welfare of souls, is analogous to this gradual clarification of doctrine.

At the time of the arrival of St. Paul's First Epistle to the Corinthians it became known that in certain circumstances a separation could be allowed between the parties to an infidel union when one of them became a convert to Christianity. The full significance of the privilege introduced by St. Paul in virtue of divine

[1] "Legitimate marriage" is here used in the sense defined in canon 1015, § 3, *i.e.*, marriage validly celebrated among the non-baptized.

authority [2] was only gradually realized. The circumstances under which the privilege can be validly used, and the preliminary steps that must be taken before that use will attain its effect of dissolving a marriage contracted while both parties were infidels, are now sufficiently well known, but the accurate determination of some important points was not made until several centuries after its promulgation. Because of an affinity between the Pauline privilege and the subject of the present dissertation a brief history of the theology of the privilege will be useful here.

Article 1. Scriptural Basis of the Pauline Privilege

The Corinthians had written St. Paul concerning marital matters. In his reply, as given in the seventh chapter of the First Epistle to the Corinthians, the Apostle first treats of the rights and duties of a Christian man and wife, next he praises virginity and celibacy to the unmarried and widows, and lastly he considers the problems arising when one party to a marriage contracted when both were infidels is now a Christian and the other remains an unbeliever. Of these latter he wrote:

"(For the rest I speak, not the Lord.) If any brother hath a wife that believeth not, and she consent to dwell with him, let him not put her away. And if any woman hath a husband that believeth not, and he consent to dwell with her, let her not put away her husband. For the unbelieving husband is sanctified by the believing wife; and the unbelieving wife is sanctified by the believing husband: otherwise your children should be unclean; but now they are holy. But if the unbeliever depart, let him depart. For a

[2] The controversy concerning the *immediate* authorship of the Pauline privilege is of long standing, with each of the two opinions supported by weighty authority. Since legitimate marriage can be dissolved only by the death of one party or by God's authority all must agree that the privilege is at least *mediately* divine. The more common opinion is that the privilege was immediately granted to the faithful by Christ, and only promulgated by St. Paul. The other opinion holds that the Apostle not only promulgated the privilege, but also instituted it by virtue of his apostolic authority. For a discussion of the question *cf.* Franciscus X. Wernz, *Ius Decretalium*, IV (2. ed., Prati, 1912), n. 702, nota 60; *infra* pp. 83-85.

brother or sister is not under servitude in such cases. But God hath called us in peace."[3]

The scope and limits of the Pauline privilege are to be found within this passage, yet even a cursory examination of the text raises questions to which the answers are not obvious. Beginning with the writings of the Fathers and continuing in the statements of the Holy See and in the works of theologians and canonists the obscurities and controverted points were studied and discussed until by the sixteenth century there was practical unanimity on the fundamental elements. By that century the important questions in the application of the privilege were satisfactorily answered, although definitive answers to some points were not to be given until the promulgation of the Code of Canon Law.

Article 2. Interpretation of the Text, 1 Cor. vii: 15

Natural law enforced by the positive law of God[4] determines that marriage even among infidels is intrinsically indissoluble. The fulfillment of the ends of the institution of marriage requires that the conjugal union be not subject to dissolution at the arbitrary will of either party nor by mutual consent. Moreover, such marriage is *per se* extrinsically indissoluble. The dissolution of a valid marriage is beyond the power of the state or any other human authority except in so far as God has granted that power for the salvation of souls.[5] For the benefit of infidels who became Christians He has granted that power through the Pauline privilege. In their context the only reasonable interpretation of St. Paul's words: "But if the unbeliever depart, let him depart. For a brother or a sister is not under servitude in such cases. But God hath called us in peace," is that a privilege is being granted to the "brother"

[3] 1 Cor. vii: 12-15.

[4] Gen. ii: 23, 24; Matt. v: 31, 32; Matt. xix: 3-9; Mark x: 2-12; Luke xvi: 18; 1 Cor. vii: 10, 11.

[5] Pius IX, *Syllabus,* prop. 67—H. Denzinger-C. Bannwart, *Enchiridion Symbolorum Definitionum et Declarationum de Rebus Fidei et Morum* (17 ed., Friburgi Brisgoviae: Herder, 1928), n. 1767; Wernz, *Ius Decretalium,* IV, nn. 30, 696; G. Payen, *De Matrimonio in Missionibus ac Potissimum in Sinis Tractatus Practicus et Casus* (Zi-Ka-Wei: Typographia T'OU-SÈ-WÈ, 1928-1929), I, nn. 96-100.

or "sister" to enter a new marriage if he or she so desires. In other words, in the circumstances stated, the bond of the original union may be dissolved. The practice of the Church founded upon the common opinion of the Fathers, of the Popes, and of all exegetes, theologians, and canonists of note has confirmed this interpretation.[6]

A. *The Privilege Applies Only to Marriages Contracted Between Infidels*

The words of St. Paul's text do not of themselves clearly indicate that he was speaking only of marriages contracted *before* the baptism of either one or the other of the parties, and not also of mixed unions entered *after* the baptism of one of them. It is impossible, however, to believe that the Apostle was here providing a basis upon which marriages to be entered between a Christian and an infidel could be dissolved if they did not prove happy. The privilege thus understood and used would in many cases encourage the abuse of the Faith whereas it is clearly intended to be a grant in its favor.[7] Hence the Church has consistently understood the text as applying to marriages between two infidels one of whom thereafter became a Catholic. This interpretation was written into the canon law in the thirteenth century when a letter of Innocent

[6] Thomas Sanchez, *De Sancto Matrimonii Sacramento Disputationes* (post. ed., Venetiis, 1712), lib. VII, disp. LXXIV, n. 4; *cf.* Ioannes Perrone, *Praelectiones Theologicae* (32. ed., Taurini, 1868), I, *Tractatus de Matrimonio,* cap. II, prop. II, pp. 432, 433; Wernz, *Ius Decretalium,* IV, n. 702, nota 61; Donald J. Gregory, *The Pauline Privilege* (The Catholic University of America, Canon Law Studies, n. 68, Washington: The Catholic University of America, 1931), p. 76.

[7] Christianus Pesch, *Praelectiones Dogmaticae* (3. ed., Friburgi Brisgoviae, 1909), VII, n. 786; Felix M. Cappello, *De Sacramentis,* III, *De Matrimonio* (3. ed., Romae: Marietti, 1933), n. 768.

The Holy See has given negative answers to *dubia* regarding the use of the privilege to dissolve the bond of marriage between a Catholic and an infidel for which a dispensation from the impediment of disparity of cult had been obtained—S. C. S. Off., resp. (Cochinchin.), 1 Aug., 1759, ad 4—*Fontes,* n. 810; S. C. S. Off., resp. (Nankin.), 5 Mar., 1852—*Fontes,* n. 918; S. C. S. Off., instr. (Siam), 4 Jul., 1855—*Fontes,* n. 931; S. C. S. Off., instr. (ad Ep. St. Alberti), 9 Dec., 1874—*Fontes,* n. 1036.

III thus describing the privilege was included in the Gregorian Decretals.[8]

It is clear also that the privilege was intended to have effect only in valid marriages among infidels. There would be need only for proof and a declaration of nullity to justify the converted party of an invalid pagan union in contracting a marriage with another Christian.

An opinion at variance with the generally accepted conclusion that the privilege applied only to marriages contracted in infidelity was given by Pope Celestine III in 1191.[9] He gave it as his view that if a party to a Christian marriage were to apostatize, abandon his Christian spouse and enter a union with a pagan, the abandoned wife might then contract a second marriage, and that she need not return to the first husband if he should repent and come back to the unity of the faith. This set of circumstances is the converse of those for which the universally accepted view considered the privilege to have been granted. It appears that this may have been only Celestine's opinion in a speculative case and not a decision for the solution of an actual case presented. In any event Celestine's successor, Innocent III, recalled the opinion and in a similar case gave a contrary decision which was later included in the Decretals of Gregory IX.[10]

B. *What Is Meant by "Departure"*

St. Paul's sentence, "If the unbeliever depart, let him depart," did not descend to particulars about the departure. The Apostle

[8] Ep., *"Quanto te magis,"* 1 Maii, 1199—c. 7, X, *de divortiis,* IV, 19. Later, when questions were presented to the Holy See from missionary countries asking if catechumens could use the privilege, the reply was in the negative. S. C. de Prop. Fide, resp. (ad C. P. pro Sin., Pekin), 16 Jan., 1803—*Fontes,* n. 4671.

[9] In ep. *"Laudabilem,"* part of which was included in the Gregorian Decretals. The part giving the above opinion was not included. *Cf. Corpus Iuris Canonici, Editio Lipsiensis II* (Richter-Friedberg, Lipsiae, 1879-1881), c. 1, X, *de conversione infidelium,* III, 33.

[10] Ep., *"Quanto te magis,"* 1 Maii, 1199—c. 7, X, *de divortiis,* IV, 19. *Cf.* Denzinger, *Enchiridion,* n. 405; Gregory, *The Pauline Privilege,* p. 31, note 94.

was content to leave to the wisdom of the Church the determination of the acts or conduct on the part of the unbeliever that could be construed as a departure. A correct understanding of the point was essential to the valid use of the privilege, hence it was of importance to know the answers to these questions: When is the unbeliever considered to have departed? Is an actual physical abandonment of the Christian party required, or may the actions of the infidel in certain circumstances be interpreted as a moral departure?

The word which has been translated into the English text as meaning "to depart," in the original text was χωρίζειν and means rather "to separate" than "to depart." It is the same term which was used in the Gospels of Matthew [11] and Mark [12] to express Our Lord's command that the marriage bond be not broken: "What therefore God hath joined together, let not man put asunder"—(μὴ χωριζέτω).[13]

In his 19th Homily on 1 Corinthians St. John Chrysostom inquires into the meaning of the phrase: "If the unbeliever depart." He answers it signifies that if the unbeliever orders his Christian spouse to offer sacrifice or to be his partner in impiety because of the marriage, or to part company, then it is better that the marriage bond be severed than that the Christian sin against religion. Further, if the infidel is continually quarrelsome on account of this matter it is better to separate. The infidel furnishes the cause for separation.[14]

Joyce points out that it is probable St. John Chrysostom understood χωρίζεται as a causative middle. On that hypothesis St.

[11] Matt. xix: 6.

[12] Mark x: 9.

[13] *Cf.* Francis E. Gigot, *Christ's Teaching Concerning Divorce* (New York, 1912), p. 102.

[14] "*Si autem infidelis discedit, discedat.* Hic enim nulla est fornicatio. Quid sibi vult autem illud: *Infidelis si discedit?* Verbi gratia si te iubet sacrificare aut sociam impietatis esse propter connubium, vel discedere, melius est dirumpi connubium quam piam religionem. Quapropter subdit: *Non enim servituti subjectus est frater aut soror in eiusdem rebus.* Si quotidie ea de causa pugnet et bellum moveat, inquit, melius est separari. Hoc enim subindicat cum dicit: *In pacem* autem vocavit nos Deus. Ille enim iam causam praebuit, ut is qui fornicatus est."—*MPG,* LXI, 155.

Paul's sentence: «εἰ δὲ ὁ ἄπιστος χωρίζεται χωριζέσθω» would mean: "If the unbeliever is the cause of separation, let him cause separation." [15] Thus understood the Apostle would not limit the use of the privilege to those unions only in which the infidel spouse went away, refusing any cohabitation; it would apply also when the infidel made it impossible for the Christian party to cohabit peacefully without injury to the Christian religion and without sin. This meant that consideration was to be given to a certain moral separation, as well as to an actual physical abandonment, as grounds for the use of the privilege. The eventual practice and legislation of the Church had necessarily to consider several aspects of the moral departure.[16]

In the latter half of the fourth century the *Commentaria in Tredecim Epistolas Beati Pauli,* which since the time of Erasmus has been attributed to Ambrosiaster or Pseudo-Ambrosius,[17] gave an unambiguous exegesis of the verse, "If the unbeliever depart, let him depart." The author stated that when the Christian party was repudiated out of hatred of God there was no sin for him in entering another marriage. In several phrases the commentary repeated that the hostility of the infidel party toward God was the reason for the freedom of the Christian. The principle, *"Contumelia creatoris solvit jus matrimonii circa eum qui relinquitur,"* was here clearly stated.[18]

[15] George Hayward Joyce, *Christian Marriage* (London and New York: Sheed & Ward, 1933), p. 483.

[16] *Cf.* Franciscus X. Wernz-Petrus Vidal, *Ius Canonicum,* V, *Ius Matrimoniale* (2. ed., Romae: Apud Aedes Universitatis Gregorianae, 1928), pp. 753-756, nota 58.

[17] *Cf.* Otto Bardenhewer, *Patrology* trans. by Thomas J. Shahan (Freiburg in Breisgau and St. Louis, 1908), pp. 435 and 440.

[18] "'Quod si infidelis discedit, discedat.' Propositum religionis custodit, praecipiendo ne Christiani relinquant conjugia: sed si infidelis odio Dei discedit, fidelis non erit reus dissoluti matrimonii; major enim causa Dei est quam matrimonii. 'Non est enim frater aut soror servituti subjectus in huiusmodi.' Hoc est, non debetur reverentia conjugii ei qui horret auctorem conjugii; non enim ratum est matrimonium, quod sine Dei devotione est, ac per hoc non est peccatum ei qui dimittitur propter Deum, si alii se junxerit. Contumelia enim Creatoris solvit jus matrimonii circa eum qui relinquitur, ne accusetur alii copulatus."—*MPL,* XVII, 231.

C. *Time at Which First Marriage Is Dissolved*

When the central fact had been established that the convert was free to enter a new marriage if his infidel spouse separated from him, the question of the time at which the bond of the first marriage was actually dissolved became important. Obviously the answer was fundamental in solving problems arising from the use of the privilege. After the Gregorian Decretals had been compiled the materials were at hand to study the arguments for the various opinions on the matter.

In view of the advice to the convert not to put away an infidel spouse if she consent to dwell with him [19] St. Paul did not consider the dissolution to be effected by the reception of baptism. He could not have advised [20] the cohabitation of couples whose marriage bond no longer existed, and there is no reason to suppose that he intended they should exchange a new matrimonial consent after the baptism of the convert. By natural law the marriage of infidels is valid and the conversion of one party does not, by that fact, destroy their matrimonial contract.[21] The question to be decided then was whether the marriage bond was dissolved immediately upon the separation that was brought about either by the physical departure of the infidel or by refusal to cohabit without insult to God, or whether something more was required. Theologians and canonists were divided among three opinions.

One opinion, based upon Ambrosiaster's principle, *"Contumelia creatoris solvit ius circa eum qui relinquitur,"* [22] held the bond to be

[19] 1 Cor. vii: 12.

[20] St. Augustine in interpreting this text considered the Apostle to be advising or counseling, rather than commanding, the continued cohabitation if the infidel was willing to do so peacefully. *Cf. De Sermone Domini in Monte*, lib. I, cap. 16—*MPL*, XXXIV, 1252; *De Adulterinis Coniugiis*, lib. I, cap. 18 sq.—*Corpus Scriptorum Ecclesiasticorum Latinorum*, XLI, 366 sq. Augustine's opinion became the view more commonly held by Latin commentators. This part of *De Adult. Coniug.* was included in the *Decretum Gratiani* under the inscription, *"Ab infidelibus coniugibus licet alicui recedere, sed non expedit."*—c. 9, C. XXVIII, q. 1.

[21] Sanchez, *De Matrimonio*, lib. VII, disp. LXXIII, nn. 2, 6.

[22] Gratian mistakenly attributed this to St. Gregory; the Roman Cor-

dissolved by the mere separation brought about by the infidel's actions and before a second marriage.

In explaining the conditions for the use of the privilege Pope Innocent III had quoted the above principle together with the text of St. Paul which established the right of the convert to enter a second marriage.[23] A gloss on the word *"contumelia"* indicated that the contumely of the infidel in refusing to cohabit without insult to the Creator was sufficient to break the bond. This opinion argued that the original matrimonial bond was an impediment to a further marriage as long as it existed, therefore it must be dissolved before the second marriage could be entered.[24]

The second opinion also held that the first marriage must be dissolved before the convert could marry again, but it required the intervention of Church authority. The infidel was to be interpellated and a period of time fixed within which to manifest willingness to cohabit peacefully with the convert spouse and without insult to God. On the expiration of the period, if the infidel had not answered, or had answered but refused to cohabit legitimately, the marriage was *ipso facto* dissolved. But if thereafter the infidel should be converted before the Christian party entered a new marriage the latter would be under obligation to renew the marriage contract and cohabit.[25]

rectors gave St. Ambrose as the author—c. 1, C. XXVIII, q. 2. In the compilation of sources from which Gratian drew his canons Friedberg lists the Commentary on 1 Corinthians as "apocryphal"—*Corp. Iuris Can.*, I, p. xxxi, under "Ambrosius."

[23] Ep. *"Quanto te magis,"* 1 Maii, 1199—c. 7, X, *de divortiis*, IV, 19.

[24] *Cf.* Sanchez, *De Matrimonio*, lib. VII, Disp. LXXV, n. 2.

[25] *Cf.* Sanchez, *ibid.*, n. 3. Sanchez here lists Hostiensis as a supporter of this second opinion on the basis of the latter's commentary on the word *"compelletur"* of Innocent's letter, *"Gaudemus in Domino"*—c. 8, X, *de divortiis*, IV, 19. *Cf.* Hostiensis, *Commentaria in Libros V Decretalium*, IV, *De Divortiis*, cap. 8, n. 13. In the previous chapter (cap. 7, n. 3), commenting on *"qui relinquitur"* of Innocent's letter *"Quanto te magis,"* Hostiensis had written *"Notabis etiam quod hic solvitur matrimonium, non per sententiam sed ipso iure propter contumeliam creatoris."* Hence, whereas it is clear that Hostiensis considered the marriage to be dissolved before the second marriage was contracted, it does not seem clear to which of the first two opinions he adhered.

The third opinion, which finally prevailed [26] and which had the greatest number of defenders among the writers on the subject, considered the first marriage to be binding up to the moment when the convert entered the second marriage. The new matrimonial consent was the cause of the dissolution of the first conjugal bond *"ita ut generatio unius fit corruptio alterius."* [27]

The ruling of Innocent III,[28] that the convert must return to his separated infidel spouse if the latter should also become a Christian before the convert had used the privilege of entering a second marriage, was a strong argument in favor of the third opinion. It indicated that Innocent did not consider the principle, *"Contumelia creatoris solvit ius circa eum qui relinquitur,"* which he had quoted in the previous letter *"Quanto te magis,"* to mean that the separation caused by the infidel *ipso facto* dissolved the first marriage. If the first marriage had been thus dissolved, then to cohabit again would be fornication unless new matrimonial consent were exchanged. Since no theologion held that parties could be made to marry against their will, the argument of those who interpreted Innocent as meaning that parties must remarry was not valid. The conclusion was that Innocent considered the bond of the first marriage to exist until the convert entered a second marriage.

St. Thomas, with many others, agreed with the conclusion and explained that the stronger bond of the *ratum* marriage of Christians loosed the weaker bond of the previous marriage in infidelity in these circumstances.[29]

The privilege, which had been granted expressly in favor of the Christian faith,[30] effected no immediate change in the obligation of the marriage bond on the infidel whose spouse had become a Christian. He could not desert the Christian consort and at once validly enter a second marriage. An attempted second marriage by the infidel would not dissolve the first marriage. If, however, the convert Christian party had legitimately used the privilege and entered

[26] *Cf.* canon 1126.

[27] Sanchez, *ibid.*, n. 4.

[28] Ep. *"Gaudemus in Domino,"* 1201—c. 8, X, *de divortiis,* IV, 19.

[29] *IV Sent.*, dist. XXXIX, q. un., art. 5, ad. 1, 2.

[30] Cc. 7, 8, X, *de divortiis,* IV, 19.

a second marriage, thus loosing the bond of the first marriage, the infidel also was then free to remarry.[31] This came to be the generally accepted opinion, but St. Thomas held the contrary view in regard to the infidel's freedom to remarry. Because the infidel had sinned against the first marriage by separating from the Christian consort, Thomas would allow him another marriage only on the condition that he too become a Christian after his consort had already entered a second marriage.[32]

D. *The Necessity of Interpellations*

The decretals of Innocent already referred to [33] determined authoritatively the actions on the part of the infidel that would constitute an objective departure or separation which would leave the convert free to enter another marriage. Innocent considered the separation to exist if the infidel refused to cohabit at all, or at least was not willing to cohabit without blasphemy of the Divine Name or without drawing the convert into mortal sin. The nature of the matter required that the infidel manifest his intention in regard to cohabitation, hence the need of learning his dispositions by interpellation.

A difference of opinion arose in regard to the freedom of the convert to enter a new marriage if the infidel was willing to cohabit peacefully without insult to the Creator and without drawing the convert into sin, but was unwilling to be converted. One opinion held that in such circumstances the Christian party was free to leave the infidel and enter another marriage. The proponents of the opinion argued from a decree of the Fourth Council of Toledo (633 A. D.) [34] which Gratian had included in the *Decretum*.[35] It directed that if Jews who had Christian wives were unwilling to be converted they were to be separated, *"quia non potest infidelis in*

[31] Sanchez, *De Matrimonio,* lib. VII, disp. LXXVII, n. 5.

[32] *IV Sent.,* dist. XXXIX, q. un., art. 5, ad 3; *Summa Theol., III Supp.,* q. 59, art. 5, ad 3.

[33] Cc. 7, 8, X, *de divortiis,* IV, 19.

[34] Capitula, 63—*Mansi,* X, 634.

[35] C. 10, C. XXVIII, q. 1.

eius permanere conjunctione quae iam in Christianam translata est fidem."

St. Thomas [36] explained the decree as being given at a time when it was not safe for a Christian to cohabit with a Jew because of the latter's obstinacy, and because in such unions there was no hope of conversion such as there was when the infidel was a gentile. By St. Thomas' time a change had come about so that gentiles and Jews were equally obstinate, hence he held that if an infidel of either type were unwilling to be converted the Christian party was not to be permitted to cohabit. This state of affairs was considered by some authors, though not by St. Thomas, to be grounds for the use of the Pauline privilege. The argument used was that if the Christian were not permitted a second marriage "he would be subject to the servitude of the former marriage without his fault." [37]

The error of this opinion seems to have begun in overlooking the fact that the decree of the Council of Toledo was merely local legislation. The inclusion of the decree in the *Decretum Gratiani* did not make it universal law.[38] Moreover, Pope Clement III (1187-1191) in a decretal given near the close of the twelfth century had directly opposed the opinion. His decretal, which was included in *Compilatio II,* legislated that if the wife of a convert Jew or Saracen was unwilling to become a Christian, but was willing to cohabit peacefully, the convert party could not use the Pauline privilege.[39]

St. Thomas [40] was among those [41] who held the opinion which alone was consonant with the the words of St. Paul, "If any brother hath a wife that believeth not and she consent to dwell with him, let

[36] *IV Sent., dist.* XXXIX, q. un., art. 3, ad 2.

[37] Sanchez, *De Matrimonio,* lib. VII, disp. LXXIV, n. 9.

[38] *Cf.* Amleto Giovanni Cicognani, *Canon Law* (2. revised ed., trans. by J. M. O'Hara and F. Brennan, Philadelphia: Dolphin Press, 1935), pp. 287, 288.

[39] C. 1, *de conversione infidelium,* III, 20, in *Compil. II.*

[40] *IV Sent.,* dist. XXXIX, q. un., art. 5, solutio: ". . . Quia si infidelis vult cohabitare sine contumelia Creatoris, vel sine hoc quod ad infidelitatem inducat, potest fidelis libere discedere; sed discedens non potest alteri nubere."

[41] *Cf.* Sanchez, *De Matrimonio,* lib. VII, disp. LXXIV, n. 8.

him not put her away," and with the decretals of Innocent III and Clement III.

It is not until after the sixteenth century that anything more definite than is given in the decretals of Innocent III is to be found in legislation concerning the interpellations.[42]

[42] Gregory, *The Pauline Privilege*, p. 65.

CHAPTER II

MISSIONS OF THE SIXTEENTH CENTURY

PERIODS of great missionary activity in the Church necessarily gave rise to a great number of matrimonial problems of which many clearly could be solved through the use of the Pauline privilege, whereas others either certainly or probably did not fulfil the conditions required for the use of the privilege. The last quarter of the fifteenth century and all of the sixteenth century, even though marked by religious unrest and great defections from the Faith in Europe, was an era of remarkable missionary activity. It was the period that witnessed the rediscovery, exploration, and beginning of colonization of the western hemisphere. Along with the early discoverers and explorers went the missionaries to carry on the conquest for souls. At the same time missionaries were active in Africa and in the Orient.

The Popes of the sixteenth century led the way in the revival of missionary zeal, and there was no lack of ardent followers. From the time of Alexander VI's Bull of Demarcation at the close of the preceding century the Holy See showed an increased determination to fulfill its duty toward the missions. Three Popes of this period, Paul III (1534-1549), Pius V (1566-1572), and Gregory XIII (1572-1585), were particularly interested in the work of spreading the Faith and in various ways manifested a keen appreciation of the needs of mission countries.[1] Pastor, the historian of the Popes, says of Paul III that his pontificate formed an epoch in the development of the hierarchy in America,[2] of Pius V that he rarely let an opportunity pass of sending exhortations or instructions to the missionaries or of transmitting briefs in their favor to the kings and

[1] Joseph Schmidlin, *Catholic Mission History*, translation by Matthias Braun (Techny: Mission Press S. V. D., 1933), p. 257.

[2] Ludwig Freiherr von Pastor, *The History of the Popes from the Close of the Middle Ages*, translation by F. I. Antrobus, R. F. Kerr, Ernest Graf (29 vols., St. Louis: Herder, 1906-1938), XX, 499.

Bishops,[3] and of Gregory XIII that he listened with great pleasure to the reports of the missionaries, gave them good advice upon their work, and was generous in his help for the missions.[4] We are here particularly interested in the legislation of these Pontiffs in regard to the matrimonial obstacles to conversion of the pagans. A review of mission countries and conditions of the time will be helpful in interpreting the legislation.

Not the least of the motives which inspired Columbus to undertake the task of finding a direct route westward to the Indies was that of zeal for the conversion of the natives.[5] It was a century when the obligation of civilizing and Christianizing the pagans was recognized on the Iberian peninsula as binding in conscience upon each Christian whether cleric or lay. It was primarily religious arguments based upon this obligation which swayed the Spanish king and queen to support Columbus' expeditions.[6] The royal instructions to him insisted on his care for the propagation of the Faith, the protection of the missionaries, and beneficent treatment of the natives. That Columbus himself later mixed his high purpose with others less worthy is well known. He was guilty of enslaving the natives and distributing them to his companions, and other early Spanish adventurers were cruel to the Indians to the point of inhumanity.[7] Nevertheless the duty and the desire of converting the Indians was too strong in the Spanish national conscience ever to escape their earnest attention.[8] The Spanish missionaries were in the vanguard of the arriving invaders of the New World and did in fact finally accomplish the task of conversion in spite of obstacles set up by the greed and cruelty of many of their lay countrymen.

[3] *Op. cit.*, XVIII, 349.

[4] *Op. cit.*, XX, 512.

[5] Joseph Schmidlin, *Catholic Mission Theory,* translation (Techny: Mission Press S. V. D., 1931), p. 11.

[6] Francis Augustus MacNutt, *Bartholomew de Las Casas* (New York and London: 1909), p. 17. See also p. 290 of this work for an article from Queen Isabella's will, in which she implores her heirs to use all diligence in seeing to the conversion and care of the Indians.

[7] Schmidlin, *Catholic Mission Theory,* p. 357.

[8] Schmidlin, *Catholic Mission History,* p. 261.

Article 1. Alexander VI's Line of Demarcation

One result of Columbus' discovery of 1492 was a controversy between the great colonizing powers, Spain and Portugal, over the newly discovered lands. In view of the activities of Portuguese subjects in Africa and the East Indies the Popes of the fifteenth century by a series of bulls had assigned the lands to be discovered south of Cape Bojador on the west coast of Africa, and as far as the Indians (*"usque ad Indos"*) to the Portuguese kings as successors of the Knights of Christ (*Christi Militia*) and of the Grand Master. The condition was that missionaries should be sent at once to convert the natives. On the basis of these bulls the king of Portugal considered himself to have exclusive rights over the southern extremity of Africa and thence eastward to India. He contested the Spanish claim to the newly discovered lands when Columbus claimed to have landed in the islands of India.[9]

The Spanish sovereigns Ferdinand and Isabella brought the matter before the Holy See. By Alexander VI's Bull, *"Inter caetera,"* of 4 May, 1493,[10] Spain was granted exclusive rights over all islands and countries (*terrae firmae*) already discovered and to be discovered by the Spanish, provided that such lands were not already occupied by a Christian power and provided that care be taken to propagate the Christian faith therein. It also established as the boundary line between the spheres of Spanish and Portuguese activity the meridian passing one hundred leagues west of the Azores and Cape Verde Islands. The islands and countries found and to be found west and south of the line, if not already actually possessed by a Christian ruler, were to belong to Spain, those to the east of it were to go to Portugal. An express condition of this bull which established Spain's authority in the newly discovered lands was that the conversion of the Indians should be a primary consideration of the government. By the Treaty of Tordesillas of the next year (1494), the line was established as being the meridian 370 leagues west of the Cape

[9] Henry Harisse, *The Diplomatic History of America—Its First Chapter, 1452-1493-1494* (London, 1897), pp. 5-10.

[10] *Bull. Rom.*, V, 361-364.

Verde Islands, thus bringing Brazil into Portugal's territory when later it was discovered.

Cyriacus Morelli (Domingo Muriel) points out that through the Bull "*Inter caetera*" Alexander VI did not intend to divide the world in such a way that the previously undiscovered parts of the western hemisphere were to belong to Spain and those of the eastern hemisphere to Portugal, but that he sought to keep peace between the two nations by sending the navigators of the one to the east and those of the other to the west. The limits on the other side of the earth would be determined by possession following upon occupation, thus although the Philippine Islands were in the Orient they were first occupied by Magellan, in the employ of the Spanish king, approaching them from the west.[11]

Article 2. Sixteenth Century Missions in the New World

A. *First Missions in the West Indies*

The Spanish sovereigns took seriously their obligation in regard to the conversion of the natives, and Franciscan and Dominican missionaries were among the first arrivals in the Greater Antilles group of the West Indies. The earliest episcopal sees in the New World were these: San Juan in Porto Rico (1511), Concepción de la Vega in Hispaniola [now Haiti] (1511),[12] San Domingo in His-

[11] *Fasti Novi Orbis et Ordinationum Apostolicarum ad Indias Pertinentiam Breviarium* (Venetiis, 1776), p. 63.

A recent author takes the following view of the Bull of Alexander: It is a feudal investiture document by which Spain is granted feudal tenure of Church property. It concerns the lands beyond the Atlantic Ocean already discovered and to be discovered by Spain. It does not constitute a transfer of *dominium*, but only of tenure. The so-called "*Divisio Mundi*" between Spain and Portugal which Alexander is supposed to have made is, in reality, only the consent of the Church to an agreement arrived at between Spain and Portugal. The agreement was in the nature of a treaty concerning navigation and commerce in the Atlantic Ocean. Alexander did not exercise the function of arbiter in this question; most likely he did not have personal knowledge of the transaction.—E. Staedler, "Die Donatio Alexandrina und die 'Divisio Mundi' von 1493," *AKKR*, CXVII (1937), 363-402. *Cf.* the summary, p. 402.

[12] Pastor, *History of the Popes*, VI, 441.

paniola (1513), and Santiago de Cuba (1522).[13] The active period for this mission field began in 1502 with the arrival in Hispaniola of twelve Franciscans under Fray Alonso del Espinal. It continued on through 1530, but in spite of strong protests by the friars, especially the Dominicans,[14] the natives were rapidly being exterminated by the Spanish colonists. The enslavement of the Indians for forced labor in the mines and sugar plantations brought death to so many that in a few years there were almost none left to convert.[15]

The missionary work was successfully continued among the Negro slaves who were brought in to replace the vanishing natives.[16]

B. *Missions in Mexico and Central America*

In the first two decades of the sixteenth century the Spanish spread from the Antilles to the mainland which proved a fertile field for the astonishingly successful missionary work of that century. Juan de Grijalva left Santiago de Cuba at the head of a fleet in 1518. He explored the coastline of what is now Mexico and Central America, landed in Mexico to treat with the natives, and gave the name "New Spain" to the territory.[17] In the following year Hernando Cortez began the conquest of Mexico. Thereafter

[13] *Annuario Pontifico (Anno 1939).*

For an account of these dioceses by which the Church was definitely established in America, and of the right of patronage in any part of the Indies granted to Ferdinand and his successors by Pope Julius II, *cf.* E. Ward Loughran, "First Episcopal Sees in Spanish America," *Hispanic American Historical Review,* X (1930), 167-187. According to Theodorus Grentrup (*Ius Missionarium* [Steyl, Hollandiae: Typographia Domus Missionum a St. Michaele Archang., 1925], I, 23) in the period from the twelfth to the seventeenth centuries the ecclesiastical order in the Spanish and Portuguese missions depended more upon the royal than upon the Papal will. *Cf.* also Maynard Geiger, *The Franciscan Conquest of Florida (1573-1619)* (The Catholic University of America, Studies in Hispanic-American History, Vol. I, Washington: The Catholic University of America, 1937), pp. 11-13.

[14] MacNutt, *Bartholomew de Las Casas,* pp. 54-66.

[15] Schmidlin, *Catholic Mission History,* p. 362.

[16] J. A. Birkhaeuser, *History of the Church* (9. ed. New York, 1893), p. 510.

[17] William H. Prescott, *History of the Conquest of Mexico* (2 vols., New York, 1843), I, 225.

the progress of the Faith was rapid and it spread from Mexico proper to the bordering lands both north and south.

Missionary work on the mainland began in earnest with the arrival of twelve Franciscans in 1524, to be followed in the next few years by large reinforcements of their own Order together with Dominicans, Augustinians, and Mercedarians. Shortly after the middle of the century a report to the Spanish king listed totals of 380 Franciscans, 210 Dominicans, and 212 Augustinians in their Mexican provinces. The baptisms administered by the Franciscans alone by 1540 numbered nine millions. In 1572 the Jesuit Fathers arrived in New Spain; four years later they established a college; and before the end of the century they had forty-four religious working in four missions.[18]

The episcopal see of Tlaxcala (Angelopoli, or Puebla de los Angeles) was erected in 1525 and the following sees within the next few years: Mexico (1530, raised to an archdiocese in 1546), Nicaragua (Leon—1534), Guatemala (1534), Panama (1534), Antequera (1535), Michoacan (Morelia—1536), Chiapas (1539), Guadalajara (1548), Tegucigalpa (1561), Yucatan (1561).[19]

C. *The Mission in Florida*

The mission to the natives of Florida proved to be one of the most difficult of those in the New World. The work was intermittent and devoid of permanent results until the Franciscans took it over in 1573. Throughout the sixteenth century it was marked by privation, arduous labor, and relatively little success in comparison with results obtained elsewhere in the same period. In the last quarter of the century, however, the groundwork was laid for later notable development.[20]

[18] Schmidlin, *Catholic Mission History,* pp. 409-422.

[19] *Annuario Pontificio (Anno 1939).* Schmidlin (*Catholic Mission History,* p. 424) mentions the see of Vera Paz as being founded in 1556. The bishop of Vera Paz is listed as one of the many in the New World to whom St. Pius V sent a letter in 1566 in regard to observing the decrees of the Council of Trent. *Cf. Annales Ecclesiastici, ab anno 1566 ubi Odericus Raynaldus desinit, auctore Jacobo de Laderchio* (Romae, 1728), XXII, 300.

[20] Geiger, *The Franciscan Conquest of Florida (1573-1618),* pp. 265, 266.

The unsuccessful attempts of the Spanish to conquer or colonize the Florida peninsula until the latter part of the century were in part responsible for the difficulties of the mission. The reluctance of the savages to give up the polygamy that was universal among them was another factor. Five friars were murdered in an uprising inspired by a convert Indian who had been reprimanded by one of them for continuing his polygamy. In the arguments he used to stir up the rebellion this Indian said: "They take away from us our women, allowing us but one, and that, in perpetuity, forbidding us to exchange them for others." Later, in the investigation, six Indians expressly declared that the friars' insistence on monogamy was the principal cause of the rebellion.[21]

D. *The Missions in South America*

South America was a field of intense and markedly successful missionary activity in the sixteenth century. The earliest results were obtained in the northwest in New Granada (Colombia), Quito (Ecuador), and in Peru.[22] The Franciscans and Dominicans supplied the greater number of missionaries in the first half of the century, and these together with the Augustinians and Mercedarians planted centers of Christianity throughout the northwest and western sections of South America. To a somewhat lesser extent they were active also in Venezuela, Paraguay, Brazil, and Argentina.

In 1549 a party of six Jesuits arrived in Brazil. On their recommendation the national see of São Salvador at Bahia was erected. By 1581 there were thirty-two large Christian settlements in Brazil, two Jesuits colleges, and 140 members of the Society. Toward the close of the century they extended their missionary activities to the natives of the interior.[23]

[21] Geiger, *op. cit.*, pp. 88-90.

[22] "The empire of Peru, at the period of the Spanish invasion, stretched along the Pacific from about the second degree north to the thirty-seventh degree of south latitude; a line, also, which describes the western boundaries of the modern republics of Ecuador, Peru, Bolivia, and Chili. Its breadth cannot so easily be determined . . . It is certain, however, that its breadth was altogether disproportionate to its length."—William H. Prescott, *History of the Conquest of Peru* (2 vols., New York, 1890), I, 1, 2.

[23] Schmidlin, *Catholic Mission History*, pp. 400-405.

After the middle of the sixteenth century the Jesuits began to arrive from Europe in considerable numbers and spread throughout the accessible parts of the continent. Together with the Dominicans and Franciscans they evangelized Argentina and also worked in the countries where the older Orders were already established. In Paraguay they were to have outstanding success with the missionary method of the "Reductions." By 1582 the Peruvian province alone had 133 members.

The following are the episcopal sees which the *Annuario Pontificio (Anno 1939)* lists as having been erected in the sixteenth century: Cartagena (1534), Santa Marta (1534), Cuzco (1536), Lima (1543, raised to the status of an archdiocese in 1546), Quito (1545), Popayán (1546), Ssma. Asunción de Paraguay (1547), La Plata or Charcas (Sucre, 1551), San Salvatore della Bahia (1551), Santiago del Chile (1561), Ssma. Concepción (in Chile, 1563), Bogotá (1564), Córdoba (in Argentina, 1570), Arequipa (1577), Trujillo (1577), Buenos Aires (1582).

Schmidlin summarizes the situation existing at a somewhat later date as follows: "As a result of these various missionary activities, there emerged an ecclesiastical life that was at least outwardly flourishing. As early as 1610 there were five archdioceses and twenty-seven dioceses, all under exemplary princes of the Church; and within these bounds there were maintained four hundred monasteries, a multitude of parishes and mission stations and millions of neophytes." He is quoting Hergenröther-Kirsch's ecclesiastical history on the numbers and adds that they evidently include Mexico. In a note he says: "According to Krose's estimate, no fewer than fourteen million pagans were won for Christianity during this period." [24]

E. *The Missions of Africa and Asia*

The missionary activities of the sixteenth century were by no means confined to the New World. Africa and the Orient were also the scenes of vast labors under the protection of the Portuguese as witnessed, among other Papal documents, by the bulls issued for the

[24] Schmidlin, *Catholic Mission History*, p. 385.

erection of dioceses. The episcopal see of Funchal on the island of Madeira, erected in 1514, embraced all Portuguese territory in Africa and India.[25] The territory of the diocese of Goa, erected in 1534 by Paul III,[26] was taken from that of Funchal and included all the places found and to be found by the Portuguese from the Cape of Good Hope through the Indies as far as China ("*per Indias usque ad Sinas*"). At the same time Paul III made provision for three other dioceses in Portuguese territory, viz., Angra in the Azores, Santiago de Caboverde, and São Thomé on the island of the same name in the Gulf of Guinea.[27] Cochin in India and Malacca were made episcopal sees in 1558.[28] In 1576 Gregory XIII [29] erected the diocese of Macao to whose bishop all China and Japan was made subject. For China this was a presage of the renewal of the apostolic work the Franciscans and Dominicans had carried on there in the thirteenth and fourteenth centuries.[30] A few years late Sixtus V [31] made a separate diocese of the kingdom of Japan. In addition to these dioceses under the direction of the Portuguese the following were erected in the Philippine Islands, which were

[25] Bull of Leo X, "*Pro excellenti praeeminentia,*" 12 Jun., 1514—*Bullarium Patronatus Portugalliae Regum in ecclesiis Africae, Asiae atque Oceaniae, Bullas, Brevia, Epistolas, Decreta Actaque S. Sedis ab Alexandre III ad hoc usque tempus amplectens* (6 tomi, Olisippone, 1868-1879), I, 100 f., *apud* Grentrup, *Ius Missionarium,* I, 197.

[26] Bull, "*Aequum reputamus,*" 3 Nov., 1534—*Bullarium Patronatus,* I, 148 f., *apud* Grentrup, *Ius Miss.,* I, 198; *Annuario Pontificio (Anno 1939)* gives 1533 as the date of erection for the diocese of Goa.

[27] Bull "*Aequum reputamus,*" 3 Nov., 1534—*Bullarum Collectio quibus serenissimis Lusitaniae Algarbiorumque Regibus terrarum omnium atque mare transcurrentium sive iam acquisitae sint sive in posterum acquirentur jus patronatus a S. Pontificibus liberaliter conceditur* (Olisippone, 1707), p. 98. *apud* Grentrup, *Ius Miss.,* I, 198. *Annuario Pontificio (Anno 1939)* gives 1534 as the date for the erection of São Thomé, and 1532 as that for Santiago de Caboverde.

[28] Pastor, *History of the Popes,* XX, 472.

[29] Bull, "*Super specula,*" 23 Jan., 1576—*Bull. Pat.,* I, 243 f., *apud* Grentrup, *Ius Miss.,* I, 204.

[30] Schmidlin, *Catholic Mission History,* pp. 232-235.

[31] By a bull, 19 Feb., 1588—*Bull. Pat.,* I, 249 f., *apud* Grentrup, *ibid.*

Spanish territory: Manila (1579), Nueva Cáceres (1595), Nueva Segovia (1595), Cebú (Nome di Gesu—1595).[32]

In view of the tenor of the bulls creating the dioceses in Portuguese territory and of a series of others issued in favor of the Portuguese kings, Portugal was given a comprehensive protectorate over the missions in Africa, Asia, and the parts of America that fell to Portugal according to the Line of Demarcation set by Alexander VI. The controversy which eventually arose between Portugal and the Holy See concerning the extension of the former's protectorate had not yet appeared in the sixteenth century.[33]

AFRICA. The west coast of Africa was visited by the Portuguese in the last quarter of the fifteenth century and Christianity was already introduced into Guinea and the Congo before 1500. Missions were continued with such satisfactory results in the Congo that by the middle of the sixteenth century the King of Portugal reported to the Pope that all the Congo was Catholic. Later developments, however, showed that Christianity was not yet solidly established. Angola, along the southern frontier of the Congo, was opened to trade by the Portuguese in 1520 on condition that the king and his people accept Christianity. Missionary results were unsatisfactory until 1578, when a chieftain was baptized. This example was followed by the king and 1,000 subjects in 1584, and by 1590 there were 20,000 Christians and 1,500 baptisms annually.[34] The episcopal see of S. Paola de Loando (Angola e Congo) was erected in 1596.[35] Missions were begun in Abyssinia in northeast Africa, and in Mozambique in the southeast during the pontificate of Paul III, but no permanent foundations were made in either section during the sixteenth century.[36]

THE ORIENT. Vasco da Gama and all the earliest voyagers to India brought missionaries with them for, like the Spanish, the Portuguese took seriously the obligation of spreading the Faith among the pagans. Vasco da Gama (1498), Cabral (1500), Al-

[32] *Annuario Pontificio (Anno 1939).*

[33] Grentrup, *Ius Miss.*, I, 195-204.

[34] Schmidlin, *Catholic Mission History*, pp. 276-282.

[35] *Annuario Pontificio (Anno 1939).*

[36] Pastor, *History of the Popes*, XX, 481, 482.

buquerque (1503), Almeida (1505), and Cunha (1506), all brought members of Religious Orders to India. After these early arrivals the missionaries came in considerable numbers. The Franciscans soon had founded a number of convents, and one of the friars was named first bishop of Goa when the vast territory assigned to that diocese was separated from Funchal.

In this Indian mission there were many obstacles to permanently successful evangelization, not the least of which was the scandalous conduct of the Portuguese settlers. A change for the better came when Francis Xavier arrived in Goa in the capacity of papal nuncio in 1542. In a short time by his wise and holy example he had put a new spirit into the entire mission.

Missionaries accompanied or followed the Portuguese discoverers and conquerors as they moved eastward to Burma, to the Malay Peninsula where Malacca became a missionary base and episcopal see, to Siam, to Annam, to the coast of China where Macao was established as a base, and to Japan, where Francis Xavier was the pioneer. Nor were the islands of the Malay Archipelago, the Celebes, or the Moluccas neglected. In all these places Christianity had been introduced by 1550 or shortly thereafter, and the missionaries continued active in them throughout the century.[37]

The success of the Jesuits in Japan during the century was particularly striking. Francis Xavier opened the campaign in 1549. By 1582 there were 150,000 converts and, in spite of a period of persecution, the number had grown to 750,000 by the close of the century.[38]

The Philippine Islands, discovered for Spain by Magellan in 1521, were at once introduced to Christianity by the discoverer himself. In 1559 the Augustinians started missionary work in the islands and in 1577 the Franciscans began to arrive, to be followed soon after by the Dominicans and the Jesuits. Their combined efforts were very fruitful. In 1585 the total number of Christians was estimated to be 400,000.[39]

[37] Schmidlin, *Catholic Mission History*, pp. 290-338.

[38] Schmidlin, *Catholic Mission History*, p. 343.

[39] Schmidlin, *Catholic Mission History*, p. 325.

Article 3. Polygamy an Obstacle to the Conversion of the Pagans

The foregoing brief outline of the expansion of the Church during the sixteenth century shows how it spread east and west from the Iberian Peninsula, through the efforts of the Spanish and Portuguese, to encircle the world. Millions of pagans from every branch of the human race were brought into contact with the Church's teaching. The stages of civilization, the kinds of social economy, and the degree of purity of the morals of the peoples were as various as the people themselves. These circumstances presented many problems to the missionary in the administration of the sacraments. One of the most troublesome and most frequently met was that of the polygamous pagan when he became a candidate for baptism.

Not all the peoples tolerated polygamy, and it was not always a general practice in those tribes in which it was tolerated. The Arawaks who inhabited the Greater Antilles in the West Indies seem not to have been polygamous as a people, though the king or chief of the tribe would have more than one wife.

Of the peoples of Mexico the Aztecs permitted polygamy which, as Prescott says, was probably confined to the wealthiest class.[40] Among the Tezcucans the princes had only one lawful wife, but kept a great number of concubines.[41] Among the Creeks in Florida marriage was not considered to be binding for more than one year, so that successive polygamy was not at all an extraordinary occurrence.[42]

In reference to the Peruvian Indians Westermarck says that polygyny, or the cohabitation of one man with more than one woman, was permitted, though probably practiced chiefly by the rich. "The first wife took precedence of the subsequent wives, or they had only one 'true and lawful wife,' though as many less legitimate wives or concubines as they liked." [43] Philip Ainsworth

[40] *Conquest of Mexico,* I, 151.

[41] Prescott, *op. cit.,* I, 185.

[42] Edward Westermarck, *The History of Human Marriage* (5. ed., 3 vols., New York: Allerton Book Co., 1922), III, 276.

[43] *Op. cit.,* III, 38, 39.

Means,[44] who relies for his information upon the careful observations of the seventeenth century Jesuit missionary and author, Bernabé Cobo,[45] agrees that in old Peru, "Among the Incas . . . practically every one was married in one way or another at least once in their lives [in his life?]; and many were married often . . . Polygamy existed; indeed among the upper classes it was general . . . The first woman whom a man received . . . was his wife in chief, remaining so until a death parted the pair . . . A woman so wedded [*i. e.*, the first wife wedded with formalities] could never be repudiated nor abandoned . . . She remained all her life his chief wife . . . Only the chief wife was so wedded, the secondary wives being no more than authorized concubines . . . [who] always remained subservient to the chief wife." On the death of the first wife the husband might marry again after a year or so but none of the secondary wives could ever take this first place.

The Araucanians of Chile likewise were polygynous, with the men usually having as many wives as they could support. Custom placed no limit to the number of consorts; some of the chiefs had as many as twenty wives, whereas necessity limited the poor to one or two.[46] Among the Araucanians also, one of the women was regarded as the principal wife with a higher social position than the others. This one was usually the first wife married.[47]

Successive polygamy was usual among the Chiriguanos of Bolivia, for after two years the husband left the first wife, moved to another village, and took a new wife.[48] Among the Guarayos of the same district it was nearly always the wife who took the initiative and separated from her husband.[49]

Nicolaus del Techo (1611-1685), Jesuit missionary and historian of the Paraguay mission, wrote of the Guarani: [50] "Matri-

[44] *Ancient Civilization of the Andes* (New York: Chas. Scribner's Sons, 1931), pp. 358-360.

[45] *Cf. Catholic Encyclopedia,* IV, 74, 75.

[46] Westermarck, *op. cit.,* III, 3.

[47] Westermarck, *op. cit.,* III, 29, 30.

[48] Westermarck, *op. cit.,* III, 276.

[49] Westermarck, *op. cit.,* III, 279.

[50] *Historia Provinciae Paraquariae Societatis Jesu* (Leodii, 1673), lib. V, cap. VII, p. 134.

monia libera sunt; quot quisque feminas alere et adipisci potens est, tot conjuges aut pellices numerat. Casiquii praesertim ius sibi in praestantissimas pagi sui puellas usurpant, quas non aegre clientibus aut hospitibus minuendas tradunt. Nuribus passim abutuntur. Dimittere uxores, et vicissim ab uxoribus dimitti, nemini admodum probro est."

Another Jesuit missionary to South America in the eighteenth century [51] gives the following account of the marriage customs of the Abipones, natives of the Chaco in the center of what was then Paraguay. "What wonder then that the custom of polygamy and divorce should be common to many savages of America, since it is upheld by the practice of the ancients? You should not however imagine that the whole nation of the Abipones follow the steps of the other nations in that respect. The major part are contented with one and the same wife, though I cannot deny that divorce is as frequent among them as the changing of the dress in Europe. Yet I have known many who kept the same wife all their lives . . . But if any Abipone marries several women he settles them in separate hordes, many leagues distant from one another, and visits first one, then the other, at intervals of a year . . . It is very common amongst them to reject wives to whom they have formerly united themselves, at their own pleasure, and with impunity, so that divines have very properly doubted the reality of the marriage of savages, as it seems to want the perpetuity of the nuptial tie. If their wives displease them, it is sufficient; they are ordered to decamp. No farther cause or objection is sought for; the will of the husband who dislikes his wife, stands in the place of reason . . . None of the men of most authority have either the right or the inclination to defend the divorced or control the divorcer."

Westermarck [52] quotes a missionary who states that of the peoples on the Orinoco there was only one to whom polygyny was unknown, whereas among the others every man had at least two or three wives. Polyandry was reported of one tribe in Ecuador

[51] Martin Dobrizhoffer, *An Account of the Abipones, An Equestrian People of Paraguay* (3 vols., trans. from original Latin, London, 1822), II, 210, 211.

[52] *Op. cit.,* III, 3.

and of two in the Guianas, but it was a much rarer form of marriage than polygyny.[53] Polygyny is described as prevailing among the tribes in which, due to devastating wars, the number of men is greatly reduced in relation to the number of women.[54]

A study correlating data obtained by various observers (missionaries, explorers, ethnologists, etc.) of the social institutions of the simpler peoples has included reports on the unity of marriage in fifty-three South American tribes. The totals show that monogamy was regular in thirteen tribes, and that polygamy was general in twelve tribes and occasional in twenty-eight. This means that polygamy was reported as practiced in 75% of the tribes. In only one tribe was marriage reported as being indissoluble, so that, including the successive type, polygamy was practically universal among these tribes.[55]

The data for the African tribes reported upon shows an even higher percentage in which polygamy was found. Out of 107 tribes listed, monogamy was regular in only four, polygamy was general in eighty-nine and occasional in fourteen. Thus 96.3% allowed polygamy.[56] A total of 438 tribes located in Asia, North and South America, Africa, Australia and Oceania are included in the tables of this work. Of these the compilers say that polygamy, either general or occasional, is the rule in approximately 90%.[57]

In view of this almost total absence of monogamy the difficulties of the sixteenth century missionary in untangling the matrimonial affairs of catechumens can easily be imagined. What was to be

[53] Westermarck, *op. cit.*, III, 107.

[54] Westermarck, *op. cit.*, III, 53.

[55] L. T. Hobhouse, G. C. Wheeler, M. Ginsberg, *The Material Culture and Social Institutions of the Simpler Peoples: An Essay in Correlation* (London: Chapman and Hall, 1930), Appendix I, pp. 176-215. The authors of this work [p. 146] define their terms thus: "Monogamy regular" is described as being the condition when both polygamy and concubinage are deemed wrong; "polygamy general" means that anyone may have more than one wife and that many in fact do; "polygamy occasional" means, (a) that it is stated as rare, or (b) that it is confined to the chiefs, nobles or wealthy, or (c) that it occurs under certain circumstances, *v. g.*, barrenness.

[56] Hobhouse, Wheeler, and Ginsberg, *op. cit.*, Appendix I, pp. 176-215.

[57] Hobhouse, Wheeler, and Ginsberg, *op. cit.*, p. 160.

done for the man who had had many wives simultaneously, or even in succession, but could not remember which of them he had first married? The validity of the first marriage, or of any of the other unions of a polygamous man could be questioned and in many instances it would be very difficult, if not impossible, to determine the true state of affairs. The important decision concerning which among many was the legitimate spouse of the catechumen must often be doubtful. It was to give authoritative solution to these cases and to simplify the problem they presented for the missionary that Paul III and St. Pius V issued their Constitutions [58] giving privileges previously unheard of and applying to the missionary countries.

[58] *"Altitudo,"* 1 Jun., 1537; *"Romani Pontificis,"* 2 Aug., 1571.

CHAPTER III

HISTORICAL NOTES ON THE CONCESSIONS FOR POLYGAMIST CONVERTS

ARTICLE 1. SOME PRELIMINARIES TO THE CONCESSIONS

BY virtue of the Pauline privilege a convert whose infidel spouse on being interpellated was unwilling to be converted, or refused to cohabit without insult to the Creator and without leading the convert into sin, was given the right to enter a second marriage. With infidels among whom the marital union of one man with one woman was the rule the application of the Pauline privilege was not difficult. It was comparatively easy to know when the conditions demanded by the privilege were verified. The polygamous conditions existing among the tribes of the New World, however, were the source of problems which either clearly could not be solved by the use of the privilege, or the marriage resulting from its use would be of doubtful validity.

In view of the considerable missionary activity in the New World in the early sixteenth century it is to be expected that the missionaries would conscientiously seek a *modus agendi* that would be in conformity with the divine law on marriage. A prelude to the legislation contained in the constitutions was the discussion of the subject in the first formal assembly of ecclesiastics held in Mexico.

In 1524 Fr. Martin de Valencia arrived in Mexico with eleven Franciscan confrères to augment the few missionaries already working there.[1] In the presence of Hernando Cortez the missionaries held Mexico's first "Apostolic Junta," as Archbishop Francisco Antonio de Lorenzana called it.[2] This assembly was considered by some

[1] Schmidlin, *Catholic Missionary History*, p. 413.

[2] *Concilios Provinciales Primero y Segundo, Celebrados en la Muy Noble, y Muy Real Ciudid De Mexico, Presidiendo El Illmo. y Rmo. Senor D. Fr. Alonso de Montufar, En los anos de 1555, y 1565* (Mexici, 1769), A2, verso.

historians to be the first Mexican synod. Francisco López de Gómara so styled it and recorded Fr. Martin de Valencia as the Pope's vicar.[3] López de Gómara, however, did not write from personal knowledge of the facts, for he was never in America. His history was composed from information received from his patron, Hernando Cortez, and it was found to contain serious errors.[4] Archbishop Lorenzana gives what is most probably the correct view of the meeting of 1524, when he says that although it came to be called the First Council of Mexico it was neither a provincial council nor a diocesan synod, because there was neither Metropolitan nor Bishop present. The first Provincial Council was not celebrated until 1555.[5]

The original record of the junta's proceedings was not available when Lorenzana was ready to publish it. He compiled the matter chiefly from documents in the archives of his church in Mexico and of the Convent of St. Francis.[6]

The record published under the heading *"Matrimonios"* stated that in regard to marriages there were major difficulties. There was question whether (any) marriages contracted by the Indians in their paganism were valid and, since they had many wives, which marriage (if any) was the valid one. The junta itself took no special action on the question, but decided to await the definition of the Apostolic See.

The report of the discussion is captioned, *"Nota."* The members of the junta who said that the marriages contracted by the Indians

Francisco Antonio de Lorenzana, Metropolitan of the Archdiocese of Mexico from 1766 to 1772, collected and published the acts of the first three provincial councils of Mexico held respectively in 1555, 1565, and 1585, and himself held the fourth Mexican provincial synod. He was recalled to Spain in 1772 to head the Archdiocese of Toledo and was created cardinal in 1789. *Cf. Catholic Encyclopedia*, IX, 357.

[3] *Hispania Victrix, Segunda Parte de la Cronica General de Las Indias* in *Biblioteca de Autores Espanoles*, edited by Manuel Rivadeneyra (71 vols., Madrid, 1846-1880), XXII, 405; *cf.* Cyriacus Morelli, *Fasti Novi Orbis*, p. 125.

[4] *Catholic Encyclopedia*, VI, 632.

[5] *Concilium Mexicanum Provinciale III* (Mexici, 1770), Praemonitio ad lectorem, A2, verso.

[6] *Concilios Provinciales Primero y Segundo*, A2, verso.

in infidelity were not valid based that opinion on the fact that there was no legitimate contract with a woman. An Indian would take many wives without knowing himself which was the principal wife and which were the concubines. Further, these Indians did not have a set formula of words with which to solemnize the contract. Hence it was not possible to elevate that contract to the status of a sacrament, after baptism. They also married without any regard to consanguinity or affinity.

On the other hand some maintained that many Indians had but one wife for several years or even for their whole life, and that others who did keep many (women) recognized only one as the principal whom they regarded as wife. The lack of a clear understanding of the Indian language and also the poverty of the language itself were factors which contributed to the belief that there was no legitimate marriage among the Indians.

The whole question was still obscure four years later when Juan de Zumarrága arrived as bishop. In the attempt to clarify the situation Cardinal Cajetan, among others, was consulted. He was inclined to believe, after studying the matter, that the Indian should declare that one to be his wife (from among those he had in his infidelity) whom he wanted as wife. In case the Indian did not take a clear stand then she whom he had had previously *"por propria"* should be his wife.[7]

Ultimately Paul III settled the matter by a brief in which he expressly commanded that when an Indian was converted to the Faith he should be given the first of the wives which he had in his paganism, and if he could not declare which one was the first he should be given the one that he wanted. Even this decision did not suffice to put an end to the dispute because after having been given one wife, some Indians declared that another was the first.[8]

[7] It is of interest to note here, in anticipation of further treatment, that as early as 1507 Cardinal Cajetan supported the view that the Pope had the power to dispense, for reasons other than religious profession, even in the bond of *ratum* marriage if it were not consummated. *Cf.* Cardinal Cajetan, *Opuscula Omnia D. Thomae de Vio in Tres Distincta Tomos* (in 1 vol., Lugdini, 1585), tract. XXVIII, *De Matrimonio*, pp. 122-124. Tract. XXVIII is dated: Romae, 24 Januarii, 1507.

[8] "Primera Junta Apostólica. MATRIMONIOS. A cerca de los Matri-

It is evident from this report of the junta's proceedings that in different tribes and different sections of New Spain [9] the missionaries were confronted with a variety of marital customs. Sometimes the marriages were monogamous; in other cases, together with a number of concubines an Indian would have one woman who clearly was

monios ocurrieron mayores dificultades sobre si eran validos entre los Indios los contrahidos en su Gentilidad, y qual de ellos lo era, porque tenian muchas mugeres, y no se resolvió cosa cierta esperando la definicion de la Silla Apostólica.

"NOTA. Los sugetos, que decian que no eran válidos los Matrimonios de los Indios en su Gentilidad, se fundaban en que no había legítimo contrato con una Muger, y que llegaban a muchas sin saberse qual era la principal, ó Señora, y las demás Concubinas; que no tenian palabras ciertas para solemnizer el contrato, y no le habiendo, no se podía elevar á razon de Sacramento despues del Bautismo; fuera de que se casaban con Parientas sin distinction.

"A el contrario otros decian, que muchos Indios solo tenian una Muger por muchos años, o por toda la vida, y aunque otros tenian muchas, era una la Señora, o principal, á la que reconocian por Muger: El no entender bien el Idioma de los Indios, la poca, o ninguna expresion de estos tocante á este assunto, hacía parecer, que no había legítimo Matrimonio entre ellos: Todos fundaban muy bien sus dictámenes, y fue tanta la obscuridad de la materia, que aun en el año de 1528, en que vino el V. Sr. D. Juan de Zumarrága por Obispo, continuamente estaba instando á sus Religiosos, y Letrados á fin de que se aclarassen estas Dudas; no lo pudo lograr, por lo que fueron Religiosos á España, y entre varios Hombres doctos, á quienes consultaron, uno de ellos fue el Cardinal Cayetano, que segun la Relacion que se le hizo, se inclinó á que se les diesse por Muger la que ellos quisiessen, en caso de no declararse bien, tocante á qual era la que por propria antes tenian.

"Ultimamente habidendose ocurrido á la Cáthedra de San Pedro, decidió el Señor Paulo III por un Breve, en que expresamente manda, que quando uno viniesse a la Fé se le dé la primera de las Mugeres, que tenía en su Gentilidad; y si no supiesse declarar qual era la primera, se le dé la que él quisiesse. Aun no bastó esta Decision para cortar disputas, porque despues de haberles dado una Muger, declararon algunos Indios, que era otra la primera; y además de esto había Matrimonios Clandestinos, hasta que se publicó el Santo Concilio de Trento."—*Concilios Provinciales Primero Y Segundo,* p. 5.

[9] The name "New Spain," in 1524, applied to the territory then occupied by the Spanish in what is now known as Mexico, together with Central America as far as, and including, Guatemala.

recognized to be his wife; in still other cases there seemed to be no criterion at all by which a determination could be made of the legitimate wife among many women. The lack of a formula or form to signify the matrimonial contract seemed to indicate that among some Indians there was no legitimate marriage. This coincides with a statement by Alphonsus a Veracruce that certain Mexican Indians married *"sicut pecora solent iungi,"* and that there was scarcely an expression of consent given. On the other hand, he said that among the pagans of the province of Michoacan there was true marriage, with man and woman legitimately joined, *"secundum mores suos."* [10]

These then are some of the facts, and obscurities, which must have been considered in forming the new legislation that applied to the marriages of polygamous infidels when they became converted. One may only conjecture how such cases were treated in the period up to 1537 when that legislation was promulgated in New Spain. Some five million Mexican Indians received baptism during that time.[11]

Lorenzana witnesses that the junta came to no decision, but left the matter to the Holy See. López de Gómara records that the junta members declared that since they were not familiar with the marriage rites, the Indian husband could marry that wife whom he wished.[12] Since Lorenzana's report of the junta was based on documents from Church archives, his statement is probably the correct one, yet in view of evidence that the missionaries of this period were *sui iuris* in the ordering of ecclesiastical discipline,[13] the *de*

[10] *Speculum Coniugiorum* (Mexici, 1556), pars II, art. 2, p. 314.

[11] Schmidlin, *Catholic Mission History*, p. 418.

[12] *Hispania Victrix, Segunda Parte de la Cronica de Las Indias*, in *Biblioteca de Autores Espanoles*, XXII, 405.

[13] "Beviter dici potest, missionarios huius periodi (a saeculo XII usque ad saeculum XVII) in ordinanda disciplina ecclesiastica fuisse sui iuris. Dum Corpus iuris canonici diversas et inter se discrepantes leges particulares in unum ius commune transformare studet, missionarii in terris remotis missionum maxima gavisi sunt libertate statuendi et abrogandi leges. Ita factum est, ut in missionibus remotis nec ius commune nec aliquod aliud ius stabile et uniforme vigeret. Cognoscitur etiam, cur Corpus iuris canonici de missionibus paene nihil dixerit."—Grentrup, *Ius Missionarium*, I, 23.

In this same place Grentrup quotes three propositions of the Franciscan

facto procedure in handling cases in which the identity of the polygamous convert's legitimate wife could not be determined may have been that which Gómara states.

Article 2. Paul III's Constitution, "*Altitudo*"

On 1 June, 1537, Pope Paul III issued the Constitution "*Altitudo*" addressed to the Bishops of West and South India. It appeared as an Apostolic bull, the most solemn form in which Papal documents are issued,[14] and contained legislation on several matters of ecclesiastical discipline in the New World. In addition to granting privileges in respect to the marriages of convert natives, Paul III prescribed the use of at least a certain minimum of ceremonies in the administration of baptism; he treated of fasts, abstinence, and holydays of obligation; he gave concessions, in view of the great distance from the Holy See, in regard to absolving the new converts from reserved cases; he ordered the bishops to expel apostates from their dioceses; and lastly, he ordered authoritative copies of the constitution to be made so that it would be available in the places where there was need of it.[15]

The section of the constitution that concerned marriage was a

Raymundus Caron in which the privileges granted to missionaries are summed up: "1. Missionarii regulares in locis Roma remotioribus (ubi scl. ad Pontificem non datur pro rei circumstantia accessus vel correspondentia, et consolatium animarum urget) habent omnimodam in utroque foro auctoritatem Pontificiam; tantam, quantam judicaverint expedire pro conversione infidelium, manutenentia atque profectu illorum in fide Catholica et obedientia Romanae Ecclesiae.

"2. Dicti missionarii possunt praeterea quaecumque facere, quae ad augmentum Divini Nominis et conversionem ipsorum infidelium populorum et ampliationem fidei orthodoxae, pro loco et tempore viderint expedire.

"3. Missionarii regulares, qui de licentia suorum Superiorum proficiscuntur ad quascumque terras infidelium et ad quamcumque mundi partem, ut eos convertant sunt tamquam legati et commissarii Papae quoad omnem potestatem in utroque foro, missioni convenientem, cum confirmatione omnium suorum privilegiorum."—Taken from Caron's *Apostolatus Evangelicus* (Antverpiae, 1653), pp. 135 sq.

[14] Cicognani, *Canon Law,* p. 91.

[15] *Cf.* complete text, *infra,* Appendix.

relatively small part of the whole. This section, together with an introductory paragraph from the constitution, as given in Document VI of the *Codex Iuris Canonici,* is as follows:

> . . . Sane cum sicut, non sine grandi et spirituali mentis nostrae laetitia, accepimus, quamplures incolae occidentalis et meridionalis Indiae, licet divinae sint legis expertes, S. Spiritu tamen cooperante, illustrati, errores, quos hactenus observarunt, penitus ab eorum mentibus et cordibus abiecerint, et secundum ritum eiusdem Romanae Ecclesiae vivere desiderent et proponant . . . Super eorum vero matrimoniis hoc observandum decernimus, ut qui ante conversionem plures iuxta eorum mores habebant uxores, et non recordantur quam primo acceperint, conversi ad fidem, unam ex illis accipiant, quam voluerint, ut cum ea matrimonium contrahant per verba de praesenti, ut moris est; qui vero recordantur quam primo acceperint, aliis dimissis, eam retineant. Ac eis concedimus, ut coniuncti etiam in tertio gradu tam consanguinitatis, quam affinitatis, non excluduntur a matrimoniis contrahendis donec huic S. Sedi super hoc aliud visum fuerit statuendum . . .

A. *Destination of the Constitution*

In view of the address of *"Altitudo"* and of the fact that three times within its subject matter it refers to West and South India, the legislation is clearly of a particular character, that is, it was enacted for the territory indicated.

In 1537 there was still considerable confusion of the newly discovered lands with India. The Pope's use of the terms *"Occidentalis et Meridionalis India"* was no doubt suggested by, and was intended to indicate the same places as, the terms used in the "Donation" of Alexander VI. In the latter's bull, *"Inter caetera,"* he assigns to Spain *"omnes insulas et terras firmas inventas et inveniendas, detectas et detegendas versus occidentem et meridiem, fabricando et construendo unam lineam a polo artico, scilicet septentrione, ad polum antarticum, scilicet meridiem, sive terrae firmae et insulae inventae et inveniendae sint versus Indiam aut versus aliam quamcumque partem. . . ."* [16] The constitution, then, was addressed to all the territory then being evangelized by the Spanish in the

[16] *Bull. Rom.,* V, 363.

New World. West and South India included the Antilles with four dioceses already erected,[17] New Spain and the adjoining lands to the south, comprising seven dioceses,[18] the north and northwestern sections of what is now South America in which three dioceses had then been erected,[19] and the Philippines, which had already been discovered for Spain.[20]

B. *The Privilege Allowing a Choice Among the Wives of a Former Polygamist*

There is a twofold privilege granted in the part of the constitution that has to do with the discipline on the sacrament of matrimony. The first is given in view of the former polygamy of the converts, and the second grants a relaxation of the prevailing discipline on the impediments of consanguinity and affinity.

The first privilege is granted to the convert natives who, before receiving baptism, had two or more wives, for the subjects are designated as those *"qui ante conversionem . . . plures habebant uxores."* [21] The constitution makes no distinction between simultaneous and successive polygamy. It seems the Pope intended to include both that class of converts who in their paganism lived with more than one wife at the same time, that is, in simultaneous polygamy, and the class who lived first with one and then with

[17] San Juan in Porto Rico, Concepción de la Vega and San Domingo in Hispaniola (Haiti), and Santiago de Cuba. *Cf. supra,* pp. 17, 18.

[18] Tlaxcala, Mexico, Nicaragua, Guatemala, Panama, Antequera, and Michoacan (Morelia). *Cf. supra,* p. 19.

[19] Cartagena, Santa Marta, and Cuzco. *Cf. supra,* p. 21.

[20] That the Philippine Islands were included in the territory to which the constitution applied is clear from a statement of a doubt made by the S. C. de Prop. Fide as to whether certain other Christian converts were obliged to the observance of fasts, yearly confession and Communion, and feasts, *"eo modo quo obligantur Indi in nova Hispania, et Insulis Philippinis, iuxta dispositionem Papae Pauli III pro Indis Occidentalibus et Meridionalibus."* The *"dispositio Papae Pauli III"* is that which the Pope made in the Constitution *"Altitudo."* Resp., 12 Sept., 1645—*Coll. S. C. P. F.,* n. 114.

[21] Reg. 40, R. J., in VI°: "Pluralis locutio duorum numero est contenta."

another, that is, in successive polygamy. Both types of polygamy were to be found among the peoples for whom the privilege was granted,[22] hence both types were *iuxta eorum mores.* The phrase, *iuxta eorum mores,* seems to indicate that the privilege was meant to extend to every convert polygamist, whatever may have been the peculiarities in the polygamous customs or practices of his particular people.

The favor granted to the subjects of the privilege is that of choosing from among the wives whom they had before their conversion that one whom they wish now to be their legitimate wife. But this choice is permitted only if the essential condition be fulfilled that the convert does not remember which wife he had first taken.

At first sight the statement of the essential condition for the use of the privilege, namely, that the convert be unable to recall which wife he had taken first, seems peculiar. In a society that has been conditioned by the Christian morality of marriage for many centuries only those with extremely defective memories, or those who have led a long life of exceptional looseness in regard to marriage ties could verify the condition. Referring again to the actual state of affairs which the missionaries found among the pagan tribes of the New World, it is quite likely that there were very many, among the millions of converts, who truthfully could say that they did not know which was their first wife.

Among some tribes the absence of any formality to designate the marriage contract would present a great difficulty. Carnal relations between a man and a woman would not necessarily make them man and wife. Even continued relations without the consent essential to marriage would be only concubinage, and meanwhile both parties might have relations with others. These would be among the marriages contracted *"sicut pecora solent iungi"* which Veracruz mentions.[23] Even among this class of Indians, however, there could be legitimate marriages and hence a first wife.

The marriage customs that were only a little less gross in certain other tribes, for example, those in which one woman was

[22] *Cf. supra,* Chap. II, Art. 3.

[23] *Cf. supra,* p. 34.

recognized as wife and the others as concubines, presented a less troublesome problem. Here the convert would have no difficulty in recalling the first wife. He may have had concubines before one woman was given the status of wife, but the others would not be numbered among those whom he, or the tribe, would consider as his wife. Lastly, there were marriages founded upon the same concept of unity that prevails in the non-Catholic western world of today.

In the light of this variety of situations, the insight which the wording of the legislation demonstrates is quite evident. The primary interpretation of Paul III's constitution would necessarily be made according to the sense of the words in the text and context, but the solution of doubts and obscurities in its application would be made according to the purpose of the law and the mind of the legislator.[24]

There is no express restriction limiting the choice which the convert may make among his wives when he does not remember which one of them he took first. Hence the woman chosen need only be one of those who according to the customs of that people, or according to his own judgment, were considered to be, or at some time to have been, his wives. In view of the uncertainty about the status of the consorts or mates, as the contemporary reports witness,[25] it would seem the ultimate criterion in many cases would necessarily be the convert polygamist's own statement.

Nor does the choice seem to have been restricted to those illegitimate wives or concubines who were still living with the convert at the time of his baptism, but it might be made also among those previously dismissed.[26] The privilege was granted to those who *according to their customs* had many wives. The customs of some Indians included successive polygamy in which wives were freely repudiated. In the nature of things the probability would favor the first woman lived with, or one of the earlier wives, as being the man's valid wife.

[24] C. 6, X, *de verborum significatione,* V, 40.

[25] *Cf. supra,* pp. 31-34.

[26] G. Vromant, "De dispensatione ab Interpellationibus in Ordine ad Privilegium Fidei," *Periodica,* XX (1931), 112*.

When the convert was able to recall the woman with whom he first contracted a valid marriage, he was obliged to dismiss the others and live with this legitimate wife. This provision, of course, did not abrogate the Pauline privilege. If the legitimate wife was unwilling to cohabit peacefully and without insult to the Creator, then the convert could invoke the privilege and by fulfilling its provisions validly marry a Christian woman.

It seems evident that the Pope meant to require the convert to retain his legitimate wife if he knew who she was. This requirement was in accord with the matrimonial discipline in force in the Church up to that time. This legitimate wife would not necessarily be she with whom the convert was first joined in any sort of carnal union, but it would be she with whom he had first entered a matrimonial contract. Whatever the mutual understanding, sign or rite expressing the matrimonial consent may have been, according to their customs, if it made the couple man and wife, the first woman with whom the convert exchanged this matrimonial consent would be the wife whom he would be required to retain, *salvo privilegio Paulino.*

C. *The Privilege Reducing the Prohibited Degrees of Consanguinity and Affinity*

The Indians' practice of marrying with little regard to the ties of consanguinity, and probably none at all to those of affinity, was one of the matters discussed by the first Mexican junta. The Pope had this difficulty in mind also when he issued the constitution. In favor of the natives of the New World he reduced the impediments of consanguinity and affinity, in the collateral line, so that they were binding only up to the second degree inclusive.[27]

Joannes de Solorzano Pereira [28] gave the impression that Fray Ioan Baptista in his work, *Advertencias Para Los Confessores,* believed only a faculty to dispense had been granted to the missionaries rather than that the impediments had been reduced. Cardinal

[27] Sanchez, *De Matrimonio,* lib. VIII, disp. XXIV, n. 35: Wernz, *Ius Decretalium,* IV, n. 409, nota 51; n. 437, nota 69.

[28] *De Indiarum Jure* (2 vols., Matriti, 1777), II, lib. I, cap. XXVIII, nn. 50, 51.

de Lugo[29] quoted Solorzano Pereira in regard to Baptista but showed that others considered the Pope to have dispensed the Indians universally and to have taken away the impediments in the third and fourth degrees. Such, in fact, was also Baptista's opinion, for he stated that the Indians in all the provinces of the Indies could marry within the third and fourth degrees of consanguinity and affinity because of the privilege of Paul III granted only to the Indians in the Bull *"Altitudo."*[30]

The concession therefore embraced both the case in which the convert remembered his first valid wife, so that he could remain with her if they were related in the forbidden degrees of these impediments beyond the second, and likewise the case in which the convert was allowed a choice and the wife chosen was related to him in one of the degrees beyond the second forbidden by the common law. If a marriage should involve an unequal impediment between Indians involving the first degree on one side, and any degree beyond the second on the other, there would be no need for a dispensation.[31]

Alphonsus a Veracruce[32] seems to have considered the conces-

[29] *Omnia Opera* (7 vols. in 4, Venetiis, 1718), vol. VII, *Responsorum Moralium Libri Sex,* lib. VI, dub. V, n. 2.

[30] *Advertencias Para Los Confessores de Los Naturales* (Mexico, 1600), fol. 87, recto et verso. The work is bound as the second part of the whole volume, *Confessario en Lengua Mexicana y Caste Llana,* Compuesto por el Padre Fray Ioan Baptista . . . En Sanctiago Tlatilulco, 1599.

Fray Baptista had stated that a Spaniard, mestizo, negro or mulatto who attempted marriage within the fourth degree inclusive without a dispensation sinned mortally, was *ipso facto* excommunicated, and the marriage was null. Shortly after came the statement on the point in question: "En las mismas penas incurrẽ los Indos q̃ asi cõtrahẽ salvo q̃ en todas las provincias de las Indias y nuevas conversiones, se puedẽ cassar dentro del tercero y quarto grado, por privilegio de Paulo 3. concedido solamẽte a los Indios. El qual Privilegio se entiende asi en el caso de consanguinidad, como de affinidad como consta claro en la Bulla de Pau. 3. que comiença "Altitudo divini consilii."

[31] Sanchez, *De Matrimonio,* lib. VIII, disp. XXIV, n. 35.

[32] *Omnium previlegiorum compendium, illorum maxime concessorum ordinibus mendicantium pro conversione infidelium* (Manuscript in John Carter Brown Library, Brown University, Providence, R. I.), fol. 69.

Cf. Seymour de Ricci—W. J. Wilson, *Census of Mediaeval and Renais-*

sion to have been made for all Indian converts absolutely, that is, without reference to previous polygamy on the part of the subject. In his list of the concessions made by Paul III in 1537 the following appears:

> Tertia concessio, idem concessit, quod Indi dictarum Indiarum etiam coniuncti in 3. gradu tam consanguinitatis, quam affinitatis possint matrimonium contrahere, donec sedes apostolica aliud statuerit.

A marginal note reads: "*Ista concessio est perpetua, donec revocetur a sede apostolica.*" He lists as number four, Paul III's concession granting the polygamous convert the right, when he does not recall the first wife whom he took, to retain one in order to make

sance Manuscripts in the U. S. and Canada (2 vols., New York: H. W. Wilson Co., 1935-1937), II, 2150, where this manuscript is listed as number twenty-six of the John Carter Brown collection. The manuscript is a bound volume of 102 leaves. A clue to the date of compilation is given on folio 92 where reference is made to Gregory XIII thus: ". . . et melius per Gregor, 13 qui nunc praeest anno 1581." There is no title page; the first folio has an "exhortatio" to the reader:

> Fratris Alphonsi a Veracruce in sacra theologia magistri ordinis haeremitarum Sancti Augustini ad candidum lectorem exhortatio—. Candide lector, omnium previlegiorum compendium, illorum maxime concessorum ordinibus mendicantium pro conversione infidelium, et profectu et manutenentia eorum in fide, a me ante triginta annos inceptum, postmodum per Reverendum patrem fratrem Alphonsus de Norena ordinis predicatorum curiose et singulariter adauctum usque ad annum 1567. Postremo tandem a me ad umbilicum (ut aiunt) deductum . . . a Gregorio 9, et Nicolao 5, incipiendo usque ad Gregorium 13, qui nunc Christi locum agit in terris co[m]pilavi, et perfeci, cui omnia, et nos subiecta esto . . .

Other internal evidence shows Alphonsus a Veracruce to have been the author of the manuscript as well as the compiler of the privileges mentioned. On folio 14, *verso*, there is a statement beginning, "Et ego Alphonsus . . ." On folio 69 a marginal reference to a point in the text, written in the same hand as that used in the text, reads: "Sic in speculo coniugiorum probatum a me late." *Speculum Coniugiorum* is the well-known work of the Augustinian friar Alphonsus Gutierez, more commonly known as Alphonsus a Veracruce (Alonso de la Veracruz), or simply Veracruz, the name under which he wrote. Dr. C. E. Castañeda, Latin American Librarian of the Lamar Library, University of Texas, expressed his opinion to the author of this dissertation that the manuscript is in the handwriting of Veracruz.

her his wife and dismiss the others.[83] Ioan Baptista's statement above gives no indication that he would differ from Veracruz that all Indian converts and not just the polygamists could use the privilege.[84]

In 1897 Leo XIII issued a brief [85] listing the privileges which were to apply to Latin America. Since some of the privileges formerly granted to *India Occidentalis* were no longer in use and others were doubtful the Pope had appointed a special congregation of Cardinals to study the matter and make a catalog of the old privileges which should still be in force. The Pope confirmed the list and granted them for a term of thirty years. Number X of the list referred to the impediments of consanguinity and affinity:

> Ut Indi et Nigritae intra tertium et quartum tam consanguinitatis quam affinitatis gradum matrimonia contrahere possint.[86]

Wernz,[87] without any reference to polygamy, held that from the time of Paul III the impediments of consanguinity and affinity were binding on the Indians and Negroes of Latin America and [on the natives?] in the Philippine Islands to the second degree inclusive only.

A problem was to arise in the application of privileges to the children resulting from unions of the European invaders with the natives. How many ancestors of an individual must be Europeans before he would cease to be considered among the "*Indi*" to whom the privileges were given? A norm seems to have been officially established on the occasion of a question that later arose concerning the use in "*Indias Orientales et Occidentales*" by Jesuit missionaries of faculties granted to them by indults of the Apostolic See, if the Bishop of the place enjoyed similar faculties. Benedict XIV in answering the question gave a definition of the "*neophyti*" in whose

[83] *Ibid.*, fol. 69.

[84] The narrow restriction to Indians alone, however, excluding the mestizo (half-Indian and half-Spanish) and the negro was to be changed.

[85] Litt. ap., "*Trans Oceanum,*" 18 Apr., 1897—*ASS,* XXIX (1896-1897), 659-663.

[86] *Ibid.*, p. 662.

[87] *Ius Decretalium,* IV, n. 409, nota 51; n. 437, nota 69.

favor the faculties of the missionaries to dispense from matrimonial impediments could be used.[38] *"Neophyti"* are not only those who have recently been baptized, but also their children even if these were baptized in infancy. The term also includes the baptized *mixti,* that is, those whose father or mother only was a native and the other parent a European. But those who have only one-quarter native blood (*quarterones*), and *a fortiori* those with only one-eighth native blood (*pucuelles*) are not to be classed as *"neophyti,"* and the missionaries may not use their faculties to dispense them from matrimonial impediments.[39] The norm thus established for granting dispensations, which are of strict interpretation, for a stronger reason should apply to privileges.

By deductions from a brief of Gregory XIV, 21 September, 1591, reported in Solorzano Pereira [40] and from a royal document also reported in Solorzano,[41] De Lugo [42] had arrived at the same principle as a norm, namely, that inhabitants of the New World who had at least one-half Indian blood could enjoy the privileges and concessions of the Indians.

D. *Summary*

To sum up it may be said that Paul III reduced to the second degree inclusive the impediments of consanguinity and affinity applying to the Indians of the New World and that all Indians, not just the polygamists, were benefited by the restricted impediments. When there became need for a determination of the subjects of the privilege all those were considered "Indians," for the use of the privilege, who had at least one-half Indian blood. The privilege

[38] Const. *"Cum venerabilis,"* 17 Jan., 1757—*Bullarium SSmi. Domini Nostri Benedicti Papae* XIV (4 vols. in 10, Venetiis, 1777-1784), IX, 226; *cf. Coll. S. C. P. F.*, n. 402.

[39] *Cf.* similar ruling by Clement IX, const. *"Animarum saluti,"* 8 Jan., 1669—*Bull. Rom.*, XVII, 754; *Coll. Hong.*, n. 1568.

[40] *De Indiarum Iure,* II, lib. I, cap. XXVIII, n. 50. The brief is here cited as that of Gregory XIII, but Gregory XIV was Pope at the date given for the brief.

[41] *Op. cit.*, II, lib. III, cap. XX, n. 4.

[42] *Responsorum Moralium Libri Sex,* lib. VI, dub. V, nn. 2-6.

was eventually extended to the Negroes, great numbers of whom were brought as slaves into the Antilles and South America in the sixteenth and following centuries. Since Fray Ioan Baptista's work was published in 1600, and he held then that Negroes who attempted marriage within the fourth degree inclusive sinned grievously and were excommunciated *ipso facto,* the extension was probably not made until after that date.

It is clear that something new in the Church's discipline on the sacrament of matrimony was introduced by the Constitution "*Altitudo.*" An essential condition for the use of the Pauline privilege had been the interpellation of the infidel wife, or a valid dispensation from the interpellation. Previous to the time of Paul III the impediment of *ligamen* bound every convert once married who had not fulfilled this condition of the privilege if his partner were still living. Paul III dissolved the existing marriage and took away the impediment of *ligamen* when the convert could not remember which wife was his first.

There is the possibility that among some polygamous Indians there were no previous valid marriages. In the other cases the definite wife with whom the convert had a true matrimonial bond was not known. But these truths do not change the fundamental fact that at least in some cases, and these would be many, the Pope's power was used to pronounce the dissolution of marriages that were valid by natural law.[43]

Article 3. St. Pius V's Constitution, "*Romani Pontificis*"

In the record of the proceedings of the first Mexican junta Lorenzana stated that even after the concession made by Paul III was put into effect there was still trouble.[44] It would seem there must have been an inquiry made to determine the identity of the convert's legitimate wife. When that could be known, then according to the grant the convert must continue to live with her, *salvo privilegio Paul-*

[43] Cappello, *De Sacramentis,* III, n. 791; Iulius De Backer, *De Matrimonio Praelectiones Canonicae* (9. ed., Louvain: Fr. Ceuterick, 1931), p. 260; Joyce, *Christian Marriage,* p. 490.

[44] *Cf. supra,* p. 32.

ino. But, as Lorenzana reports, after having been given one wife some of the Indians would declare that another was their first wife. In the Mexican mission, whatever the method or the practice may have been in determining the two parties who were previously legitimately married, this report shows that the results were not entirely satisfactory. It is not surprising to see that one of the causes impelling St. Pius V to grant a privilege which allowed a simpler procedure in the case of polygamous converts was consideration for the grave scruples of the missionaries. The responsibility rested upon the Bishops and priests to prevent adulterous unions among the converts, yet under the existing conditions they could not be certain that they were not tolerating many such unions.

St. Pius V issued the Constitution *"Romani Pontificis"* in 1571. By that time the missionary zeal of this sixteenth century had encircled the world with active mission centers, many of which were established dioceses. In Mexico and the adjacent territory to the south there were then twelve flourishing dioceses and millions of Catholics. South America had as many dioceses and the missions had spread throughout the continent.

As has been seen, it was not only the western world that had benefited by this apostolic zeal. From Africa eastward to the Philippines Catholic doctrine was being taught. In the second half of the century inhabitants of all the great nations and of the myriad islands in the Orient were being baptized. The solicitude of the Popes was as marked for this section of the globe as for the newly discovered lands to the west. In a brief dated 7 October, 1567,[45] St. Pius V urged the archbishop of Goa, Gaspar de Leam Pereira, not to resign the archbishopric, as he had expressed a desire to do, and granted the faculty to dispense those who had contracted marriage, or in the future would do so, within the degrees prohibited by law. Later in the same year in a brief [46] addressed to the General and other superiors of the Jesuits, he granted to the general provincials or their vicars, in Ethiopia, Arabia, Persia, India, China, Japan, Brazil, and in other regions of the Orient or of the islands

[45] *"Pervenisse ad te"—Annales Ecclesiastici,* XXII, 442, 443.

[46] *"Cum gratiarum,"* 20 Decembris, 1567—*Annales Ecclesiastici,* XXII, 444, 445.

of the Ocean, the faculty to dispense in any degree of consanguinity or affinity not prohibited by divine law.

These grants for the missions in the Portuguese sphere of influence were similar to that made by Paul III for the Spanish New World colonies, except that the latter Pope was considered to have reduced the impediments to include only the first and second degree of the collateral line, whereas St. Pius left the impediments intact but granted the faculty to dispense beyond the second degree. There is an indication here that missionaries throughout the world were encountering similar difficulties in regard to the marriages of their converts.

A. *The Text and Destination of the Constitution*

PIUS PAPA V

Ad futuram rei memoriam.

Romani Pontificis aequa et circumspecta providentia (1*), ne ea quae pro salubri (2*) Indorum noviter ad fidem conversorum (3*) directione sanciri debent et terminari, alicuius haesitationis (4*) scrupulo subiaceant, declarationibus et aliis opportunis consuevit providere remediis. Cum itaque, sicut accepimus, Indis in sua infidelitate manentibus plures permittantur uxores, quas ipsi etiam levissimis de causis repudiant, hinc factum est quod recipientibus baptismum permissum sit permanere (5*) cum ea uxore, quae simul cum marito baptizata existit; et quia saepenumero contingit illam non esse primam coniugem, unde (6*) tam ministri quam Episcopi gravissimis scrupulis torquentur, existimantes illud non esse verum matrimonium; sed quia durissimum esset (7*) separare eos ab uxoribus, cum quibus ipsi Indi baptismum susceperunt, maxime quia difficillimum foret primam coniugem reperire: ideo Nos, statui dictorum Indorum paterno affectu benigne consulere, atque ipsos Episcopos et ministros ab (8*) huiusmodi scrupulis eximere volentes, motu proprio et ex certa scientia Nostra (9*), ac apostolicae potestatis plenitudine (10*), ut Indi, sic ut praemittitur (11*) baptizati, et in futurum baptizandi, cum uxore, quae cum ipsis fuerit baptizata et baptizabitur, remanere valeant, tamquam cum uxore legitima, aliis dimissis, apostolica auctoritate, tenore praesentium, declaramus, matrimoniumque huiusmodi inter eos legitime consistere (12*),[47] sic que per quoscumque Judices et (13*) Commissarios quavis auctoritate fungentes, sublata eis et eorum cuilibet quavis aliter iudicandi (14*) et interpretandi facultate et auctoritate judicari ac (15*) diffiniri debere et si secus super his a quoquam (16*) quavis auctoritate scienter vel ignoranter contigerit attentari irritum et (17*) inane decernimus, non obstantibus quibusvis Apostolicis ac in Provincialibus et Synodalibus Conciliis editis generalibus vel specialibus Constitutonibus et Ordinationibus (18*), ceterisque contrariis quibuscumque.

Datum Romae apud Sanctum Petrum sub annulo Piscatoris, die 2 Augusti, 1571.[48]

[47] *Codex Iuris Canonici,* Documentum VII.

[48] *Appendix ad Bullarium Pontificium S. C. P. F.* (Romae), I, 45. The compiler of the *Appendix* advises in general of its contents that the constitutions of the Roman Pontiffs were found in the archives of the Sacrum Consilium "Christiano nomini propagando," and gives no other source for the individual constitutions.

The references marked with an asterisk, 1*, 2*, etc., indicate variations found in a transcription of the constitution in the *Bullarium Ordinis Fratrum Minorum Capucinorum* (ed. a Michaele a Tugio in Helvetia, 7 vols., Romae, 1740-1752), VII, 103. A note to the transcription in the *Bullarium* gives the source: "Ex Bullario Romano edit. antiquae." The variations:

1* "prudentia" for "providentia"
2* "salutis" for "salubri"
3* "ad fidem conversorum et convertendorum directione" for "ad fidem conversorum directione"
4* "dubitationis" for "haesitationis"
5* "manere" for "permanere"
6* "inde" for "unde"
7* "est" for "esset"
8* "ab" does not appear
9* "Nostra" does not appear
10* "ac de apostolicae potestatis plenitudine" for "ac apostolicae potestatis plenitudine"
11* "(sicut praefertur) baptizati" for "sic ut praemittitur baptizati"
12* "matrimonium huiusmodi inter eos consistere" for "matrimoniumque huiusmodi inter eos legitime consistere"
13* "ac" for "et"
14* "et cuilibet aliter iudicandi" for "et eorum cuilibet quavis aliter iudicandi"

Unlike Paul III's Constitution *"Altitudo,"* the Constitution *"Romani Pontificis"* was not addressed to the Bishops of a determined territory, but rather it had reference to that class of converts who could be included under the term "Indi." Before the discovery of the New World *indus* used as a substantive meant an inhabitant of India;[49] it was frequently applied also to many peoples living in the lands south and east of the Mediterranean, because they were considered to have had their origin in India.[50] Columbus' error in thinking that he had arrived in the islands of India by sailing westward from Europe was the basis for an extension of the name to the inhabitants of the New World. His correspondence constantly referred to his discoveries as being the Indies, and to the inhabitants as being Indians. Before the first quarter of the sixteenth century was over it was known that these discoveries were not the sought-for India, as became clear when Magellan in 1521 sailed westward ocross the Pacific Ocean and landed in the Philippine Islands. Common usage by that time, however, had permanently attached the name Indian to the natives of the New World. This, of course, did not mean that those to

15* "definiri" for "diffiniri"

16* "quocumque" for "quoquam"

17* "ac" for "et"

18* The transcription in the *Bullarium* indicates its omission of the part from "non obstantibus" to "ceterisque" by putting "etc." after "obstantibus."

Rayanna notes that the constitution as given in the *Bullarium Ordinis Fratrum Minorum Capucinorum* was taken from the same typical text as that used for the copy found in the collection, *Constitutiones Apostolicae, Brevia, Decreta, etc., pro Missionibus Sinarum, Tunquini, etc.* (Parisiis, 1676).

Rayanna lists a third typical text, copies of which were used by Veracruz in his *Speculum Coniugiorum* (Mediolani, 1599), by Ludovicus Cerqueira in his *Manuale ad Sacramenta Ecclesiae Ministranda* (Nangasaquii, 1605), and by Claudius Aquaviva in regard to a request to the Holy See for an extension of the privilege to Angola. Puthota Rayanna, "De Constitutione S. Pii Papae V *Romani Pontificis* (3 [2?] Augusti, 1571)," *Periodica,* XXVII (1938), 304.

[49] All oriental Asia including China and Japan, at the time of the Portuguese discoveries in the East and for some years thereafter, was called India. *Cf.* Grentrup, *Ius Missionarium,* I, p. 201, nota 2.

[50] *Cf.* Morelli, *Fasti Novi Orbis,* p. 282.

whom the name originally applied were no longer called Indians, but that the name now included both groups.

In the constitution itself there is no clue as to whether the privilege was granted to all Indians, to those of *India Occidentalis* only, or to those of *India Orientalis* only.[51] Some authors have declared that it was given for the Indians of New Spain,[52] and others that it was a grant for India.[53] Whatever the original destination of the constitution may have been, it was in use in both the Indies within thirty-five years from its date. The provincial council of Lima held in 1582-1583, and called the first of that city,[54] listed

[51] Alexander VI's Bull of Demarcation was the authority for this division of the vaguely known India. *Cf. supra*, pp. 16, 17. Gregory XIII, for the use of the privileges of the Society of Jesus, gave a more definite delineation of the two geographical terms. According to an *oraculum vivae vocis* of 11 October, 1579, reported in the *Compendium Indicum* of 1585, the Pope declared that by the name *India Orientalis* were understood all the regions and islands to the south and east beyond Mauretania (comprising modern Morocco and a part of Algeria) which pertained to the king of Portugal by right of ownership, or conquest, or commerce and navigation. By *India Occidentalis* were understood the lands which lay beyond the Fortunate (Canary) and Tertian islands to the west, whether they pertained to the king of Spain or to the king of Portugal. *Cf.* Didacus de Avendano, *Thesaurus Indicus* (Antverpiae, 1668), tit. XII, Cap. VI, n. 129; Morelli, *Fasti Novi Orbis*, p. 281. When the original line of demarcation was moved by treaty from the meridian 100 leagues west of the Cape Verde Islands to the meridian 370 leagues west, Brazil was brought within Portugal's sphere of influence, hence the reference Gregory XIII made to lands in *India Occidentalis* which pertained to the king of Portugal.

[52] *Gabriel Vasquez (Commentariorum ac Disputationum in Primam Secundae Sancti Thomae Tomus Primus* [Lugdini, 1620], q. XIX, art. VI, disp. LXVI, cap. V, n. 25) cites Veracruz; *cf.* also Sanchez, *De Matrimonio*, lib. VII, disp. LXXIV, n. 13; Basilius Pontius, *Tractatus de Sacramento Matrimonii* (2. ed., Bruxellis, 1627), lib. IX, cap. IV, n. 22. It is likely that these authors were all following Veracruz.

[53] Augustinus Lehmkuhl, *Theologia Moralis* (5. ed., Friburgi Brisgoviae, 1888), II, n. 707; A. DeSmet, *Tractatus Theologico-Canonicus De Sponsalibus et Matrimonio* (4. ed., Brugis: Beyaert, 1927), n. 353, not. 1, p. 300. *Cf.* Rayanna, "De Constitutione S. Pii Papae V, etc.," *Periodica*, XXVII (1938), 306, 307.

[54] Provincial councils had been held at Lima in 1552 (1553) and in 1567. The first seems to have been lacking in due authority, the second was legiti-

among the privileges granted to the Indians by the Popes the one contained in the Constitution *"Romani Pontificis."* The statement of it in the acts of the council is a summary of the dispositive part of the constitution.[55] The constitution was also in use in *India Orientalis* by 1605, if not previously, for in that year Ludovicus Cerquera, bishop of Japan, included it in his *Manuale ad Sacramenta Ecclesiae Ministranda* published in Nagasaki.[56]

Rayanna suggests the twofold communication of favors and privileges at that time effective among Regulars as the reason that the privilege of St. Pius V was in use in both the Indies.[57] The first communication was that existing among the Orders whether or not they were Mendicant.[58] St. Pius V had revised and restated the canonical institute on this matter to bring it into conformity with the provisions of the Council of Trent.[59] The same Pontiff had is-

mately convened, celebrated, and promulgated, yet the council of 1582-1583 is commonly called the First Provincial Council of Lima. *Cf.* Morelli, *Fasti Novi Orbis*, p. 173; Mansi, 36 *bis*, 193-195. The Council of 1582-1583 was approved by the Holy See, 31 October, 1588. Josephus Saenz de Aguirre, *Collectio Maxima Conciliorum Omnium Hispaniae et Novi Orbis* (4 vols., Romae, 1693-1694), IV, 262.

55 "Privilegia Indis per pontifices . . . Quae uxor ex pluribus retinenda. Pius V concedit, quod Indi ad Fidem conversi, qui in sua infidelitate plures habebant uxores, eam pro legitima retineant, et cum ea contrahant, quae simul cum ipsis ad Fidem conversa et baptizata fuerit, quamvis non fuerit prima uxor eorum adhuc viventium, quas in infidelitate duxerint, et quod eiusmodi matrimonium absque ullo scrupulo habeatur pro legitimo. Ex litt. Apost. 1571, die 2. Augusti. In archivo Ecclesiae civitatis Regum." Aguirre, *op. cit.*, IV, 269; *cf.* Franciscus Haroldus, *Lima Limata Conciliis, Constitutionibus, Synodalibus, et aliis Monumentis Quibus Venerab. Servus Dei Toribius Alphonsus Mogroveius, Archiepisc. Limanus Provinciam Limensem, seu Peruanun Imperium elimavit et ad normam SS. Canonum Composuit* (Romae, 1673), p. 111; Mansi, 36 *bis*, 251.

56 Rayanna, "De Constitutione S. Pii Papae V, etc.," *Periodica*, XXVII (1938), 304.

57 "De Constitutione S. Pii, Papae V, etc.," *Periodica*, XXVII (1938), 309, 310.

58 *Cf.* A. Van Hove, *Commentarium Lovaniense in Codicem Iuris Canonici*, Vol. I, Tom. V, *De Privilegiis—De Dispensationibus* (Mechliniae et Romae: Dessain, 1939), n. 137.

59 Const., *"Etsi Mendicantium,"* 16 Maii, 1567—*Bull. Rom.*, VII, 573.

sued a constitution declaring the Society of Jesus to be a Mendicant Order and that therefore it could enjoy the favors and privileges of the Medicants.[60] The second communication was that granted by Gregory XIII in a brief, 10 February, 1579, to the effect that all privileges, faculties and favors which had been granted in the past or would be granted in the future to *India Orientalis* and *India Occidentalis* separately, were communciated by this brief to each of the regions reciprocally. Moreover, the religious of the Society of Jesus in New Spain could use all the privileges, faculties and favors given to either of the Indies, just as though they had been *specialiter et nominatim* given to the Jesuits.

In his commentary on Gregory XIII's brief of 10 February, 1579, which he notes as being contained in the *Compendium Indicum* of the Society, Avendano says that although the concession was directed to the religious, yet it seems to have been the mind of the Pope that the privileges granted to *India Orientalis* and *India Occidentalis* individually now be considered as common to both, for the privileges were granted not so much for the religious as for the Indians themselves. The Pope seems to have referred not to special grants made to provinces or communities of the religious, but to the general concessions made for the two great mission fields to the east and to the west. Avendano admits, however, that the less universal sense, that is, that the Pope may have been referring only to grants made directly to the religious, may, without violence to the wording of the brief, be sustained.[61] Morelli favored the interpretation that, although the concession made by this brief was directed to the Jesuits, the Pope sufficiently declared his will of communicating the general privileges between the two Indies. *"Saltem religiosi alii iure communicationis gaudentes illis uti poterunt indiscriminatim."* [62]

[60] *"Dum indefessae,"* 7 Jul., 1571—*Bull. Rom.*, VII, 923.

[61] *Thesaurus Indicus*, tit. XII, cap. V, n. 114.

[62] *Fasti Novi Orbis*, p. 279; *cf.* A. Vermeersch, "Commentaria de Formulis Facultatum Quas S. Congr. De Propaganda Fide Concedere Solet," *Periodica*, XI (1922), n. 4, p. (37) where he states that the wide faculties found in *Compendio Indico Societatis Iesu*, by virtue of communication of privileges, benefited all [missionary religious].

In view of the fact that missionaries were confronted with the problem of convert polygamists throughout the world, it is quite probable that St. Pius V intended to grant the privileges of the Constitution "*Romani Pontificis*" to both the Indies and for that reason did not limit it geographically. If, however, he originally meant the privilege to apply in only one or the other of the Indies, within a decade there were juridical reasons for its valid use in both.

B. *Interpretation of the Constitution by Authors From the Sixteenth Century to the Eighteenth*

In the constitution St. Pius V first gave a résumé of the difficulties in regard to the marriages of convert polygamists. He had been informed that as pagans the Indians were permitted many wives whom they repudiated for the slightest reasons. When they became Christians they had been permitted to remain with that wife who received baptism with them. But this convert wife frequently was not the first wife, and hence the missionary priests and bishops became greatly troubled. They were fearing, no doubt, and with reason, that they were tolerating adulterous unions among their Christians. If they had been demanding that the convert make the interpellations of the first wife as required for the use of the Pauline privilege there could have been no cause for anxiety. Hence it seems evident they were not requiring the interpellations.

It would be of interest to know upon what grounds the missionaries and Bishops had been allowing the Indians to retain the wife who would be baptized even if she was not the first wife. The experience of the Jesuit missionaries in the province of Paraquaria [63] may be typical of what had happened in other mission fields. The

[63] Paraquaria was the great mission of the Paraguay district in the central part of South America between Brazil and the Peruvian district which spread along the west coast.—Nicolaus del Techo, *Historia Provinciae Paraquariae,* lib. I, cap. XVI, p. 12. *Cf.* also Nicolaus del Techo (alias du Toict), *Relatio Triplex De Rebus Indicis* (Antverpiae, 1654), p. 45: "Porro de caelo istarum regionum ut aliquid etiam dicam, et glebae fertilitate, id scire oportet, hanc nostram, quam Paraquariam appellamus, provinciam, tres Praefecturas complecti; Paraquariam, Tucumanicam, et quam a flumine Argenteo vocarunt, quae omnes uti soli feracitate diversae sunt . . ."

following account [64] was given at a later date when the privilege of "*Romani Pontificis*" could have been in force, but for some reason does not seem then to have been used in Paraquaria. The chiefs of the Guarani natives, accustomed in their paganism to keep many concubines, found the obligation of Christian monogamy a great hindrance to their conversion. Some missionaries required them on becoming Christian to keep the first wife but others permitted them to take whichever of the concubines they wished for a wife. Because of the difference of opinion Joannes de Lugo, later Cardinal de Lugo, laid the matter before Pope Urban VIII.[65] He explained to the Pope that frequently when the natives took a wife they would also take her daughters or sisters if she had any, and that they dismissed their wives as easily as the Europeons would dismiss servants. As a consequence of these and like practices many missionaries thought that, at least commonly, the unions were not marriages but concubinage and when the natives were converted they allowed them to keep a baptized partner.[66] But other missionaries "*scrupulum habeant,*" and require the converts to return to the first wife, hence the following inconveniences: many are turned away from baptism "*hoc terrore*"; some are untruthful, saying they have no other wife,

[64] "Guaranae gentis primores solebant tot pellices alere, quot eorum libido et authoritas a popularibus suis impetrabat: nec aliud erat maius capessendae religionis nostrae impedimentum, quam cum monerentur unica uxore Christianos ex lege Divina contentos esse debere. Accessit huic obstaculo nimia quorumdum Sociorum religiositas, eiusmodi homines ad primam uxorem adigere volentium. Alii dempto scrupulo, religionem Christianam ineuntibus, quam cumque vellent, ex pellicibus pro uxore permittebant. Ob eorum opinionum diversitatem, inde natam, quod Doctores scholastici de ea re inter se dissentiant, ad summum Legum interpretem recursum est, et Ioannes de Lugo, post modum Cardinalis, rem totam his verbis Urbano VIII Pontifici Maximo exposuit. . . ." —Techo, *Historia Provinciae Paraquariae,* lib. X, cap. XV, pp. 277 (misnumbered 279), 278. Joannes de Cardenas (*Crisis Theologica* [Venetiis, 1696], dissert. II, cap. VIII, nn. 552, 553) and also Henricus Feije (*De Imped. et Disp. Matrimonialibus* [3. ed., Lovanii, 1885], n. 486, nota 4, pp. 358-361) transcribe this whole section from the *Historia.*

[65] This would have been done not later than 1643 since it was in that year that Joannes de Lugo was raised to the Cardinalite.

[66] ". . . atque ideo permittunt, quod coniugem baptizatum [sic] accipiant, quando ad fidem convertuntur . . ."

and contract marriage in bad faith with another; some pretend that they return to the first wife but in fact have another and do not trouble themselves about the first. Frequently, too, it is extremely difficult to determine the first because they scarcely remember which was the first among so great a number. Moreover, having found the first it would be necessary to carry on an inquiry to see if she previously had had husbands, and if so whether they had other wives before her. To these difficulties are added the fact that frequently in their unions the natives do not use any special external sign different from that by which they take a concubine for a week or a month so that often no external sign is given to express the consent required for marriage.[67]

Such were the convert matrimonial problems troubling the missionaries in the province of Paraquaria even after the date of the Constitution "*Romani Pontificis.*" As will be seen, the early interpretations of the constitution greatly restricted the concession granted in it, which probably explains why it was not applied in Paraquaria to aid in solving the above difficulties.

One may conjecture that in the New World as a whole the practice of allowing the convert to remain with the wife who received baptism with him, as related by St. Pius V, grew out of the privilege granted by Paul III. In that large mission field the status

[67] In view of all this De Lugo petitioned Urban for a faculty for the Jesuits to dispense the converts so that they could contract a true marriage before the Church. Among the cases for which he asked the faculty was that in which it would be very difficult for the convert to go back to a first wife already dismissed. Urban replied that there did not seem to him to be need of a special dispensation, which opinion he evidently based on the doubtful validity of all the marriages: "Urbanus VIII indicto Sapientium virorum super ea re consulto, pronunciavit non videri sibi speciali sua dispensatione opus esse, sed ubi Doctorum sententiae utrimque probabiles intercederent, sequerentur opiniones pro conditione locorum ac hominum Barbaris favorabiliores salva interim utriusque partis authoritate, sinerent doctis hominibus sentiendi libertatem. Constans igitur Sociorum plerorumque in his terris degentium opinio praxi confirmata fuit, horum Barbarorum matrimonia ob rationes supra relatas nulla esse, et posse Barbaros ad fidem conversos quamcumque baptizatam, reiectis aliis, in conjugem sumere. Quamquam eam semper adhibuere cautelam, quam rei gravitas postulabat." Techo, *Historia Provinciae Paraquariae*, lib. X, cap. XV, p. 278.

of the marriages among the pagan natives, although sometimes clear, more often was so involved that to make a determination of the legitimate wife was very difficult when not actually impossible. Such certainly would not be a juridical interpretation of the privilege in "*Altitudo,*" but it may have been an expedient application in view of the hundreds of thousands of pagans, mostly polygamists, who were flocking to baptism. Whatever may have been its basis, St. Pius V confirmed the practice by declaring valid both the past and future marriages entered in conformity with it.

A more detailed interpretation of the privilege will be given later,[68] but it may be noted here that in the statement of the privilege itself there is no restriction to those cases only in which the first wife cannot be found. Nor is there, in reference to the first wife, any mention of interpellations to be made or to be dispensed from. The unconditional statement of it seems to grant the privilege absolutely.[69]

Authorities in the missions of the New World truncated the privilege to make it conform with Innocent III's decretal, "*Gaudemus in Domino,*" [70] and therefore considered it as an application of the Pauline privilege to particular circumstances.

Veracruz paraphrased the constitution [71] and then warned that its use should conform with the decretal, "*Gaudemus in Domino.*" He interpreted St. Pius V as referring only to cases in which the first wife could not be found.[72]

[68] *Cf. infra,* Chap. IX.

[69] *Cf.* Vermeersch, "Commentaria de Formulis Facultatum, etc.," *Periodica,* XI (1922), (139).

[70] C. 8, X, *de divortiis,* IV, 19.

[71] "Pius 5. ad instantiam religiosorum commorantium apud indos anno 1571 circa matrimonium indorum, et facilitatem repudiandi ipsorum, sit in quodam brevi: Et quibus fuit consuetum repudiare facile in tempore infidelitatis, et cum baptizantur, manent cum illa cum qua tempore conversionis ad fidem, habitabat sine diligentia praevia, an illa fuerit prima, an alia, quae fuerat repudiata, ad quietandas conscientias episcoporum, et religiosorum, illa, cum qua infidelis ad fidem conversus est, habeatur, ut vera et legitima uxor. Et sic vult per alios iudicari . . ." *Compendium omnium previlegiorum, etc.* (Mss. in John Carter Brown Library), fol. 85 v.

[72] "Haec pontificis decisio debet cum iudicio recipi, si quidem si absolute intelligatur, quod in quocumque eventu, etiam si sit alia prima, quae fuit

In the first edition (1556) of the *Speculum Coniugiorum* Veracruz held that it seemed to be the true conclusion of all theologians, with a few exceptions, that *matrimonium ratum,* even though not consummated, could only be dissolved by the entrance of one party into religion, and not by Papal dispensation.[73] Further, he said that the Church dissolved the consummated legitimate marriages of infidels in the three cases outlined in the decretal of Innocent III, *"Quanto te magis,"* [74] on the authority of Christ, speaking through St. Paul.[75] It follows, Veracruz continues, that if marriage is truly dissolved, it is not by precept of the Church, but through the dispensation of God.[76]

The failure of Veracruz to recognize any other power in the Church to dissolve legitimate marriage, except that connected with the Pauline privilege, undoubtedly explains his restricted interpretation of St. Pius V's constitution.

Jose de Acosta likewise sought to make the constitution conform to Innocent III's decretal *"Gaudemus in Domino."* Fr. Acosta, a member of the Society of Jesus and a lecturer in theology at

repudiata, est contra expressam iuris canonici determinationem, c. gaudemus, extra. de divortiis. quae fundatur in iure divino, et naturali; Oportet ergo intelligere Pium 5., tunc verum tenere, ad quietandas conscientias, quando non potest inveniri illa prima repudiata, accepta affectu maritali, quia tunc possidentis melior est conditio. De quo vide in appendice speculi coniugiorum."—*Ibid.* The *Appendix ad Speculum Coniugiorum* here referred to was first published as a separate volume in 1571 and then included in the 1572 and 1599 editions of *Speculum Coniugiorum. Cf. Bibliotheca Ibero-Americana de la Orden de San Augustin* (El Escorial, 1913-1931), VIII, 167.

[73] Pars II, art. 28, p. 482.

[74] "Si enim alter infidelium coniugum ad fidem catholicam convertatur, altero vel nullo modo, vel saltem non sine blasphemia divini nominis, vel ut eum pertrahat ad mortale peccatum, ei cohabitare volente: qui relinquitur, ad secunda, si voluerit, vota transibit . . ." C. 7, X, *de divortiis,* IV, 19.

[75] 1 Cor. vii: 15.

[76] "Alioquin, nisi ex Christi vel Apostolorum verbis haberet ecclesia, non posset ipsa dissolvere matrimonium quod semel fuit contractum inter legitimas personas." *Op cit.,* pars II, art. 28, p. 483; *cf.* Rayanna, "De Constitutione S. Pii Papae V, etc.," *Periodica,* XXVII (1938), 312, 313, for similar matter from the 1572 and 1599 editions of *Speculum Coniugiorum.*

Ocaña in Spain, was sent to Lima, Peru, in 1569. He was elected provincial of the Jesuits in 1576, and was a consultor in the provincial council at Lima in 1582-1583. It was he who translated the proceedings of the council into Latin and took them to Rome for approbation.[77]

Since a copy of the Constitution "*Romani Pontificis*" was in the ecclesiastical archives at Lima,[78] Acosta may be presumed to have seen it, especially in view of his important part in the provincial council. In the section of his *De Procuranda Indorum Salute* in which he treats of the marriage of polygamous converts, he states first the privilege granted by Paul III in the Constitution "*Altitudo.*" If the convert remembers which of his wives was the first he will retain her only, but if he does not know which of them was first he may take the one he desires. The grant made by St. Pius V immediately follows, but Acosta limits it. If that first wife "*abest et baptizari differt,*" he says, then the convert may choose whom he wishes from the other wives of his polygamous unions. This concession is stated as being not at all contrary to the legislation of Innocent III. There is a marginal note at this point, "*Eodem ca. Gaudemus.*" After that there is the provision that whenever an infidel wife is converted to the faith, the convert husband must receive her, if he has not already married another Christian woman.[79]

It seems evident that Acosta was striving to bring the concession of St. Pius V within the scope of the Pauline privilege. There is the difficulty of explaining, however, how such an interpretation can be in conformity with Innocent III's decretal "*Gaudemus in Domino,*" since both St. Paul and Innocent forbid a convert to dismiss an

[77] *Cath. Ency.*, I, 108; Morelli, *Fasti Novi Orbis*, p. 173.

[78] *Cf. supra*, p. 51, note 55.

[79] Josephus Acosta, *De Procuranda Salute Indorum Libri Sex* (Salmanticae, 1588), lib. VI, cap. XXI. This work is the second part of a volume: *De Natura Novi Orbis et de Promulgatione Evangelii apud Barbaros sive De Procuranda Indorum Salute Libri Sex* (Salmanticae, 1589). A later edition, *De Natura Novi Orbis Libri Duo et De Promulgatione Evangelii apud Barbaros, sive De Procuranda Indorum Salute, Libri Sex* (Coloniae Agrippinae, 1596), does not differ from the 1588 edition, at least in so far as lib. VI, cap. XXI, is concerned.

infidel spouse who is willing to cohabit peacefully. In other words, how explain the omission of the interpellation in regard to cohabiting peacefully?[80]

In the same chapter Acosta had previously quoted a decree of the Fourth Council of Toledo (633) which Gratian had included in the *Decretum*.[81] The decree stated that Jews who have Christian wives must be admonished by the Bishop of that city that if they desire to remain with them they are to become Christians. But if, after having been admonished, they refuse to do so they are to be separated: for an infidel cannot remain united with her who has passed over to the Christian faith. Acosta stated that the synod of Lima had followed the authority of the Toledo council and had decreed what was to be done if one spouse refused to be baptized. The priest with a notary and witnesses was to advise him to become a Christian and be baptized within six months. If at the end of that time he refused, he was to be considered as resolved on remaining in the Jewish religion and the pastor was to advise the bishop so that the later could decide what should be done.[82] Then follows an opinion by Acosta which seems to explain why he could disregard an interpellation in regard to peacefully cohabiting, and yet consider his interpretation of St. Pius V not to be contrary to the decretal *"Gaudemus in Domino."* He held that the separation provided for in the decree of the Council of Toledo meant not only separation from bed, but also dissolution of the bond, so that the Christian party

[80] *Cf.* Rayanna, "De Constitutione S. Pii Papae V, etc.," *Periodica*, XXVII (1938), 321.

[81] C. 10, C. XXVIII, q. 1.

[82] There is a marginal note to this, *"Conc. Lim. const. 36."* In reference to the Council of Lima to which Acosta refers in the marginal notes, Morelli says that it cannot be that of 1582-1583, since Acosta's work was written before then, and it cannot be the second (1567), since that was divided not into constitutions, but into sessions and chapters; therefore it was the first (1552). *Fasti Novi Orbis*, p. 173.

Substantially the same provision as this which Acosta quotes from a previous Council of Lima is found in Actio Secunda, Caput X, of the Provincial Council of 1582-1583, and a footnote refers it to "Conc. 2. Lim. 2, C. 38." *Cf.* Aguirre, *Collectio Maxima Conciliorum*, etc., IV, 235, 236.

would thereafter be free to marry again.[83] Sanchez was among the Spanish theologians who in the sixteenth and seventeenth centuries maintained that a convert could use the Pauline privilege if his spouse even refused only to be baptized.[84] It is not clear therefore that Acosta saw in the constitution anything more than an application to the polygamous Indians of the Pauline privilege interpreted in the light of the decree of the Council of Toledo.

For other writers also of the sixteenth and the following century the decretal *"Gaudemus in Domino"* was the Procrustean bed into which the constitution must fit. Thus, Vasquez explains that according to the decretal a convert whose partner is unwilling to cohabit, or will not cohabit without insult to the Creator, may dissolve the marriage by contracting with, or remaining with, another wife. He interprets the constitution of St. Pius V as being applicable when the first wife cannot be found, even if there be no certainty of her death. He brings the constitution into conformity with the decretal by stating that when that (first) wife cannot be found, she is presumed by law to be unwilling to cohabit, or will not cohabit without insult to the Creator. For that reason, Vasquez holds, the Pope declared that the first marriage can be dissolved and thus the convert may remain with a wife other than his first.[85]

Sanchez, treating the question of whether or not interpellation (*monitio*) is required in the use of the Pauline privilege when there is moral certainty of the obstinacy of the infidel, cites the constitution of St. Pius V in favor of the negative opinion. Sanchez, also, considers that the constitution has reference to those cases in which the infidel cannot be found, and then quotes the reason Vasquez

[83] "Separationem autem illam Concilii Tolentani ego non solum quoad torum intelligo, sed etiam quoad vinculum. Itaque licebit, ut graves quoque autores confirmant, fideli iam tunc alias nuptias conciliare sibi. Contumelia enim creatoris et periculum fidei intelligitur, cum coniugis infidelis adeo est in sua superstitione obstinatus." *Op. cit.*, lib. VI, cap. XXI.

[84] *De Matrimonio,* lib. VII, disp. LXXIV, n. 9. For a résumé of the development of this opinion from the time of the Fourth Council of Toledo, *cf.*, Joyce, *Christian Marriage,* pp. 484, 485.

[85] Vasquez, *Commentariorum ac Disputationum in Primam Secundae Sancti Thomae Tomus Primus,* q. XIX, art. VI, disp. LXVI, cap. V, nn. 25, 26.

gives why interpellation is not required in such circumstances. The reason being, as above, that the obstinacy of the absent infidel may be inferred as a moral certainty. Sanchez adds that when the infidel is at such a distance that the interpellation cannot be duly (*commode*) made, there is no need of it. It may then be considered as morally certain that the infidel wife would be unwilling to be converted and to leave her present connections to return to her former husband. If she had previously left her husband and entered another marriage, that fact would be a sufficient indication of her refusal to cohabit peacefully; hence the interpellation need not be made. If her husband had repudiated her, however, then even though she had married again the convert husband would be required to make the interpellations, for in these circumstances the new marriage did not provide a moral certainty of her obstinacy.[86] Thus Sanchez seems to have considered the constitution only as affecting the interpellations required for the use of the Pauline privilege. He was not subject to the prejudice that the Pope did not have the power to dissolve infidel marriage, for he favored the opinion that the Pope could dispense in the consummated marriage of infidels even after both parties were baptized, provided they had not thereafter consummated the marriage.[87] This was a highly controverted opinion at the time, however, and he applied the constitution according to the more conservative opinion.

Pontius' certainty that the consummated marriage of infidels could not be dissolved by the Pope [88] necessarily induced him to interpret the concession in the more limited sense. His interpretation concentrated upon the phrase *"maxime quia difficillimum foret primam conjugem reperire"* in *"Romani Pontificis,"* and he distinguished two kinds of cases in which the infidel wife could not be found. There was that in which the interpellation could not be made because of certain danger of great harm. The other case existed if the whereabouts of the infidel were not known, or if she lived at so great a distance that the difficulty of the journey was an obstacle to making the interpellation. He interpreted the constitu-

[86] *De Matrimonio*, lib. VII, disp. LXXIV, nn. 13-15.

[87] *Op. cit.*, lib. II, disp. XVII, n. 2.

[88] Pontius, *De Matrimonio*, lib. IX, cap. II, n. 8.

tion of St. Pius V as dispensing from and supplying the interpellation in either of these events. Moreover, he held that Gregory XIII granted the like dispensation in the Constitution "Populis,"[89] hence he seems to have thought that the two constitutions had the same object. Like the others Pontius was mindful of the decretal *"Gaudemus."* He explained that the Popes in granting the dispensations presume that the infidel who cannot be found is unwilling to cohabit at all, or will not cohabit without insult to the Creator.[90]

The opinions of these outstanding authors on the subject of matrimony had a great influence on the subsequent interpretation of the constitution among other writers. Thus Benedict XIV, treating together the constitutions of St. Pius V and Gregory XIII, considered the Popes to be only tempering the discipline on interpellations to the extent that extrajudicial knowledge would satisfy the requirement of the Pauline privilege in certain circumstances.[91]

A recognition of the fact that at least in some of the marriages of the polygamous Indians the Pope was granting a dissolution of the bond of valid infidel marriage had to wait upon the acknowledgment among authors of his power to do this. When it became the common opinion that he had the power, the use of it by St. Pius V was as generally recognized, although those canonists who denied such a power still maintained that the constitution had reference only to milder requirements under the Pauline privilege.[92]

Gregory XIII's Constitution *"Populis"* contained a provision of greatest importance in the study of the whole question, since a conclusion that the Pope was actually using such a power to dissolve marriage could only be avoided by very unlikely explanations. The Constitution *"Populis"* will be considered in the following chapter.

[89] *Op. cit.*, lib. IX, cap. IV, n. 22.

[90] *Op. cit.*, lib. X, cap. XV, n. 10.

[91] *De Synodo Dioecesana* (2 vols., Romae, 1767), lib. XIII, cap. XXI, n. 4.

[92] *Cf. infra*, Chap. V.

CHAPTER IV

GREGORY XIII'S CONSTITUTION *"POPULIS"*

THE institution of Negro slavery, both as it affected Africa as the source of supply, and the New World as the destination of the slaves, was the cause of a problem for the missionaries perhaps even more difficult than that of polygamy among the Indians.

The Portuguese began the modern slave trade in the first half of the fifteenth century shortly after their discoveries on the west coast of Africa. The first slaves were taken to Portugal and there sold readily as laborers. Thenceforward through the fifteenth century between seven and eight hundred slaves were supplied annually to Portugal and Southern Spain. [1]

In the New World in the islands of the Antilles and on the north coast of South America, the Spanish colonists needed labor for their plantations and mines. When the native Arawaks of the Antilles died by the hundreds of thousands under the work that was forced upon them,[2] Negro slaves were imported to take their places. The first contingent came in 1502 from southern Spain and Portugal as the original intention was to import only Christian Negroes. Soon, however, slaves were being brought in great numbers directly from Africa. In 1516 Charles V struck a bargain with a Flemish agent to supply 4,000 Negroes to Cuba, Hispaniola, Jamaica, and Porto Rico. This concession was eventually controlled by the Portuguese with British slavers also taking part. Together they transported thousands of slaves from Africa in the sixteenth century.[3]

The problem which the slave trade created for the missionary both in Africa and in the New World is easily seen. Within Africa the stronger tribes raided the weaker, took as many captives as possible regardless of sex, and delivered them to the foreign slave

[1] MacNutt, *Bartholomew de Las Casas*, p. xiv.

[2] Schmidlin, *Catholic Mission History*, p. 362.

[3] Harry H. Johnston, *The Negro in the New World* (London, 1910), pp. 36-40.

traders. Little if any attention was paid to family ties, and in the crowded and unhealthy slave ships the death rate was extremely high. Shipments to the New World often separated husbands and wives irretrievably. When the missionary finally converted the slave or a Negro who had escaped captivity in Africa but whose partner had been taken, it was often impossible to say what had happened to the convert's legitimate spouse. In view of these and similar difficulties in regard to captives in other parts of the missionary world, Gregory XIII issued the Constitution "*Populis,*" 25 January, 1585.

ARTICLE 1. TEXT OF THE CONSTITUTION "*Populis*"

Document VIII of the Code of Canon Law gives the text of the constitution with the exception of the closing two sentences. In the *Codicis Iuris Canonici Fontes* [4] the reference given for Document VIII of the Code is the 1907 edition of the *Collectanea S. Congregationis de Propaganda Fide.*[5] It is also to be found in the 1893 edition of the *Collectanea,*[6] and the complete text of the constitution appears in the *Appendix ad Bullarium S. Congregationis de Propaganda Fide.*[7] In transcribing the constitution from the *Collectanea* to Document VIII of the Code Cardinal Gasparri changed the word "*contracti*" to "*transacti*" in the phrase, "*et ad fidem etiam tempore transacti secundi matrimonii conversos fuisse.*" The authority given for the change [8] is the fact that Benedict XIV has the word "*transacti*" rather than "*contracti.*"[9]

[4] N. 155.

[5] N. 400, nota 1.

[6] N. 1307.

[7] I, 103, 104.

[8] *Cf.* Petrus Gasparri, *Tractatus Canonicus de Matrimonio* (editio nova ad mentem Codicis I. C., Romae; Typis Polyglottis Vaticanis, 1932), n. 1159, nota 1.

[9] *Cf. De Synodo Dioecesana,* lib. XIII, cap. XXI, n. 3. Gasparri's note gives the reference as lib. XIII, cap. XXI, n. 5, but the passage in question is to be found in n. 3. In this same place Benedict XIV gives Pontius, *De Matrimonio,* lib. VII, cap. XLVIII, n. 23, as the source from which he took the constitution.

In the first two editions of his *De Matrimonio* Gasparri had retained *"contracti."* [10] The change to *"transacti"* was made in the third edition. He considered it to be the better reading, for the passage could then be interpreted in a way to avoid the conclusion that Gregory XIII meant to dissolve a consummated marriage between Christians. Gasparri objected to Benedict XIV's interpretation of the constitution, as meaning that the second marriage would be valid even if the absent wife had been converted *before* the second marriage of her husband. He explained that the passage with *"transacti"* meant that if it were later discovered that the absent wife was converted *after* her husband, who was then a Christian, had married again, this latter marriage would nevertheless be valid.[11] This is the same effect that would result from a use of the Pauline privilege with a valid dispensation from the interpellations. At that time Gasparri seemingly did not see the distinction between dissolving a consummated marriage between infidels which had later become *ratum* through the baptism of both parties and not subsequently consummated (*consummatum et ratum*), and dissolving a marriage between Christians which was subsequently consummated (*ratum et consummatum*). In his latest edition, although he retained the

[10] *Tractatus Canonicus de Matrimonio* (Parisiis, 1891), n. 1101; (2. ed., Parisiis et Lugduni, 1900), n. 1101.

[11] "Nonnulli habent: *tempore contracti secundi matrimonii,* sed melius legitur: *tempore transacti secundi matrimonii.* Et sensus est matrimonium valere, etsi postea innotuerit conjugem priorem infidelem baptizatum fuisse *post* contractum a fideli secundum matrimonium. E contrario, Benedictus XIV, *De Syn.,* lib. XIII, cap. XXI, n. 5, ita verba Gregorii XIII intellexit ut matrimonium valeret, etsi postea innotuerit conjugem priorem infidelem baptizatum fuisse *ante* contractum a fideli secundum matrimonium; qui intellectus est manifeste erroneus, tum quia Gregorius XIII loquitur de conversione ad fidem *tempore transacti secundi matrimonii,* quod tempus, stricte loquendo, tum incipit, cum secundum matrimonium contractum fuit, tum quia secus sequeretur Gregorium XIII, momento secundi matrimonii, solvisse matrimonium etiam consummatum inter duos fideles." *Tractatus Canonicus de Matrimonio* (3. ed., Parisiis, 1904), n. 1349, nota 1.

D'Annibale interpreted the controverted clause thus: "... quamvis postea apparuerit priores conjuges *tempore secundi matrimonii conversos fuisse.*"—*Summula Theologiae Moralis* (3. ed., Romae, 1892), pars III, n. 470, nota 20.

word "*transacti,*" Gasparri recognized that the constitution of Gregory XIII meant that even if the absent wife had been converted *before* the second marriage of her husband, this latter marriage would be valid, and that this result did not follow from an application of the Pauline privilege but rather from the use of Papal power.[12]

The phrase "*alias tamen rite contrahere*" which appears in Pontius' and therefore also in Benedict XIV's copy of the constitution, is given in the *Collectanea S. C. P. F.* copy as "*alterius etiam ritus contrahere.*" In preparing Document VIII of the Code Gasparri did not change the phrase as he found it in the *Collectanea* to make it conform with Benedict's copy, as he did in regard to the word "*contracti.*"

An author writing in the *Archiv für Katholisches Kirchenrecht*[13] quoted the Constitution "*Populis*" in full, giving the *Appendix ad Bullarium S. C. P. F.* as the source. This copy has both "*alterius etiam ritus contrahere*" and "*contracti.*" The pre-Code authors who quote the constitution and use as their source either the *Appendix ad Bullarium,* the article in the *Archiv,* or the *Collectanea,* have the wording of the two questionable parts as here given. Pesch,[14] however, cites the *Archiv* article as his source, but nevertheless has "*alias tamen rite contrahere.*" The pre-Code authors who quote Pontius or Benedict XIV have "*alias tamen rite contrahere*" and "*transacti.*" Joyce[15] has "*alterius etiam ritus contrahere*" and "*contracti,*" as found in the *Appendix ad Bullarium,* but cites Document VIII of the Code as his source.

Woods[16] found the readings "*alias tamen rite contrahere*" and "*contracti*" in a copy of the constitution as it appeared in a book of

[12] *Tractatus Canonicus de Matrimonio* (ed. 1932), n. 1159.

[13] Karl Ludwig Braun, "Zur Lehre von der Natur des paulinischen Privilegiums. 1 Cor. VII," *AKKR,* LI (1884), 209-227, *cf.* pp. 218, 219 for the constitution.

[14] *Praelectiones Dogmaticae,* VII, n. 794.

[15] *Christian Marriage,* Appendix, p. 621.

[16] Francis F. Woods, *The Constitutions of Canon 1125 and Their Application in the United States* (Milwaukee: Bruce, 1935), pp. 60-63.

Jesuit faculties for 1585,[17] the year in which the constitution was issued. As Woods states, that copy has a particular claim to authenticity because of its date and because the Jesuits were authorized in the constitution itself to make official copies. Avendano[18] and Morelli,[19] quoting the *Compendium*,[20] agree with the copy as quoted by Woods. Both have *"alias tamen rite contrahere"* and Avendano has *"contracti."* Morelli summarizes parts of the constitution rather than giving it *verbatim,* and interprets the latter part of it thus:

> Et etiamsi priores conjuges infideles post contractum secundum matrimonium aut ad fidem convertantur, aut ostendant se juste impeditos fuisse ad declarandam suam voluntatem; nihilominus praedicta matrimonia rescindi non debere, sed valida et firma.

This is similar to Gasparri's earlier view that the Pope meant that if the absent wife was converted *after* the second marriage of her husband then that marriage would nevertheless be valid.

The alternate wording for the two points in question is indicated below in the text of the constitution as given in Document VIII of the Code together with the necessary complementary parts taken from the *Appendix ad Bullarium S. C. P. F.*[21]

[17] *Literae Apostolicae qubius Variae Facultates et Indulgentiae Religiosis Societatis Jesu et Aliis Christi Fidelibus in Indiarum Orientalium et Occidentalium, Provinciis Concenduntur.* Woods, *op. cit.,* p. 60, note 3.

[18] *Thesaurus Indicus,* tit. XII, cap. XIV, n. 398, p. 114.

[19] *Fasti Novi Orbis,* p. 298.

[20] Avendano: ". . . in *Compendio Indico,* verb. 'Matrimonium.'" Morelli: "Ita habet *Compendium Priv. Soc." Compendium Privilegiorum et Gratiarum quae Reliosis Societatis Jesu et aliis Christi Fidelibus in Utriusque Indiae regionibus commorantibus a Summis Pontificibus conceduntur* (Romae, 1937), is the revised edition of *Compendium Indicum* (Romae, 1580), according to Rayanna, "De Constitutione S. Pii Papae V, etc.," *Periodica,* XXVII (1938), p. 298.

[21] It should be noted that authors before the Code frequently referred to the constitution not as *"Populis"* or *"Populis ac nationibus,"* but as *"Quoniam saepe contingit"* which are the opening words of the part of it quoted by Pontius *(De Matrimonio,* lib. VII, cap. XLVIII, n. 23; lib. IX, cap. IV, n. 22), and after him by Benedict XIV and others.

GREGORIUS PAPA XIII

Ad futuram rei memoriam.[22]

Populis ac nationibus nuper ex gentilitatis errore ad fidem catholicam conversis expedit indulgere circa libertatem contrahendi matrimonia, ne homines, continentiae servandae minime assueti, propterea minus libenter in fide persistant, et alios illorum exemplo ab eius perceptione deterreant. Quoniam igitur saepe contingit multos utriusque sed praecipue virilis sexus infideles, post contracta gentili ritu matrimonia, ex Angola, Aethiopia, Brasilia, et aliis Indicis regionibus, ab hostibus captos, a patriis finibus et propriis coniugibus in remotissimas regiones exterminari, adeo ut tam ipsi, captivique qui in patria remanent, si postea ad fidem convertantur, coniuges infideles tam longo locorum intervallo disiunctos, an sine contumelia Creatoris secum cohabitare velint, ut par est, monere nequeant, vel quia interdum ad hostiles et barbaras provincias ne nuntiis quidem accessus pateat, vel quia ignorent prorsus in quas regiones fuerint transvecti, vel quia itineris longitudo magnam afferat difficultatem: idcirco Nos attendentes huiusmodi connubia inter infideles contracta, vera quidem, non tamen adeo rata censeri, ut necessitate suadente dissolvi non possint, talium gentium infirmitatem paterna pietate miserati, universis et singulis dictorum locorum Ordinariis et parochis, et presbyteris Societatis Iesu ad confessiones audiendas ab eiusdem Societatis Superioribus approbatis et ad dictas regiones pro tempore missis vel in illis admissis, plenam auctoritate Apostolica, tenore praesentium, concedimus facultatem dispensandi cum quibuscumque utriusque sexus Christifidelibus incolis dictarum regionum et serius ad fidem conversis que ante baptisma susceptum matrimonium contraxerunt, ut eorum quilibet, superstite coniuge infideli, et eius consensu minime requisito, aut responso non expectato, matrimonia cum quovis fideli alterius etiam ritus contrahere (*alias tamen rite contrahere*) et in facie Ecclesiae solemnizare, et in eis postea carnali copula consummatis quoad vixerint remanere licite valeant: dummodo constet etiam summarie et extraiudicialiter, coniugem, ut praefertur, absentem moneri legitime non posse, aut monitum intra tempus in eadem monitione praefixum

[22] *Appendix ad Bullarium S. C. P. F.*, I, 103.

suam voluntatem non significasse; quae quidem matrimonia, etiamsi postea innotuerit coniuges priores infideles suam voluntatem iuste impeditos declarare non potuisse, et ad fidem etiam tempore transacti (*contracti*) secundi matrimonii conversos fuisse, nihilominus rescindi nunquam debere, sed valida et firma, prolemque inde suscipiendam legitimam fore decernimus. Non obstantibus [23] Constitutionibus et ordinationibus Apostolicis ac conciliis etiam generalibus editis caeterisque contrariis quibuscumque. Et quia difficile esset praesentes literas ubicumque usus venerit, ostendi et publicari volumus, ut earum exemplis etiam impressis manu Notarii publici vel dictae societatis Secretarii subscriptis et personae in dignitate Ecclesiastica constitutae seu Praepositi generalis eiusdem societatis pro tempore existentis sigillo munitis eadem fides habeatur, quae eisdem praesentibus haberetur si essent exhibitae vel ostensae.

Datum Romae apud S. Petrum sub annulo Piscatoris die 25 Januarii 1585. Pontificatus nostri anno tertiodecimo. Jo. Bapt. Canobius.[24]

Article 2. Destination and Force of the Constitution

Although Angola and Ethiopia in Africa, and Brazil in the New World, were the countries specifically mentioned, the constitution had a much wider application through the phrase "*et aliis Indicis regionibus.*" According to Gregory XIII's definition of the terms "*India Orientalis*" and "*India Occidentalis,*" Angola and Ethiopia were included in the former, and Brazil in the latter.[25] It seems, then, that by the other countries of the Indies referred to, Gregory intended to include the two great fields to the east and to the west in which the missionaries of the sixteenth century were active. The Antilles, New Spain, and the countries of South America were the usual destination for the shiploads of captives taken from the west coast of Africa. Thus the missionaries of *India Occidentalis* would have considerable use for the new legislation, as would also the missionaries of Africa. The faculties granted by the constitution could also be used in other parts of *India Orientalis* when the conditions

[23] *Codex Iuris Canonici, Documentum VIII.*

[24] *Appendix ad Bullarium S. C. P. F.,* I, 103, 104.

[25] *Cf. supra,* p. 50, note 51.

required were present. This seems almost certainly to have been true, if not because of the phrase *"aliis Indicis regionibus,"* then because of the communication of privileges, faculties, and favors established previously between the two Indies by Gregory XIII.[26] It may be noted here that Benedict XIV[27] considered that the faculties granted could not be extended to regions other than those for which the constitution was given, whatever similarity of reason there may have been for such an extension. Benedict XIV gives no indication that by this statement he meant to exclude any of the regions that could be included under the term "Indies." His purpose was probably to emphasize that the constitution did not apply to European countries.

In the preamble the reasons which moved Gregory XIII to issue the constitution are stated. Infidels of both sexes, especially men, were being captured and taken to distant lands. As a consequence, when one or the other party was converted there was great difficulty in making the interpellations. Often it was not known where the other party was living; sometimes communication with a former partner was not possible because of enmity between the districts; at other times the great distance separating the two parties was an obstacle.

The dispositive part is prefaced with the statement that, although marriages contracted in infidelity are true marriages, they are not so absolutely binding that in case of necessity they cannot be dissolved.[28] The following are then mentioned as recipients of the special faculties of the constitution: Ordinaries and pastors in the countries mentioned, and Jesuit priests who are in those countries and are approved for confessions by the Superiors of the Society of Jesus.[29] These may dispense the native converts who were married while still pagan, so that without interpellating the absent party even though he or she be alive, or without waiting for a reply, the

[26] *Cf. supra,* p. 52.

[27] *De Synodo Dioecesana,* lib. XIII, cap. XXI, nn. 3, 6.

[28] *Cf.* St. Thomas, *IV Sent.,* dist. XXXIX, q. un., art. 5, ad 1, in which the principle is stated that the firmer bond of the perfect marriage of the baptized dissolves the less firm bond of infidel marriage if it is contrary to it.

[29] St. Pius V had declared the Society of Jesus to be a Mendicant Order. *Cf. supra,* pp. 51, 52. By reason of communication of privileges, therefore, all the Religious then working in the Indies who participated in the communication

convert may marry a Catholic even of another rite.[80] The condition under which the dispensation could be given validly was that there be certainty, from a summary and extrajudicial investigation, either

of Mendicant Order privileges also enjoyed the habitual faculty here given to the Jesuits. It seems that practically all Religious at that time participated in the communication of privileges. *Cf.* Bernardus a Vasto, *De Communicatione Privilegiorum Praesertim Inter Religiones* (Aquilae in Vestinis: Auctor, 1936), n. 28. With reference to pre-Code law Honestus Tatjer has the following: "Ordines mendicantes omnes habent ad invicem absolutam, perfectam et plenissimam communicationem privilegiorum, prout omnes Doctores de ea disserentes unanimiter docuerunt . . . de facto, fere omnes [Ordines non mendicantes] participationem obtinuerunt privilegiorum Mendicantium."—"De Communicatione privilegiorum inter Religiones," *Apollinaris,* V (1932), 460.

Avendano treated the question of communication of privileges among the Religious in the Indies. He held that members of the institutes participating in the communication could use the privileges granted to the Indies if these Religious came to the Indies with the permission of the king and Superiors *(Praelatorum).* His opinion was that among the institutes which were working in the Indies, that of B. John of God, and those of the Orders of Knights, did not participate in the communication; he does not list the institutes which did participate.—*Thesaurus Indicus,* tit. XII, cap. VII, n. 131-137. Clericatus considered those who could grant the dispensation provided for by the Constitution *"Populis"* to be the following: "Ordinarii, parochi, tum etiam confessarii regulares." *Cf.* Joannes Clericatus, *Decisiones de Matrimonio* (Augustae Vindelicorum, 1730), dec. XI, n. 29, p. 66.

80 If the words *"alterius etiam ritus contrahere,"* as given in Document VIII of the Code, were in the original constitution rather than *"alias tamen rite contrahere,"* the reference may have been to the Syrian Thomas Christians whom the sixteenth century missionaries found in India. The Portuguese missionaries had a certain amount of success in winning these people to unity with Rome, but the Nestorianism with which their prelates were infected was an element which made the status of the Thomas Christians questionable. *Cf. Catholic Encyclopedia,* XIV, p. 684. Gregory XIII showed interest in their case, hence it is possible that he had them in mind as the "faithful of another rite" whom the convert could marry, that is, if *"alterius etiam ritus contrahere"* was in the Constitution *"Populis"* as originally given. Gregory was very zealous in his efforts to preserve the faith of the Oriental Catholics and in every way to foster their best interests. (*Cf.* B. Ojetti, *De Curia Romana* (Romae, 1910), n. 69; Pastor, *History of the Popes,* XX, 486, 487.) If the alternate *"alias tamen rite contrahere"* was in the original Constitution *"Populis,"* its purpose would seem to be to emphasize that all other points of Church discipline in regard to the sacrament of matrimony must be observed.

that the absent party could not be interpellated, or that having been interpellated the party had failed to answer within the prescribed time. If possible, therefore, the requirements of the Pauline privilege were to be fulfilled; only if this were not possible could the dispensation be given. Its effect was the same as would have followed from a negative reply to interpellation.

The concessions of Paul III and St. Pius V had been made directly to the convert polygamous Indians. In the Constitution *"Populis"* Gregory XIII granted to Church authorities the faculty of dispensing, but attached a condition that required an investigation before the party could be allowed to enter the new marriage.

The singular importance in the history of the Papal power—the power, namely, to effect the dissolution of a marriage—which attaches to the Constitution *"Populis"* arises from Gregory XIII's affirmation of the validity of the marriages entered by virtue of the previous exercise of that power. He decreed that even if it should later become known that the absent party was hindered by a just cause from answering the interpellation, and at the time of the second marriage had already been converted to the Faith, nevertheless the second marriage was never to be rescinded, but was valid and firm, and the children born of it were legitimate. Only through the dissolution of the bond of the first marriage could this second valid marriage take place. Obviously this does not happen through the exercise of the Pauline privilege which can be invoked only if one party, but not both, have been baptized. The Pope here legislated that a dispensation may be given in the bond of marriage contracted and consummated in infidelity, even if it had later become *ratum* through the baptism of both parties. A dissolution is thus allowed in a marriage that is *consummatum et ratum*, which is quite different from *a ratum et consummatum* marriage. Only by a distortion of the sense of his words can the conclusion be avoided that the Pope was here using a power to dissolve consummated marriage between infidels who had later become Christians, and that this was not an application of the Pauline privilege.[31]

[31] *Cf.* T. Lincoln Bouscaren, "An Inquiry into the Practical Application of Canon 1125 Outside of Mission Territory," *Miscellanea Vermeersch* (2 vols., Romae: Pontificia Universita Gregoriana, 1935), I, 281-283.

Article 3. Interpretation of the Constitution by Authors of the Seventeenth and Eighteenth Centuries

The Papal power involved in the dissolution of a marriage which had been contracted and consummated in infidelity and had later become *ratum* had been considered in a case treated by Navarrus (1493-1586).[32] The wife of a Jew, Lazarus, had become a convert. She had not made use of the Pauline privilege when Lazarus married a second wife and had children by her. While the first wife was still living and had not yet married, both Lazarus and his second wife were also converted. In answer to the doubts proposed, Navarrus held that by the common law, without a dispensation from the Pope, Lazarus could not justly remain with the second wife, but if a Papal dispensation were given for a just cause he could do so. Navarrus also held that in the case, as reported to him, there was a just cause to grant the dispensation. Hence, it was Navarrus' opinion that outside the Pauline privilege the Pope had the power to dissolve the bond of a *consummatum et ratum* marriage.

Sanchez favored the opinion of Navarrus in regard to the Pope's power,[33] but he did not mention Gregory XIII's constitution.[34] His opinion in regard to interpellations when it is morally impossible to make them can be gathered from his treatment of the constitution of St. Pius V. In such circumstances the obstinacy of the absent party is to be presumed and there is then no need to make the interpellations. He does not say that a dispensation from the interpellations is required, but only that the obligation to make them ceases. If, however, there is a doubt about the obstinacy of the infidel, then the

[32] Martinus Azpilcueta (Navarrus), *Consilia seu Responsa, in Quinque Libros iuxta Numerum et Titulos Decretalium, Distributa* (2 vols., Venetiis, 1621), lib. III, *De conversione infidelium,* cons. III. For the Florentine Case involving similar circumstances and which came before the S. Cong. of the Council in 1726, *cf.* Joyce, *Christian Marriage,* pp. 479, 480.

[33] *De Matrimonio,* lib. II, disp. XVII, n. 2.

[34] There seems to be nothing in Sanchez' *De Matrimonio* to indicate that he knew of the constitution at the time he wrote. Augustinus Lehmkuhl (*Cath. Ency.,* XIII, 428), gives the following information on Sanchez' *De Matrimonio.* "The first edition is said to have appeared at Genoa in 1602, but this can have been only the first folio volume, for which permission to print was secured in 1599, as the two succeeding volumes contain both in their preface and the author's dedication the date 1603."

convert may not enter a new marriage without having previously made the interpellations.[35]

Pontius quoted Gregory XIII's constitution substantially complete, but failed to see that it contained anything more than was granted by St. Pius V. He interpreted both constitutions as granting dispensations from the interpellations. In both cases the Popes were only interpreting divine law and declaring that in the circumstances the unwillingness of the infidel to cohabit was verified. The dispensation from the interpellations was granted on that presumption, and there was no reason to hold that either Pope intended to dissolve the consummated marriage of infidels.[36] This view of the constitution, in harmony with the more common opinion on the absence of any power over these marriages except that given by the Pauline privilege, had considerable influence. Clericatus [37] held that the dispensation from the interpellations was necessary in missionary countries. Benedict XIV [38] quoted Verricellus as interpreting both St. Pius V and Gregory XIII to be truly dissolving the bond of these marriages, but he himself approved of Pontius and refused to retreat from the position that the Pope did not have the power to dissolve the bond. Avendano [39] considered that there was nothing granted by Gregory's privilege which had not previously been allowed, and that the missionaries, on the Pope's authority, were to grant the dispensation from the interpellations. A general realization of the full force of the grant had to wait upon a clearer understanding of the full powers of the Vicar of Christ.

Within fifty years of the date of the Constitution *"Populis"* Urban VIII (1623-1644) issued briefs dated 20 October, 1626, and 17 September, 1627, in which he used almost the same words as Gregory in regard to the dissolution of the marriages of infidels.[40]

[35] *Op. cit.,* lib. VII, disp. LXXIV, nn. 12-16.

[36] *De Matrimonio,* lib. IX, cap. IV, n. 22.

[37] *Decisiones de Matrimonio,* dec. XI, n. 29, p. 66.

[38] *De Synodo Dioecesana,* lib. XIII, cap. XXI, n. 5.

[39] *Thesaurus Indicus,* tit. XII, cap. XIV, nn. 403, 404.

[40] "Nos attendentes huiusmodi infidelium matrimonia non ita censeri, quin necessitate suadente dissolvi possunt, etc. . . ."—Techo, *Historia Provinciae Paraquariae,* lib. X, cap. XV, p. 278. Joannes de Lugo made reference to these briefs in his petition to Urban VIII for faculties for the missionaries to dispense polygamous converts.—*Cf. supra,* p. 54, nota 64.

CHAPTER V.

THE PAPAL AUTHORITY TO DISSOLVE MARRIAGE *"IN FAVOREM FIDEI"*

There can be nothing in the established and continued discipline of the infallible Church that is not in harmony with divine law. In the Papal constitutions that have just been considered it was seen that the bond of marriages contracted and consummated in infidelity was dissolved by the Popes in circumstances different from those to which the Pauline privilege could apply. Moreover, Gregory XIII provided that a marriage of this type could be dissolved even after it had become *ratum* through the baptism of both parties. Gregory's declaration was not made for some very extraordinary and isolated case, but for all the instances in certain large districts which would fulfill the conditions imposed. The Pope *de facto* dissolved the bond of those marriages, therefore he had the authority to dissolve them. Today, because of the use that various Popes have made of it, there can be no question about the existence of the Papal power, but it was a controversial matter at the time the constitutions were given.

Article 1. Statement of the Controversy

As has been seen, the use of Papal power to dissolve the bond of legitimate marriage *in favorem fidei* was something new to the sixteenth century. In the subsequent controversy those canonists who were opposed to admitting such a power in the Papal office offered other solutions to explain the grants of the constitutions. Some considered the Popes to be merely dispensing from the interpellations when, because of the absence of the valid wife in an unknown place, they could not be made. Others held that the Popes were tempering the canonical laws, so that when it could be presumed from the circumstances and extrajudicial knowledge that the infidel was unwilling to be converted or refused to cohabit peacefully there was no necessity to make the interpellations. Another view considered the Popes to be declarring that in certain circumstances the obligation of the divine law to retain the first wife ceased, even though she were willing to cohabit peacefully, and indeed even if she had been baptized.[1] In a word, according to these opinions, the Popes were doing nothing more than declaring that the Pauline privilege was applicable to those marriages contracted in infidelity which the constitutions considered. Other authors held, on the contrary, that the dissolution which was effected in at least some of the marriages for which the constitutions had been given could not be explained as a use of the Pauline privilege. The dissolution in these latter cases was therefore made by Papal dispensation.[2]

All authors agreed that after the baptism of one of the parties the Pope could dissolve a marriage contracted in infidelity which was not consummated either before or after the baptism of the one party. Likewise, all agreed that the Pope could *not* dissolve an infidel marriage if both parties remained unbaptized, or if both parties received baptism and thereafter consummated their marriage. The question at issue was whether or not, outside the Pauline privilege, the Pope had the power to dissolve a marriage contracted and consummated in infidelity if, after the baptism of only one party, the marriage remained simply disparate without a new consummation, or if it was again consummated. There was a further question concerning the power of the Pope to dissolve, *in favorem fidei,* a marriage contracted and consummated in infidelity, if after the reception of baptism by both the parties their marriage, having the status of a *matrimonium consummatum et ratum,* was not again consummated.[3]

Article 2. Differences Between the Marriage of Infidels and That of Christians

Natural law, together with the positive law of God expressed in both the Old and the New Testament,[4] determines that even the

[1] *Cf.* Henricus Ioannes Feije, *De Impedimentis et Dispensationibus Matrimonialibus* (2. ed., Lovanii, 1874), nn. 489, 494, 602.

[2] *Cf.* Wernz, *Ius Decretalium,* IV, n. 705.

[3] *Cf.* Cappello, *De Sacramentis,* III, nn. 789-792.

[4] Gen. ii: 23, 24; Matt. v: 31, 32; Matt. xix: 3-9; Mark x: 2-12; Luke xvi: 18; 1 Cor. vii: 10, 11; *cf.* exegesis of texts by William R. O'Connor, "The Indissolubility of a Ratified Consummated Marriage," *ETL,* XIII (1936), 696-701.

legitimate marriage of infidels is intrinsically indissoluble.[5] The especial reason for its indissolubility is its relation to the primary end of marriage, namely, to beget children and to educate and conduct them to their perfect state. In these legitimate marriages, once the matrimonial bond exists through the mutual consent of a man and a woman neither of whom is hindered by divine law from giving consent, consummation adds only a certain perfection to the quality of indissolubility already proper to the bond. This added perfection has its basis in the change from a remote to a proximate relation to the *bonum prolis* which is the principal norm according to which the natural indissolubility is measured.[6]

Christ raised to the dignity of a sacrament the contract arising from the exchange of matrimonial consent between two baptized persons.[7] Sacramental marriage, as a contract, is *per se* indissoluble, but it is more than a contract. It is a title to grace, and it is a symbol of the union of Christ with the human soul in the state of grace and of His indissoluble union with the Church.[8] Before it is consummated, Christian marriage signifies the union of Christ with the human soul through grace. But that union can be broken, for the soul can lose the state of grace through the commission of mortal sin. Therefore the symbolism that exists between non-consummated marriage and the union of Christ with the soul would not suffer if such merely *ratum* marriage, although it is a sacrament, could be dissolved in some circumstances. In fact, in the twelfth century Alexander III (1159-1181) in two decretals[9] stated that the entrance into religion of one party to a non-consummated Christian marriage dissolved the matrimonial bond so that the other party was free to enter another marriage. In the second of these decretals, "*Ex publico*," he explained that our Lord's teaching that it is not lawful for a man to put away his wife save for the cause

[5] *Cf.* Sanchez, *De Matrimonio,* lib. II, disp. XIII, n. 7.

[6] Ludovicus Billot, *De Ecclesiae Sacramentis Commentarius in Tertiam Partem S. Thomae* (6. ed., 2 vols., Romae, 1922), II, 413, 414.

[7] Canon 1012, § 1.

[8] Eph. v: 29-32; St. Thomas, *Suppl.,* Q. LXI, art. II, ad 1; c. 5, X, *de bigamis non ordinandis,* I, 21.

[9] Cc. 2, 7, X, *de conversione coniugatorum,* III, 32.

of fornication is to be understood of those whose marriages have been consummated. Although it is true that this principle was not immediately accepted in its full import,[10] from the time of Martin V in the fifteenth century the Holy See granted dispensations in *ratum non consummatum marriages.*[11]

The principle was common before the sixteenth century that the bond of marriage among infidels is weaker than that of the sacramental marriage of Christians.[12] When it was determined that the Pope had the power to dissolve the latter if the marriage had not been consummated, there was an *a fortiori* argument for his power to dissolve the marriages contracted between infidels when one of them later became a convert. This would be true even though the infidel marriage had been consummated. Gregory XIII mentioned the relative weakness of infidel marriages in the preamble to his concession.

Although the question of the extrinsic indissolubility of consummated Christian marriage is not involved in the present subject, a few points on it will be mentioned to avoid a lacuna which otherwise would appear. Merely *ratum* marriage may be dissolved; therefore the sacrament alone is not the basis of extrinsic indissolubility.[13] Nor can the basis be consummation alone since the consummated non-ratum or legitimate marriage is dissoluble. The two elements,

[10] Innocent III (1198-1216) followed Alexander III's precedent of allowing a dissolution of the bond of non-consummated sacramental marriage in view of the religious profession of one party, but he seemed to do it reluctantly. Moreover, he gave as his opinion that marriage once contracted between legitimate persons *per verba de praesenti* could not be dissolved except there be a divine revelation to that effect. C. 14, X, *de conversione coniugatorum,* III, 32.

[11] Joannes Perrone, *De Matrimonio Christiano* (3 vols., Romae, 1858), lib. III, cap. VI, art. IV, § I. *Cf.* for the opinions of theologians and canonists: Cardinal Cajetan, *Opuscula Omnia D. Thomae de Vio in Tres Distincta Tomos* (in 1 vol., Lugdini, 1585), tract. XXVIII, *De Matrimonio,* pp. 122-124; Benedict XIV, *Quaestiones Canonicae,* q. 479, in *Opera Benedicti XIV* (Prati, 1845), XIII, 166.

[12] St. Thomas, *IV Sent.,* dist. XXXIX, q. un., art. 5, ad 1.

[13] However, *cf.* canon 1013, § 2: "Essentiales matrimonii proprietates sunt unitas ac indissolubilitas, *quae in matrimonio christiano peculiarem obtinent firmitatem ratione sacramenti.*"

sacramentalitas et consummatio, must be present to effect the absolute indissolubility of marriage.[14]

Christian marriage after it has been consummated is a symbol of the inseparable union of Christ with the Church [15] and theologians have stressed the symbolism in treating of the basis for the absolute indissolubility of such a marriage. It has been pointed out,[16] however, as an objection to symbolism as its basis that the indissolubility must be proved before the symbolism can be seen. The symbolism is apart from the indissolubility which precedes it by a priority of nature. From Scripture it is clear that all marriages are intrinsically indissoluble by divine law, and that Christ held up as a norm the ideal of primitive marriage in which there was no divorce even by extrinsic authority. Nowhere, however, does there appear a command in the strict sense which could make *ratum et consummatum* marriages and no others extrinsically indissoluble. Viewed in this light the argument for the Power of the Keys, used in this instance for binding rather than for loosing, seems more conclusive than any other in its potentiality to supply the real and proper basis for the indissolubility of a Christian consummated marriage. In view of the symbolism that exists between consummated Christian marriage and the union of Christ with the Church, and mindful of our Lord's wish that Christian marriage be like primitive marriage in its stability, the Church from the beginning and without any exceptions has exercised its divine power of binding and loosing to declare *ratum et consummatum* marriage absolutely indissoluble.[17]

Article 3. Opinions on the Nature of the Constitutions

The Pauline privilege is the one dispensation explicitly granted by the common law as promulgated in the New Testament by which the bond of marriage contracted and consummated between infidels may be dissolved. When the constitutions of Paul III, St. Pius V,

[14] Cappello, *De Sacramentis,* III, n. 755.

[15] St. Thomas, *Suppl.,* Q. LXI, art. II, ad 1: *cf.* Cappello, *ibid.,* for other citations.

[16] *Cf.* O'Connor, "The Indissolubility of a Ratified, Consummated Marriage," *ETL,* XIII (1936), 695.

[17] O'Connor, *op. cit.,* pp. 718-722.

and Gregory XIII began to be studied by theologians and canonists it was to be expected that comparisons with the Pauline privilege would be made.

At the opening of the seventeenth century the opinion that the Pope had power to dissolve infidel marriage *in favorem fidei* was only just beginning to gain adherents. Pontius was utterly opposed to the opinion. He held [18] that the indissolubility of marriage came entirely from the natural law and that the symbolism of Christian marriage gave no added firmness to it. Infidel marriage once consummated was as indissoluble as consummated Christian marriage in so far as any Papal power was concerned.[19] As was seen above, Pontius explained the grants of the constitutions of St. Pius V and Gregory XIII as coming within the scope of the Pauline privilege, that is, they were nothing more than dispensations from the interpellations.

Pontius' view was approved by Cardinal Lambertini (later Pope Benedict XIV). The authority and arguments of this great canonist no doubt did much to recommend the opinion to the later writers who adopted it with some modifications. Benedict XIV understood the grants as "tempering the practice of rigorous interpellation" by allowing dispensations from the interpellations.[20] Benedict used the phrase especially in reference to the constitution of Gregory XIII and his opinion was the same in regard to that of St. Pius V.[21]

In the light of present day understanding of the Pope's power to dissolve legitimate marriage *in favorem fidei,* the effort made to bring under the Pauline privilege all the cases comprehended by the constitutions seems forced and without justification. A comparison of the grants with the fundamental requirements of the Pauline privilege shows irreconcilable differences.

The constitution of St. Pius V made no reference to interpellations or to dispensations from them. The Pope simply decreed that the convert Indian who had been a polygamist could retain as his

[18] *De Matrimonio,* lib. I, cap. XIII.

[19] *Op. cit.,* lib. IX, cap. II, nn. 11, 12.

[20] *Quaestiones Canonicae,* q. 546, n. 38, in *Opera Benedicti XIV,* XIII, 253.

[21] *De Synodo Dioecesana,* lib. XIII, cap. XXI, nn. 4-6.

valid wife that one who would be baptized with him. No requirement was made that it be impossible to find or to know the first and legitimate wife. In some instances there would be that difficulty, but in the great variety of matrimonial customs among the polygamous Indians there were circumstances in which the first wife could easily be found. It could happen that the first wife would be willing to cohabit peacefully with her convert husband and thus eliminate the *discessus* required for the use of the Pauline privilege, yet St. Pius V allowed the convert validly to marry another.

If the Popes were only intending to dispense from the necessity of doing that which could not possibly be done, then their use of the fortifying clauses, "*motu proprio et ex certa scientia Nostra, ac Apostolicae potestatis plenitudine*" and "*sublata . . . cuilibet . . . aliter iudicandi atque interpretandi facultate,*" as employed in the Constitution "*Romani Pontificis,*" and "*plenam auctoritate Apostolica, tenore praesentium, concedimus facultatem dispensandi . . .* " as used in the Constitution "*Populis,*" was indeed superfluous.[22] It can scarcely be presumed that the Popes, when using such terms, were only legislating that when it was impossible to make the interpellations they need not be made. The objective was one of greater significance.

In the Constitution "*Populis,*" Gregory XIII required that the normal procedure for the use of the Pauline privilege be followed when circumstances were such that the interpellations could be made. In the other cases he granted the right to dispense converts whose absent wives could not be interpellated, with the effect that they might be free to enter second marriages. The object and force of the dispensation is shown in the provision affirming the validity of the new marriage even if it should later be discovered that the absent first wife had already been baptized when her husband married again. This provision sets up a case that is not comprehended by the Pauline privilege, for that privilege has never been considered to be applicable when both parties to the original marriage are baptized. St. Paul's words were, "*Si infidelis discedit, discedat.*" To

[22] *Cf.* Gury-Ballerini, *Compendium Theologiae Moralis,* II, 522, 535; Cappello, *De Sacramentis,* Vol. III *De Matrimonio* (4. ed., Taurinorum Augustae-Romae: Marietti, 1939), n. 787.

hold that the *discessus* of a baptized party is also a cause under the privilege for dissolving the marriage bond is to include *fidelis* with *infidelis,* which would be extending the privilege beyond its original limits.

If Christ has provided no other means by which the bond of consummated legitimate marriage may be dissolved except the Pauline privilege immediately granted by Him and promulgated by St. Paul, as some authors insisted,[23] then the Popes in their constitutions were giving only a declarative interpretation of the privilege. An authentic extensive interpretation would in reality have been impossible, for the Pope was unable then, as he is unable now, to extend or restrict divine law by his interpretation. The privilege would need to be strictly interpreted.[24] If the other opinion about the privilege be held, namely, that it is of mediate divine origin, both instituted and promulgated by St. Paul in virtue of his participation in apostolic authority, any extension of it must require the same apostolic authority and the extended privilege is no longer the Pauline, but a new law applying to the cases outside the ambit of the former privilege.

Further, if the Popes were intending to give an authentic interpretation of the Pauline privilege, that interpretation would be valid everywhere. It would be as universal as the privilege itself. But they limited their grants to apply only to the people of particular places. They could not, then, have considered themselves to be merely interpreting the Pauline privilege.

The only explanation that is adequate for all cases covered by the three constitutions is that, at least in so far as the privileges of the constitutions applied to marriages which could not come within the recognized limits of the Pauline privilege, new laws were established granting or permitting a dispensation in the bond of marriage contracted in infidelity and consummated before, but not after, the baptism of both parties. There would, of course, be no place for such a dispensation before at least one of the parties became a subject of the Church through baptism.

[23] *Cf.* Wernz, *Ius Decretalium,* IV, n. 705; Wernz-Vidal, *Ius Canonicum,* V, n. 635.

[24] *Cf.* Wernz, *Ius Decretalium,* IV, n. 702, nota 62.

Article 4. Basis of the Papal Power

The controverted question of the immediate origin of the Pauline privilege enters into any inquiry concerning the basis for the dissolution in favor of the Faith of marriage contracted by the unbaptized. The more common opinion has been that Christ immediately instituted the privilege and St. Paul only promulgated it.[25]

St. Paul's introductory sentence, "For the rest I speak, not the Lord," strongly favors the opposite opinion that the privilege is only of mediate divine origin. There is an exegesis, however, which refers the sentence not to the verses which follow, in which the privilege is contained, but as a conclusion to verses eight to eleven which precede.[26] In verses ten and eleven St. Paul had given instructions to the married which he said, " . . . not I but the Lord commandeth." In verses eight and nine he had given advice to the widows and the unmarried. "For the rest I speak, not the Lord," is referred by this exegesis to verses eight and nine and the sense is that the commandment to the married is imposed by the Lord, not by St. Paul, but that it is St. Paul and not the Lord who speaks to the widows and the unmarried. With the passage thus understood verse fifteen which contains the privilege for converts would not be controlled by the sentence, "For the rest I speak, not the Lord."

[25] Sanchez, *De Matrimonio,* lib. VII, disp. LXXIV, n. 4; Benedict XIV, *De Synodo Dioecesana,* lib. VI, cap. IV, n. 3; Perrone, *De Matrimonio Christiano,* lib. II, sect. I, cap. VII, art. I; Petro Giovine, *Consultationes Canonicae De Dispensationibus Matrimonialibus* (2 vols., Neapoli, 1863), I, 508, cons. XVIII, § CCLXXI, n. 2; Henricus Feije, *De Impedimentis et Dispensationibus Matrimonialibus* (3. ed., Lovanii, 1885), n. 471; Pesch, *Praelectiones Dogmaticae,* VII, n. 790; H. Noldin, *De Matrimonio* (5. ed., Oeniponte, 1904), n. 30; Wernz, *Ius Decretalium,* IV, n. 702; Ludovicus Billot, *De Ecclesiae Sacramentis Commentarius in Tertiam Partem S. Thomae* (6. ed., 2 vols., Romae, 1922), II, 429; Th. M. Vlaming, *Praelectiones Iuris Matrimonii* (3. ed., 2 vols., Bussum in Hollandia: Sumptibus Societatis Editricis Anonymae, 1919-1921), II, n. 718; Wernz-Vidal, *Ius Canonicum,* V, n. 631, nota 56; *Payen, De Matrimonio,* II, n. 2210; G. Vromant, *Ius Missionariorum,* V, *De Matrimonio* (Louvain: Museum Lessianum, 1931), n. 272; Gabrielus Huarte, *Tractatus de Ordine et Matrimonio* (3. ed., Romae: Aedes Universitatis Gregorianae, 1931), n. 335.

[26] Cornelius A. Lapide, *Commentaria in Scripturam Sacram* (ed. Parisiis, 1866), XVIII, 306; *cf.* Dominicus Palmieri, *Tractatus de Matrimonio Christiano* (Romae, 1880), p. 216; Billot, *op. cit.,* II, 427, 428.

Two instructions of the Holy Office have had considerable influence in favor of the opinion for the immediate divine origin. The statements are clear that the privilege was granted by Christ and promulgated by St. Paul, thus: "... *privilegio in favorem fidei a Christo Domino concesso et a Paulo Apostolo promulgato*";[27] "... *virtute privilegii in favorem fidei a Christo Domino concessi, et per Apostolum Paulum promulgati.*"[28] The fact that in its instructions the Holy Office does not treat *ex professo* of the origin of the privilege[29] does not entirely destroy the force of the statements.[30]

Authors who hold, or are inclined toward, the opinion that the Pauline privilege is only *mediately* divine, that is, that St. Paul in virtue of his apostolic power both instituted and promulgated the privilege,[31] consider that the Apostle's sentence, "For the rest I speak, not the Lord," is an introduction to what follows rather than a conclusion to what went before, and that it refers to the authority by which St. Paul gives both the instruction in the following verses twelve to fourteen and the privilege in verse fifteen.[32]

The obvious sense of the words should be followed, say these authors, since it does not exclude the necessary divine basis for the privilege. The opinion is considered to be more in harmony with Christ's plan of giving a broad general spiritual authority to the Church, and leaving to it the details of sacramental discipline.

[27] S. C. S. Offic., instr. (pro Vic. Ap. ad Gallas), 20 Jun., 1866, "Prima dubiorum classis"—*Fontes,* n. 994.

[28] S. C. S. Offic., instr. (Natal), 11 Jul., 1866, ad 8—*Fontes,* n. 996.

[29] Petrus Gasparri, *Tractatus Canonicus de Matrimonio* (3. ed., Parisiis, 1904), II, n. 1329.

[30] *Cf.* Wernz, *Ius Decretalium,* IV, n. 702, nota 60.

[31] Cornely, *Commentarius in Primam Epistolam ad Cor.,* p. 181; Augustinus Lehmkuhl, *Theologia Moralis* (5. ed., Friburgi Brisgoviae 1888), II, n. 709; A. Vermeersch, *De Casu Apostoli* (Brugis, 1911), n. 2; A. De Smet, *Tractatus Theologico-Canonicus De Sponsalibus et Matrimonio* (4. ed., Brugis: Beyaert, 1937), n. 341; Gasparri, *Tractatus Canonicus de Matrimonio* (ed. nova ad mentem Codicis I. C., Romae: Typis Polyglottis Vaticanis, 1932), II, n. 1166; Cappello, *De Sacramentis,* III, n. 767; Woods, *The Constitutions of Canon 1125,* p. 27; Gregory, *The Pauline Privilege,* p. 49; Louis Chaussegros de Léry, *Le Privilège de la Foi* (Montreal: Collection des Studia, 1938), n. 126.

[32] Lehmkuhl, *ibid.*

Thus, the only positive laws which He gave in the New Testament were the necessary precepts of faith and the sacraments.[33]

If the privilege was instituted only mediately by Christ through St. Paul there is no need to postulate any special and immediate intervention of Christ in the matter of the dissolution of marriage: St. Paul would have made use of the apostolic authority granted to St. Peter in the Power of the Keys and shared by the other Apostles and St. Paul. The argument urges the convenience of basing in the same apostolic authority both the power used by St. Paul and that used by the Popes in dissolving marriage.[34] "If . . . the Church has, of itself, more than sufficient power, there is no apparent reason for the intervention of immediately divine power in the case of the Apostle." [35]

The controversy is of long standing and each opinion is supported by solid arguments proposed by authors of note. As has been seen, the single clue given by St. Paul to the correct answer is open to interpretations which will favor either one or the other opinion. Perhaps no one after apostolic times could satisfactorily answer the question of fact involved. Moreover, in itself, the controversy is not of great moment since the privilege, from the nature of the matter must be of at least mediate divine origin. There will be no difference in the use of the privilege as such, whether it be considered that St. Paul both instituted and promulgated it by virtue of his apostolic authority, or that he only promulgated that which Christ instituted.[36]

The Pauline privilege is a specific entity within the generic and more comprehensive *privilegium fidei* which also includes, for example, those cases comprehended by Gregory XIII's grant in which, in certain circumstances, a dispensation in the bond of marriage is allowed although both parties were baptized after the marriage was contracted. Stated briefly, the object of an inquiry into the basis for dissolution in favor of the Faith of marriages either certainly or

[33] Vermeersch, *ibid.*

[34] Cappello, *ibid.*; Woods, *ibid.*; Gregory, *ibid.*

[35] De Smet, *Betrothment and Marriage,* n. 341; *cf.* De Smet, *De Spons. et Matr.*, n. 341.

[36] Payen, *De Matrimonio,* II, n. 2210.

doubtfully contracted by the unbaptized, is the answer to the question: What is the source of power used for the *privilegium fidei?* To accept the hypothesis of mediate divine origin for the Pauline privilege and found it upon the divinely granted apostolic authority would not be to regard it as synonymous with the *privilegium fidei.* For there would be no difficulty in holding the other opinion that the Pauline privilege was immediately granted by Christ, and then finding in another divine grant the source of the power used for cases which are within the ambit of the *privilegium fidei* and yet do not fulfill the conditions necessary for the use of the Pauline privilege. These propositions are not mutually exclusive and Sanchez in fact embraced both.[87] The opinion, however, for the mediate divine origin, that is, that St. Paul both instituted and promulgated the privilege, although less generally held, seems to have the stronger arguments in its favor and will be followed here.

The Papal power of dispensing in the bond of a *ratum non-consummatum* marriage has long been unquestioned. The convincing proof that the power of dispensing in the bond of a *legitimum consummatum* marriage is proper to the Pope rests upon the *de facto* use which has been made of it,[88] not only in the three constitutions here being considered, but in other instances also. The well-known Helena case [89] is an example. The case involved C. G. M., an unbaptized man, and F. E. G., a woman baptized in the Anglican sect. In September, 1919, and therefore at a time when disparity of cult did not hinder a valid marriage between an infidel and a baptized non-Catholic, C. G. M. married F. E. G. before an Anglican minister. Later C. G. M. obtained a civil divorce from the woman and she thereafter entered another union. When C. G. M. desired to become a Catholic and to marry a Catholic woman Pius XI granted the petition *"pro gratia dissolutionis vinculi naturalis primi matrimonii contracti a C. G. M. cum F. E. G. in favorem fidei."* That this was not just an isolated case in which extraordinary circumstances could explain the dissolution is evident from the *"Normae"*

[87] *De Matrimonio,* lib. II, disp. XVII, n. 2; lib. VII, disp. LXXIV, n. 4.

[88] De Smet, *De Spons. et Matr.,* nn. 333, 355; Cappello, *De Sacramentis,* III, n. 791.

[89] *Cf. AER,* LXXII (1925), 188; Bouscaren, *Canon Law Digest,* I, 552, 553.

issued by the Sacred Congregation of the Holy Office, 1 May, 1934, for conducting the process of investigation in such cases, and from other similar dissolutions that have been granted.[40]

The existence of the Papal power to dissolve legitimate marriage is also shown in the provision of canon 1127. Through application of the canon, *in favorem fidei* a marriage contracted in infidelity may be considered null if its validity remains doubtful after due inquiry. It is clear that doubt, which is in the subjective order, even though grave and positive, does not change the objective order, that is, it does not make a doubtful marriage *de facto* null, yet the Church pronounces it such in favor of a convert.[41] It can no longer be questioned that the Popes have used the power. The immediate problem is to see wherein the power was granted.

The indissolubility of the bond of marriage *in genere* has its basis in the precepts of the natural law, for the indissoluble marriage bond best serves the primary end of marriage which is the procreation and education of children.[42] It is divine law that all marriages are intrinsically indissoluble, for whether they be unbaptized or Christian the parties to a valid marriage cannot on their own authority dissolve the bond of their union. But all marriages are not extrinsically indissoluble. Among the precepts of natural law are some that are absolute and bind every human being, for example, the precept that God must be worshiped. There can be no possible circumstances which would release a person from the obligation of obeying these absolute precepts. But there are other precepts of the natural law which oblige only after some act or determination on the part of the individual. The obligation to observe the indissolubility of the matrimonial contract is among these, as also the obligation to keep a vow. These *praecepta conditionata* are found antecedently in the natural law, but they do not bind until the individual voluntarily places the act which begets the obligation.

[40] *Cf.* v.g., Bouscaren, *Canon Law Digest,* II, 157; *AKKR,* CVII (1927), 183.

[41] *Cf.* G. Vromant, "De Applicatione Canonis 1127," *Ius Pontificium,* XII (1932), 114, 115, vel *De Matrimonio* (2. ed.), n. 368; Payen, *De Matrimonio,* II, n. 2448; Wernz, *Ius Decretalium,* IV, n. 702, nota 66.

[42] *Cf.* Gasparri, *Tractatus Canonicus de Matrimonio* (ed. 1932), II, n. 1126.

Man cannot always foresee the circumstances that may occur in which it would be for his greater good that the obligations he thus takes upon himself should cease to bind, hence it is expedient that it be within the jurisdiction of a superior sometimes to grant dispensations in these matters. It is to be noted, however, that a dispensation in any matter which takes its obligations from the natural law is not properly a dispensation, that is, it is not a relaxation of the law itself. The natural law, comprehending in its precepts all that is consonant with human nature, cannot be changed even by divine power except human nature first be changed.[43] The effect of the dispensation here is to loose from the obligation that followed upon the free exchange of marriage consent. The act, once placed, cannot be recalled, but God can release man from the obligation He has attached to the act. In effecting the release He employs the Church acting "*potestate vicaria, nomine Dei.*"[44] Cicognani states the matter thus: "In such cases (vows, oaths, ratified unconsummated marriages) the Roman pontiff has power to dispense and he exercises this power with respect to the action of the human will rather than to the law, by freeing a person, for a just cause, from the obligation of a promise freely made, and he does this in virtue of a power divinely delegated to him."[45]

Christ endowed the Church with a broad jurisdiction which it exercises either as principal, or as instrumental or ministerial cause. By the will of its Founder the Church is a juridically perfect and supreme society[46] and therefore in its own right and as principal cause it exercises the functions necessary for its government. In its canon law, for example, and in the jurisdiction which it exercises in ecclesiastical courts, the Church acts as principal cause. But in addition to the powers flowing from its nature as a society the Church has been granted the exercise, in God's Name, of unique

[43] *Cf.* Suarez, *De Legibus*, lib. II, cap. XIV, n. 11; lib. II, cap. XV, nn. 16-19, 26-28.

[44] *Cf.* Franz Triebs, *Praktisches Handbuch des geltenden kanonischen Eherechts in Vergleichung mit dem deutschen staatlichen Eherecht* (Breslau: Ostdeutsche Verlagsanstalt, 1933), pp. 213, 214.

[45] *Canon Law*, p. 589, *cf.* also, p. 836.

[46] *Cf.* Alaphridus Ottaviani, *Institutiones Iuris Publici Ecclesiastici* (2. ed., 2 vols., Romae: Typis Polyglottis Vaticanis, 1936), I, 167 sq.

powers. They were given in the first place to St. Peter: "And I will give to thee the keys of the kingdom of heaven. And whatsoever thou shalt bind upon earth, it shall be bound also in heaven. And whatsoever thou shalt loose on earth, it shall be loosed also in heaven," [47] and then to all the Apostles: "Amen I say to you, whatsoever you shall bind upon earth, shall be bound also in heaven; and whatsoever you shall loose upon earth, shall be loosed also in heaven." [48] In the internal forum where it exercises the Power of the Keys in forgiving the offenses of man against the laws of God the Church acts as instrumental or ministerial cause. Moreover it understands that in the wide power of loosing which is unrestricted—"Whatever you shall loose"—granted to it in the person of St. Peter and his successors, there is included the ministerial power of dispensing in certain of those matters which derive their obligation from the natural law after the human act has been placed. Thus the Church may dispense in vows made to God. The dissolution of marriage granted by the Papal constitutions is to be attributed to the use of the same ministerial power. In the plenitude of their apostolic authority as Vicars of Christ, the Popes grant dispensations from the bond of marriages contracted in infidelity even though the marriages have been consummated.[49] St. Paul as a participant in the apostolic authority made use of it, according to the opinion defending the mediate divine origin position, in granting the privilege which takes its name from him.[50]

The Popes dispensing as instrumental or ministerial cause in a matter which was of obligation by divine law needed a just cause in order to act with valid effect.[51] The Pauline privilege had already demonstrated that the natural bond of marriage could be loosed in view of a good so excellent as that of conversion to the Faith, or perseverance in it, if the continuance of that bond after conver-

[47] Matt. xvi: 19.

[48] Matt. xviii: 18.

[49] Billot, *De Sacramentis,* II, 434, 435; Vromant, *De Matrimonio,* n. 271.

[50] Vermeersch, *De Casu Apostoli,* n. 2; Gasparri, *Tractatus Canonicus de Matrimonio* (ed. 1932), II, n. 1166; *cf.* O'Connor, "The Indissolubility of a Ratified Consummated Marriage," *ETL,* XIII (1936), 716.

[51] *Cf.* Cappello, *De Sacramentis,* III, n. 762.

sion would necessitate the heavy burden of perfect chastity. The same purpose as that for which St. Paul used his participation in the apostolic authority to grant the Pauline privilege could be considered also as just cause for the Popes to exercise their authority to the same effect.

To this same instrumental or ministerial power, then, is to be attributed the dispensation granted by Gregory XIII in marriage that had become *ratum* by the baptism of both parties and not thereafter consumated, as also the dispensations granted by Paul III and St. Pius V.[52]

[52] Billot, *op. cit.*, II, 439; *cf.* Suarez, *op. cit.*, lib. II, cap. XIV, n. 20; Vlaming, *Praelect. Iuris Mat.*, II, nn. 731, 732; G. Arendt, "Quomodo in favorem fidei solvatur a S. Pontifice matrimonium in infidelitate contractum, Nota theologico-canonica circa canonem 1127," *ETL*, I (1924), 174-184. See especially pp. 180 and 184 of this article in *ETL*.

CHAPTER VI

NECESSITY OF INTERPELLATIONS IN THE PAULINE PRIVILEGE

APOSTOLIC FACULTIES RELATED TO THE CONSTITUTIONS

THE similarity between the object of the privileges of the constitutions and that of the Pauline privilege, namely, the dissolution of a marriage bond in favor of a convert to the faith, makes it of interest to inquire further into the Pauline privilege especially in regard to the necessity of the interpellations in its use. Moreover, as there is a relation between the privileges of the constitutions and certain of the Apostolic faculties granted through the Congregation for the Propagation of the Faith, these latter also should be given some attention. The present chapter therefore considers the necessity of interpellations in the use of the Pauline privilege, and the relevant Apostolic faculties.

I. The Necessity of Interpellations in the Pauline Privilege

In the use of the Pauline privilege the separation of the infidel party—the *discessus*—is a fundamental condition and cannot be presumed but must be demonstrated.[1] The normal way in which the demonstration will be made is by the formal declaration of the infidel party in answer to the interpellations, first as to whether or not he desires to be converted and receive baptism, or at least whether he will cohabit with his convert spouse peaceably and without insult to the Creator.

ARTICLE 1. NECESSITY FOR LICIT USE

The necessity, at least in ecclesiastical law, of making both interpellations for the *licit* use of the privilege is unquestioned. Canon

[1] Vermeersch, *De Casu Apostoli*, n. 51.

1121, § 2, states that they must always be made unless the Holy See shall have declared otherwise. With reference to the ecclesiastical law, it is certain from many decrees and responses that however great the distance or the difficulty of making the necessary journey, whatever the danger involved, or whatever persuasion or certainty may exist that it will be useless to make the interpellations, their omission will not be licit without the declaration of the Holy See.[2]

Something should be said here about the terminology used to designate a permitted omission of the interpellations. Previous to the Code the common expression used was that of *dispensing* from them. Gregory XIII in his Constitution *"Populis"* has *"concedimus facultatem dispensandi"* which, from what follows, clearly refers to interpellations: faculties granted through the Holy Office [3] also used the term *"dispensandi super interpellatione"*: it was the normal expression among the authors. D'Annibale, however,[4] held that in regard to interpellations the Roman Pontiff *"improprie dispensare dicitur."*

The legislator in the Code in canons 1121-1123 refrains from using terminology indicating a dispensation and provides that the interpellations may be omitted on the *declaration* of the Holy See.

[2] *Cf.* Payen, *De Matrimonio,* II, n. 2351; Vromant, *De Matrimonio,* n. 327; De Smet, *De Spons. et Matr.*, n. 351; De Becker, *Praelectiones Can. De Matr.*, p. 245; Vermeersch-Creusen, *Epitome,* II, n. 434.

But *cf.* Vermeersch, *De Casu Apostoli,* n. 53, to the contrary in a case in which an infidel man, *after* the baptism of his wife, had shown great anger, cursed the woman and the Christian faith, attempted to force her to apostatize, and finally dismissed her. Vermeersch (here writing before the Code) held no further interpellation to be necessary. He considered that two responses of the S. C. de Prop. Fide ([C. P. pro Sin.], 5 Mar., 1816—*Coll. S. C. P. F.*, n. 705; [Portland], 18 Jun., 1884—*Coll. S. C. P. F.*, n. 1620) requiring a dispensation from interpellation, even in the face of evident departure of the infidel, were not applicable to the present case, since in the cases to which the responses applied the departure had taken place *before* the baptism of the convert party.

[3] *Cf. supra,* p. 105.

[4] *Summula Theologiae Moralis* (3. ed., 3 vols., Romae, 1892), III, n. 476. After the Code, *cf.* Van Hove: "Num sit facultas dispensandi facultas concessa parochis et confessariis circa omittendas interpellationes de quibus in can. 1121-1125, dubitari licet."—*Commentarium Lovaniense,* Vol. I, Tom. V, *De Privilegiis —De Dispensationibus* (Mechliniae-Romae: Dessain, 1939), n. 147.

The first drafts of the canons followed the old expression: the change was made in the final draft.[5]

The usual term "dispensation" will be followed here, but with the connotation that it may apply to any case for which the Holy See declares the interpellations may be omitted. For the use of the Pauline privilege as ordinarily understood the Holy See grants faculties which so declare[6] in certain circumstances when the departure of the infidel party is manifest from other evidence, as also when the departure is not certain but grave difficulties are an obstacle to making the interpellations. In addition to these the full extent of canon 1125 comprehends cases that are outside the limits of the Pauline privilege and for these also the declaration of the Holy See, as made in the constitutions and now become universal law by the canon, states that the interpellations may be omitted.[7]

An instruction of the Holy Office[8] recalls to missionaries the statements of Benedict XIV,[9] which declare that opinion not sufficiently safe in practice which holds that the judicial interpellation may be omitted as often as it is really impossible, or when it is foreseen to be useless if made. Benedict maintained that even when it was impossible to make the interpellation because the infidel party had gone to a distant country or to parts unknown, a dispensation was necessary, given by the authority of the Supreme Pontiff to whom it pertains to declare under what circumstances the interpellations need not be made.[10]

[5] *Cf.* Rayanna, "De Constitutione S. Pii Papae V, etc.," *Periodica,* XXVIII (1939), pp. 123, 124, nota 133. *Cf. ibid.* for the arguments of Cardinals Billot and Lorenzelli against using *"dispense"* in the canons.

[6] Yet "dispense" is still used in the faculties. *Cf. infra,* p. 108.

[7] *Cf.* Gregory, *The Pauline Privilege,* p. 77: Bouscaren, "An Inquiry into the Practical Application of Canon 1125, etc.," *Misc. Ver.,* I, 290.

[8] (Ad. Archiep. Quebecan.), 16 Sept., 1824, ad 3—*Fontes,* n. 866.

[9] *De Synodo Dioecesana,* lib. VI, cap. IV, n. 3; lib. XIII, cap. XXI, n. 6.

[10] *Cf.* S. C. S. Off. (Ex Litter. S. C. de Prop. Fide ad N. Mission Pondicher.), 5 Jan., 1757, ad 5—*Coll. Hong.,* n. 1428, which required interpellation of the infidel husband even though he had entered a second union and there was solid reason to fear that out of revenge he would kill the first wife who now wanted to be baptized. *Cf.* also, S. C. S. Off., resp. in *Analecta Ecclesiastica,* year 1901, pp. 154, 155, in which a dispensation from the Holy See was required in the case in spite of insuperable difficulties attached to making the interpellations.

It is controverted whether or not the Church's insistence upon the interpellations has its basis in the divine law. Statements of the Roman Congregations [11] have favored the opinion that they are simply of divine law. If the privilege is considered to be of mediate divine origin [12] the opinion may follow that the interpellations are only of ecclesiatical law with the Church determining the manner in which the *discessus* shall be proved. In the opinion that the privilege is of immediate divine origin the formal interpellations must be considered to be of divine law if the *discessus* can be known in no other way. The requirement for licit use of the privilege that, unless there is a dispensation, they be made also in the cases in which the will of the infidel to separate can be known from other circumstances is then considered to be founded in ecclesiastical law. Since in any event the privilege is of at least mediate divine origin this latter explanation seems preferable.

An additional reason for the necessity of interpellations in a licit use of the privilege is the danger that without sufficient grounds some authorities inferior to the Holy See might conclude that the infidel party had manifested the will to separate.[13] Since the *discessus* understood in its full significance, as a separation caused by the infidel party, is a *conditio sine qua non* for the use of the privilege, the Supreme Pontiff reserves to himself the judgment of the grave difficulty, the danger to the faithful or to the *interpellans*, the impossibility, or the inutility of using the normal means of determining the *de facto* separation.[14] The Pope may, and does, declare that in certain circumstances the interpellations need not be made,[15] and the licit omission depends upon such declaration.

Article 2. Necessity for Validity

The distinction between divine and ecclesiastical law is also to be made in resolving the question of the necessity of interpellations, or

[11] S. C. S. Off., instr. (Ad Archiep. Quebecen.), 16 Sept., 1824, ad 3—*Fontes*, n. 866; S. C. S. Off., resp. (Cochinchin. Occident.), 12 Jun., 1850, ad 1—*Fontes*, n. 910; *cf.* also S. C. de Prop. Fide, resp. (C. P. pro Sin., Tunkin. Occident.), 5 Mar., 1816, ad 1—*Fontes*. n. 4697.

[12] *Cf. supra*, pp. 84-86.

[13] *Cf.* Wernz, *Ius Decretalium*, IV, n. 705, nota 92.

[14] *Cf.* Cappello, *De Sacramentis*, III, n. 776, 3°.

[15] Canons 1121, § 2: 1123.

of a dispensation from them, for the *valid* use of the Pauline privilege. With reference first to the necessity from divine law, opinions vary from that which holds the only requirement is that the *discessus* actually have taken place after the baptism of the convert party, though there be no proof of it, to that which considers the interpellations (or a dispensation) to be always necessary.[16]

Separation of the parties in this matter may be physical or moral. The infidel separates physically if he refuses to cohabit with his convert spouse, or if *de facto* he cannot cohabit with her. He is considered to separate morally if he is certainly willing to cohabit, but not without blasphemy of the Creator or without attempts to induce the convert to apostatize or to commit other grave sins,[17] in other words if he will cohabit but not *"pacifice sine contumelia Creatoris*.[18]

Deduction from St. Paul's words [19] show the separation caused by the infidel to be necessary for valid use of the privilege. But it does not seem that the same can be said of any one particular kind of proof that the separation has been effected by the infidel. Hence so long as it is clear, either from adequate questions privately asked or from other evidence, that the *discessus* has certainly taken place after the baptism of the convert party, divine law does not require the formal interpellations.[20] It would seem that for valid use of the

[16] *Cf.* Payen, *De Matrimonio,* n. 2353.

[17] *Cf.* cc. 7, 8, X, *de divortiis,* IV, 19; Vromant, *De Matrimonio,* nn. 309, 317.

[18] Canon 1121, § 1, 2 °.

[19] 1 Cor. vii: 15.

[20] Cappello, *De Sacramentis,* III (4. ed.), n. 776, 3°: But *cf.* De Becker, A Recension in *ETL,* II (1925), 274, in which, after stating that it is at least doubtful whether the interpellations are not of obligation by divine law, he seems to argue from the ecclesiastical requirement of interpellations (or a dispensation from them) for the valid use of the privilege to the possibility of a like requirement in divine law: "Et quia certum est multos et graves Doctores olim et hodie adhuc uti saltem probabiliorem tenere sententiam quod, ex jure divino, ad validitatem novi matrimonii requiratur interpellatio (vel dispensatio), optime intelligitur legislatorem nostrum practice solvisse casum exigendo, saltem ex jure ecclesiastico, in omni casu et ad validitatem, praedictam interpellationem." In his *De Matrimonio, cf.* p. 245, De Becker does not express an opinion on the question of requirement of interpellations by divine law for validity.

privilege when it is impossible to make the formal interpellations and the *discessus* is not certain from other evidence, as also when it is possible to make them and from other evidence the fact of the *discessus* is only doubtful, by divine law the judgment of the case must be left to the Church and expressed by declaration that the interpellations need not be made.[21]

It is clear that the Church always considers the use of the privilege illicit when the interpellations have been omitted without dispensation, but it is not so clear that it *always* considers such use to be invalid. By far the predominating sense of statements of the Congregations is that it is invalid, but these together do not give incontrovertible proof. In addition to statements made both in general instructions and in particular responses insisting upon the interpellations or a dispensation from them,[22] the Holy Office has refused to grant requested *sanationes in radice* for marriages in which the interpellations or a dispensation from them was omitted,[23] the reason being that the marriage in infidelity was an impediment to a new valid marriage until the interpellations had been provided for. The petitioners were instructed to dispense from the interpellations (in the first document cited, in view of the causes present, and in the second, if it were determined that there was cause) and procure renewal of consent. There is, however, at least one case to the contrary.[24] An infidel having left his first, and presumably validly married wife, married another in a place distant from where the first

[21] But *cf.* Cappello, *De Sacramentis,* III (4. ed.), n. 776, 3°: "Non liquet utrum, spectato iure divino seu rei natura, interpellatio duplex requiratur, aut in casu quo discessus sit dubius."

[22] Vg., S. C. S. Off. (Ex Litter. S. C. de Prop. Fide ad N. Mission Pondicher.), 5 Jan., 1757, ad 5—*Coll. Hong.*, n. 1428; S. C. de Prop. Fide, resp. (C. P. pro Sin.-Tunkin Occident.), 5 Mar., 1816, ad 1 et 3—*Fontes,* n. 4697; S. C. S. Off., instr. (Ad Archiep. Quebecen.), 16 Sept., 1824, ad 3—*Fontes,* n. 866; S. C. de Prop. Fide, instr. (ad Vic. Ap. Siam), 20 Mar., 1836—*Fontes,* n. 4762; S. C. S. Off. (Siam), 4 Jul., 1855, *prope finem*—*Fontes,* n. 931; S. C. S. Off., resp. 11 Aug., 1855—*Fontes,* n. 954; S. C. S. Off., resp. (Portland), 18 Jun., 1884—*Fontes,* n. 1088; S. C. S. Off., resp., 13 Mar., 1901—*Analecta Ecclesiastica,* year 1901, pp. 154, 155.

[23] S. C. S. Off., resp. (Coreae), 11 Sept., 1878, ad 1—*Fontes,* n. 1057; resp. (Curatus Dioecesis N.), 19 Jan., 1900—*Coll. Hong.*, n. 2288.

[24] S. C. de Prop. Fide, resp. (C. P. pro Sin.—Sutchuen.), 5 Mar., 1787, ad 2—*Fontes,* n. 4615.

was living. Upon becoming a catechumen with the second woman, he heard that the first wife was opposed to his conversion and even exhorted him not to become a Christian. The missionary baptized the man and the second woman and with no provision for interpellations, or dispensation from them, married the two. Later the man having returned to the place where his first wife was staying found she had changed her mind and was altogether disposed to become a Christian. The doubt proposed was whether the marriage with the second woman was valid since the missionary had no faculty to dispense from the interpellations. The statement of the doubt adverts to the opinion of many missionaries (in that place) that the marriage was illicit but not certainly invalid. The response given seems to favor the opinion, at least it does not correct it: *"Attentis circumstantiis in facto concurrentibus, coniuges de quibus agitur, non esse inquietandos: sed caveant missionarii dispensationem ab interpellatione coniugis impertiri, si careant huiusmodi facultate."*

The wording of canons 1121, 1122 and 1123 strongly favors the invalidity of a marriage contracted in view of the Pauline privilege but without the interpellations having been made or dispensed from, but the wording is not so explicit that authors are willing to hold as indisputable that every such marriage is invalid.[25]

In practice, at least for a licit use of the Pauline privilege, before the marriage the interpellations must *always* be made or a dispensation from making them must be obtained. This is true whatever may be the impossibility or the danger or the uselessness of making them, or however certain the *discessus* may be from other sources of information.[26] Such was also the discipline before the Code.[27]

[25] *Cf.* Vlaming, *Praelect. Iuris Mat.*, II, n. 722, nota 1, p. 322; Chelodi, *Ius. Matrimoniale*, n. 158; De Smet, *De Spons. et Mat.*, n. 352; Payen, *De Matrimonio*, II, n. 2355; Wernz-Vidal, *Ius Canonicum*, V, n. 632, nota 68, *in fine*; Vermeersch-Creusen, *Epitome*, II, n. 430; Cappello, *De Sacramentis*, III (4. ed.), n. 777.

[26] *Cf.* can. 1121, § 2; Payen, *De Matrimonio*, II, n. 2356; Vromant, *De Matrimonio*, nn. 327, 331. For the *ratio agendi* after the marriage, if the interpellations have certainly been omitted without dispensation, or if it is doubtful whether they were properly provided for, *cf.* Payen, *De Matrimonio*, nn. 2358, 2359.

[27] *Cf.* Vermeersch, *De Casu Apostoli*, n. 51; De Smet, *De Spons. et Mat.* (2. ed., Brugis, 1910), n. 195, D.

II. *Apostolic Faculties Having a Relation to the Privileges of the Constitutions*

Article 1. Résumé of the Origin of the Formulas of Faculties in Use Prior to the Code

The peculiar needs of the missionary countries evangelized in the sixteenth and following centuries, and the distance of these countries from the Holy See made it imperative that the missionaries be furnished with special faculties. Previous to the formation of the Sacred Congregation for the Propagation of the Faith in 1622, the faculties were given directly by the Pope through briefs or constitutions, or indirectly through the Holy Office, or through Cardinals or Superiors of religious institutes. All Superiors General of the Orders enjoyed the power of establishing missions and of granting faculties to missionaries.[28] The *Compendium Indicum Societatis Jesu* (1580) contained wider faculties than were to be found elsewhere and because of the communication of privileges existing among the religious Orders these could be granted by the Superiors of missionaries other than the Jesuits. The advisability of having the special faculties of the Orders suppressed was considered by the Cardinals of the Cong. for the Propagation of the Faith in anticipation of the new faculties to be given by that Congregation. Vermeersch states, however, that there is no trace of any brief or bull having been issued to that effect, and that a prudent use of the privileges was foreseen in the simultaneous existence of the faculties of the Regulars and those of the Congregation.[29]

As could be expected, the special faculties needed in the various missionary countries were more or less similar, and yet no general formulas of these had been drawn up. Moreover, faculties additional to those previously given were needed in view of the great diversity of places and peoples coming under the influence of Christianity during the extraordinary missionary activity of the sixteenth and seventeenth centuries. In the constitution providing for the erection of the Cong. for the Propagation of the Faith broad

[28] *Cf. Coll. S. C. P. F.*, n. 101.

[29] "Commentaria de Formulis Facultatum, etc.," *Periodica*, XI (1922), n. 5, p. (38).

powers respecting all mission matters were entrusted to the members of the Congregation;[80] nevertheless, in order prudently to provide for the required faculties Urban VII in 1633 instituted a particular Congregation made up of two Cardinals from the Holy Office and three Cardinals from the Cong. for the Propagation of the Faith. In 1637 the Congregation on faculties presented its recommendation of seven general rules to govern the granting of faculties, and five formulas of faculties. With a few changes the Pope approved the rules and formulas.[81]

Formula I listed the faculties for bishops in Africa, Asia and America; Formula II provided for bishops in those parts of Europe subject to infidels and remote from the Roman Curia; Formula III gave the faculties which could be used in certain parts of Europe where heresy was flourishing; Formula IV gave greater or extraordinary faculties for the Prefects of the missions in Asia, Africa and America and for their associates and the Guardian of Jerusalem. These four formulas after a few changes came to be known as "ordinary." Formula V proposed by the Congregation on faculties seems to have had no specific destination and fell into disuse as a complete formula. Many bishops and missionaries were given a formula of faculties called Formula V, but the faculties contained varied according to the needs of the places and their distance from the Holy See.[82]

At about the same time five additional special formulas, which came to be known as Formulas VI, VII, VIII, IX and X, were prepared for particular places through selection, from the five general formulas according to the seven general rules, of faculties needed in the territories in question. These special formulas drawn from the approved formulas and according to the rules approved by the Holy See were not given approval proper to themselves. In the

[80] Gregory XV, const. "*Inscrutabili,*" 22 Jun., 1622—*Coll. S. C. P. F.*, n. 3.

[81] Vermeersch, *op. cit.*, n. 9, p. (41).

[82] Vermeersch, *op. cit.*, n. 20, pp. (61), (62). *Cf.* Antonius Konings-Joseph Putzer, *Commentarium in Facultates Apostolicas* (4. ed., New York, 1897), n. 97, where the faculties of the various Formulas V are called "extraordinary," although the statement is made that many of these faculties are the same as those in the other formulas which were designated as "ordinary."

nineteenth century a number of formulas additional to the "ordinary" formulas of Urban VIII were granted. Known as "extraordinary," these were designated by letters of the alphabet as a, aa, b, C. D, etc., and contained extraordinary faculties to be used in addition to the faculties of the "ordinary" formulas granted.[33]

It was not until 1765 that the Cong. for the Propagation of the Faith through its Secretary, *"ex audientia Sanctissimi,"* began to provide the faculties directly to its missionaries. Previously it had referred the missionaries to the Holy Office to obtain the formulas and, indeed, continued to do this frequently up to 1790.[34]

Both the Holy Office and the Cong. for the Propagation of the Faith took part in the interpretation of the faculties. In reference to the position taken by some missionaries in the Philippine Islands, namely, that the resolutions and decrees of the Cong. for the Propagation of the Faith had only the force of probable opinion, that is, that they were pure and simple declarations of the Cardinals and hence that a contrary opinion could be defended, Innocent X (1644-1655) confirmed a decree of Urban VIII that the decrees of the Congregation when issued with certain stated formalities had the force of an apostolic constitution and were to be observed by all.[35] About twenty years later on the authority of Clement X (1670-1676) it was decreed that resolutions of doubts made by the Holy Office or the Cong. for the Propagation of the Faith were sent to missionaries and other ministers of the Congregation not as definitions but as simple instructions by which those concerned could and ought to be governed.[36]

In his reformation of the Roman Curia in 1908 Pius X made a more exact determination of the jurisdiction of the Dicasteries than

[33] *Cf.* Van Hove, *De Priv.—De Disp.*, n. 162, p. 153, nota 3.

[34] Vermeersch, *op. cit.*, nn. 23, 24, pp. (65)-(67).

[35] S. C. de Prop. Fide, instr., 30 Jul., 1652—*Coll. S. C. P. F.*, n. 119.

[36] "De Mandato Sanctissimi (Clementis X), injunctum fuit quod quotiescumque Missionariis, caeterisque S. C. de Prop. F. ministris, mittuntur resolutiones dubiorum factae a S. C. S. Offic. et Propag. Fidei, non mittantur tanquam definitiones, sed tanquam simplices instructiones, quibus in occurrentibus dubiis gubernari valeant et debeant." 19 Sept., 1671—*Collectanea Constitutionum, Decretorum, Indultorum ac Instructionum S. Sedis ad usum Societatis Missionum ad exteros* (2. ed., Hongkong, 1905—*Coll. Hong.*), n. 6.

was previously observed. Thus he decreed that the Cong. for the Propagation of the Faith should refer to the proper Congregation of the Curia matters having regard to faith, matrimony, or the discipline of the sacred rites.[37] This provision gave rise to a doubt concerning the competence of the Cong. for the Propagation of the Faith to grant to the ordinaries of places subject to it the formulas of faculties, since some of these faculties pertained to matrimony. The Sacred Consistorial Congregation[38] answered: *"Affirmative, re tamen agitata et composita cum S. Congregatione de Sacramentis."*

Pius X confirmed a later decision of the Consistorial Congregation that the Holy Office had competence in all matters which directly or indirectly, *in iure* or *in facto,* had reference to the Pauline privilege and to dispensations for marriages between a Catholic and a non-Catholic, with due regard to the power of the Holy Office to remit a question concerning such marriages to another office of the Holy See if it saw fit. Moreover, the Pope commanded that in the future every question concerning mixed or disparate marriage was to be referred to the Holy Office which, in its decisions on such questions, was to observe the provisions of the decree *"Ne Temere"* in regard to the form of marriage for Catholics.[39]

Article 2. Dispensations from the Impediments of Consanguinity and Affinity

The faculty which was treated of in article six of Formulas I and II, in article three of Formula III, in article four of Formula IV, and in article nine of Formula V, had a relation to that privilege in the Constitution "*Altitudo*" of Paul III which referred to the impediments of consanguinity and affinity. For the benefit of the natives of the New World, Paul III had reduced these impediments to include only the first and second degrees.[40]

The article containing the grant of the faculty in Formulas I, II and IV reads as follows:

[37] Const. *"Sapienti consilio,"* 29 Jun., 1908, § 1, n. 6°, 4—*AAS,* I (1909), 12. *Cf.* canon 252, § 4.

[38] Resp., 12 Nov., 1908, ad II—*AAS,* I (1909), 149-151.

[39] S. C. Consist., 21 Jan., 1910—*AAS,* II (1910), 56. *Cf.* canon 247, § 3.

[40] *Cf. supra,* p. 40.

> Dispensandi in tertio et quarto consanguinitatis et affinitatis gradu simplici et mixto tantum, et in secundo, tertio et quarto mixtis, non tamen in secundo solo quo ad futura matrimonia, quo vero ad praeterita etiam in secundo solo cum iis qui ab haeresi, vel infidelitate convertuntur ad fidem catholicam, et in praedictis casibus prolem susceptam declarandi legitimam.

The faculty in Formula III was slightly different. In Formula V the additional words *"cum pauperibus"* appeared after *"dispensandi,"* but otherwise the wording was the same as above.[41] A few changes were subsequently made in the articles. Thus, for example, in the second to last formularies of Formulas I and II issued before the Code, after the words *"quo vero ad praeterita etiam in secundo solo"* the phrase *"dummodo nullo modo attingat primum gradum"* was added. The words *"in praedictis casibus"* were changed to *"in praefatis casibus."* In those formularies of Formulas I and II which were in use immediately before the Code article six read as follows:

> Dispensandi in tertio et quarto consanguinitatis et affinitatis gradu simplici et mixto tantum, et in secundo, tertio et quarto mixtis tam in contractis quam in contrahendis; et etiam, quoad contracta, in secundo solo, dummodo non attíngat primum, cum iis qui ab haeresi, vel schismate, vel infidelitate convertuntur ad fidem catholicam, datis, si una pars tantum convertatur, cautionibus ab Ecclesiäe praescriptis et in praefatis casibus, prolem susceptam declarandi legitimam.[42]

The "ordinary" formulas, therefore, gave the power to dispense converts who were either already married or who were yet to be married, but who were subject to an impediment of consanguinity or affinity even if it involved the second degree mixed with the third or fourth. Moreover, if it were a question of a marriage already contracted before the conversion of the parties or of one of them, by this faculty the parties or party could be dispensed from an impediment in the second degree equal, as between first cousins. Hence the ordinary faculties allowing the dispensation of converts from the impediments of consanguinity and affinity in territories subject

[41] Vermeersch, *op. cit.*, nn. 15-19, pp. (48)-(59), *passim.*

[42] Vermeersch, *op. cit.*, n. 22, pp. (63)-(65).

to the Cong. for the Propagation of the Faith went beyond the concession in regard to these same impediments made by Paul III for the Indians of the New World. It is to be noted here that the Holy Office refused to grant a requested abrogation of the impediment arising from the third and fourth degrees of affinity and consanguinity—in effect a territorial extension of Paul III's concession—which was sought in favor of the natives of India.[43] The tenor of the Holy Office reply was that such a general dispensation was not needed since the Vicars Apostolic and their delegates already had sufficient power in regard to these impediments.

ARTICLE 3. THE FACULTY OF DISPENSING CONVERT POLYGAMISTS

The faculty which was contained in article eleven of the original Formulas I and II, in article nine of Formula IV, and in article fourteen of Formula V[44] had a close relation to the privileges granted to convert polygamists in the Constitutions "*Altitudo*" and "*Romani Pontificis.*"[45] In the course of time the wording of the articles on several other faculties was altered in one way or another, but it appears that in no document where this faculty in favor of polygamist converts was granted has there even been any change in the text except, perhaps, for a transposition of words which effected no change in meaning. The wording in the formula of faculties granted after the Code[46] and, to note only one other example out of many, in the faculties granted in 1895 to the Bishops and Vicars Apostolic of the Paris Foreign Mission Society,[47] is the same as in the early manuscript Codex of Formula I[48] where it reads as follows:

[43] S. C. S. Off., resp. (ad Vicar. Ap. Maysourensis), 14 Dec., 1865—*Coll. S. C. P. F.*, n. 1278.

[44] Vermeersch, *op. cit.*, nn. 15-19, pp. (48)-(60), *passim*.

[45] This faculty was absent from Formula III which provided faculties to be used in certain parts of Europe where heresy was flourishing.

[46] *Formula tertia (maior)*, art. 24—*Sylloge*, n. 209.

[47] *Coll. Hong.*, n. 58 ad 11.

[48] Vermeersch, *op. cit.*, n. 15, p. (48), ad 11.

Dispensandi cum gentilibus [49] et infidelibus plures uxores habentibus, ut post conversionem et baptismum, quam ex illis maluerint, si etiam ipsa fidelis fiat, retinere possint, nisi prima voluerit converti.

An interesting point about this faculty is the interpretation given the phrase *"nisi prima voluerit converti."* The jurisprudence of the Cong. for the Propagation of the Faith at first did not expressly require the interpellation of the first wife.[50] At the beginning of the nineteenth century the faculty was construed in the Synod of Su-tchuen (1803), the decrees of which were approved through the Congregation, as meaning that it was sufficient to interpellate the first wife as to whether or not she wished to be converted.[51] The Congregation emphasized in a letter to the Vicar Apostolic of Siam [52] that the concession of making the interpellation on only the one point did not apply to those who were monogamists as pagans, but that it applied only to polygamist converts, *"tunc enim sufficit ut primam interpellat num velit converti, secus eam retineat ex aliis, quae fidelis fiat."*

A response of the Holy Office to the Archbishop of Quebec [53] excluded from the jurisdiction of the Archbishop the concession of asking only the one question of the first wife. After reviewing the faculty and its accepted sense that the convert polygamist was required to keep the first wife if she desired to be baptized, the Archbishop had asked for a "new concession" which he considered to be contained in the Constitution *"Romani Pontificis"* of St. Pius V. He asked that the convert polygamist be allowed to choose whichever of his former wives he desired, provided that the one chosen would be baptized, without the obligation of choosing the

[49] *Sylloge,* n. 209 ad 24 has *"gentibus"* instead of *"gentilibus."* Although not listed in the *Errata corrigenda,* this is probably a typographical error.

[50] Ex instr., 15 Feb., 1756—*Fontes,* n. 4520; resp. (C. P. pro Sin.—Tunkin. Orient.), 14 Jan., 1806—*Fontes,* n. 4686.

[51] Cap. IX, § 8, Synodus Sutchuensis—*Collectio Lacensis,* VI, col. 623, *ad calcem; cf. Coll. S. C. P. F.,* II, p. 481, nota 1; S. C. de Prop. Fide, letter of approbation of the Synod, 22 Jun., 1822—*Coll. Lac.,* VI, col. 638, 639.

[52] 30 Sept., 1837—*Coll. S. C. P. F.,* II, p. 481, *ad calcem.*

[53] 8 Jun., 1836—*Fontes,* n. 874.

first. The Holy Office answered that when there was question of a valid marriage the Congregation had no doubt that polygamists after their conversion must retain the first wife if she would receive baptism or at least would consent to cohabit without injury to the Creator. In effect this nullified the faculty since it insisted upon the common law requirements for the use of the Pauline privilege.

Later when the Vicar Apostolic of Siam asked if it would be sufficient, in a case in which the second wife desires to be converted, to interpellate the first wife on the one point of her desire to be converted and omit the question about whether she would cohabit peacefully, the Holy Office, referring to the faculty for polygamist converts which the Vicar Apostolic enjoyed, said that before it would reply to the case proposed it wanted to know the reason why the Vicar Apostolic doubted about using his faculty.[54] Implicitly contained in the response therefore is the answer that the faculty permits interpellation on the one point only—whether the first wife wishes to be converted. Such was the sense in which the faculty was understood up to the promulgation of the Code.[55]

Another faculty which is relevant to the present subject because it has a close relation to the concession granted in Gregory XIII's Constitution "*Populis*" is that which allowed a dispensation from interpellations in what were called "ordinary cases":

> Sancta Sedis benigne concedit "facultatem dispensandi super interpellatione coniugum in infidelitate relictorum, pro omnibus casibus ordinariis, dummodo scilicet, adhibitis antea omnibus diligentiis, etiam per publicas ephemerides, ad reperiendum locum ubi coniux infidelis habitat, iisque in irritum cessis, constet saltem summarie ex extrajudicialiter, coniugem absentem moneri legitime non posse, aut monitum infra tempus in monitione praefixum, suam voluntatem non significasse."[56]

[54] Resp., 4 Jul., 1855, ad tertiam secundi dubii questionem—*Fontes*, n. 931.

[55] S. C. S. Off., instr. (ad Vic. Ap. Gallas), 28 Mar., 1860, ad 8—*Fontes*, n. 957; *cf.* S. C. S. Off., resp., 5 Sept., 1855—*Fontes*, n. 933; Konings-Putzer, *Commentarium in Fac. Apos.*, n. 127, d; Vermeersch, *De Casu Apostoli*, n. 81.

[56] S. C. S. Off., resp. (Ep. Vhrbosnensis), 16 Aug., 1895—*ASS*, XXIX (1896-1897), 565, 566. This is a type of the faculty granted previously to many Ordinaries. *Cf.* Konings-Putzer, *op. cit.*, n. 130, e.

Cap. IX, § 8, of the decrees of the Synod of Su-tchuen[57] insisted that those missionaries who enjoyed the faculty to dispense from interpellation must use it according to the norm of Gregory's Constitution. Reference to the various responses of the Roman Congregations which made clear the practical application of the norm will be reserved for the commentary on the Constitution *"Populis."*

Article 4. Apostolic Faculties After the Code

By a decree of the Consistorial Congregation,[58] faculties granted to the Ordinaries of places other than those subject to the Cong. for the Propagation of the Faith were discontinued from the 18th of May, 1918. Faculties granted by the Sacred Penitentiary were excluded from the effect of the decree. It was explained that the new Code, which became universal law on that day, rendered the former faculties superfluous, and since some of the faculties contained in the old formulas were at variance with the new law confusion would result if they continued in force. Provisions were made for temporary extraordinary faculties for remote regions and for regions from which recourse to the Holy See would be difficult because of the World War. The continued use of the old faculties through ignorance was pronounced valid. Canon 1125 in the new Code was of notable effect, as will be seen, in rendering juridically superfluous certain former faculties having regard to the *privilegium fidei.*

Not long after the Code went into effect it became evident that in addition to the powers given them by the Code, Bishops still had need of at least some of the quinquennial faculties which they formerly enjoyed. Before the Code even many Bishops who were not subject to the Cong. for the Propagation of the Faith obtained the quinquennial faculties through that Congregation. After the Code provision was made for the faculties by the various Congregations according to their competence, but in order to obviate the necessity of applying to each Dicastery separately, in 1923 Pius XI[59] decreed that all Bishops not subject to the Cong. for the

[57] *Coll. Lac.*, VI, col. 623; *Coll. S. C. P. F.*, II, p. 481, nota 1

[58] 25 Apr., 1918—*AAS*, X (1918), 190-192.

[59] Motu Proprio, Post datum, 20 Apr., 1923—*AAS*, XV (1923), 193, 194;

Propagation of the Faith or the Cong. for the Oriental Church were to procure their quinquennial faculties through the Consistorial Congregation.[60]

The pre-Code faculties for Ordinaries in the regions subject to the Cong. for the Propagation of the Faith were in effect until the first day of January, 1920, when all formulas of faculties, "ordinary" and "extraordinary" were superseded by new formulas prepared in view of the provisions of the Code.[61] The new faculties are provided in three formulas not distinguished like previous formulas as "ordinary" and "extraordinary," but each has *"maior"* and *"minor"* forms so that there are six formulas in all. Originally only the second and third had the two forms.[62] But now the first is also contradistinguished.[63]

For reference, the faculties of the post-Code formulas which

cf. Periodica, XII (1923), 65-67. Vermeersch-Creusen (*Epitome,* I, n. 874), give the index of quinquennial faculties for 1932-1937.

60 The Index of Faculties granted after the Code by the Holy See to Nuncios, Internuncios, and Apostolic Delegates is given in Vermeersch-Creusen, *Epitome,* I, n. 872. *Cf.* Vermeersch, "Facultatum quae, post Codicem, Legatis Apostolicis concedi consueverunt breve Commentarium," *Periodica,* XII (1923), (69)-(98), (125)-(159), and the notation in regard to faculty n. 30 in *Periodica,* XIII (1924), (28).

61 Vermeersch ("Commentaria de Formulis Facultatum, etc.," *Periodica,* XI [1922], n. 29, p. (70)), refers the reader to the letter of the S. C. de Prop. Fide, 1 Jul., 1919, protoc. 1522/19.

An exception was made for the Ordinaries of Jugoslavia who, by special disposition of the Holy See still subject to the S. C. de Prop. Fide, temporarily were allowed the use of an extraordinary formula. *Cf.* Vermeersch-Creusen, *Epitome,* I, n. 873, pp. 641, 648-654. *Sylloge,* n. 213, under the heading, "S. Congregatio de Propaganda Fide, (n. 2267-31 prot.)," gives the "Formula extra ordinem," with the notation, "Pro dioecesibus: Sarajewo, Banjaluca, Mostar, Antivari, Scopia."

62 Vermeersch, *ibid.*

63 *Cf. Sylloge,* nn. 207, 208, 209—Formula prima (maior), formula secunda (maior), formula tertia (maior); nn. 210, 211, 212—Formula prima (minor), formula secunda (minor), formula tertia (minor).

For distribution as to regions and Ordinaries, *cf.* Vermeersch, *op. cit.,* n. 31; G. Vromant, *Facultates Apostolicae Quas Sacra Congregatio de Propaganda Fide Delegare Solet Ordinariis Missionum, Commentaria in Formulam Tertiam* (2. ed., Bruxelles et Paris: Museum Lessianum, 1938), nn. 3, 4.

have a relation to the concessions of the constitutions of canon 1125, as also the additional faculty for dispensing from interpellation, are given here. The numbers are those given the articles containing the faculties in *formula tertia* both *maior* and *minor*,[64] which are accommodated to mission territories among the pagans[65] and have the broadest faculties.

F III et F 3, *24. Dispensandi cum gentilibus et infidelibus *plures uxores* habentibus, ut post conversionem et baptismum, quam ex illis maluerint, si etiam ipsa fidelis fiat, retinere possint, nisi prima voluerit converti.

F III et F 3, *25. Dispensandi super *interpellatione* coniugum in infidelitate relictorum pro omnibus *casibus* ordinariis, dummodo scilicet adhibitis antea omnibus diligentiis, etiam per publicas ephemereides ad reperiendum locum ubi coniux infidelis habitat, iisque in irritum cessis, constet saltem summarie et extrajudicialiter coniugem absentem moneri legitime non posse, aut monitum infra tempus in monitione praefixum suam voluntatem non significasse.

F III et F 3, *26. Itemque dispensandi super *interpellatione* coniugis in infidelitate relicti, siquidem certo constiterit, saltem summarie et extrajudicialiter, interpellationem fieri non posse sine evidenti *gravis damni* aut coniugi iam ad fidem converso, aut christianis inferendi periculo.

It will be noted that articles nn. 24 and 25 are worded the same as the corresponding pre-Code faculties. In his commentary on the new formulas Vermeersch stated that nn. 24 and 25 granted faculties *"quae omnibus competere videntur vi can. 1125 qui ad alias regiones extendit CC. Pauli III, S. Pii V et Gregorii*

[64] The *maior* formulas are usually designated, F I, F II, F III; the *minor*, F 1, F 2, F 3. Those faculties which may be subdelegated by the Ordinaries to whom they are granted are indicated by an asterisk. For the text of F III *cf.*, in addition to *Sylloge*, n. 209; Vermeersch-Creusen, *Epitome*, n. 873; Vromant, *op. cit.*, text and commentary.

[65] Briefly, for China, Indo-China, Japan, India, Malakka, the islands in the Pacific, parts of Africa, the Vicariates and Prefectures of America. *Cf.* Vromant, *Facultates Apostolicae*, n. 4.

XIII . . . ,"[66] the advantage of the faculties being to prescribe norms for the prudent application of the constitutions.

The treatment of the history of the legislation in canon 1125 which has been attempted in the first part of the dissertation closes here; the second part will be concerned with the practical application of the canon.

[66] "Commentaria de Formulis Facultatum, etc.," *Periodica*, XI (1922), n. 120, p. (139), nota 1.

Part Two

Canonical Commentary

CHAPTER VII

DISCUSSION PRELIMINARY TO COMMENTARY ON THE CONSTITUTIONS

Canon 1125

Ea quae matrimonium respiciunt in constitutionibus Pauli III *Altitudo,* 1 Iun. 1537; S. Pii V *Romani Pontificis,* 2 Aug. 1571; Gregorii XIII *Populis,* 25 Ian. 1585, quaeque pro peculiaribus locis scripta sunt, ad alias quoque regiones in eisdem adiunctis extenduntur.

Article 1. The Extensive Force of the Canon

Unanimity of opinion on the import of the phrase "*in eisdem adiunctis*" was not immediate after the promulgation of the Code. Did the phrase mean that the application of the constitutions' provisions to other countries was dependent upon the presence *in those countries* of the same local (and social) circumstances which gave rise to the necessity for the legislation in the particular places? Or did it mean that the provisions were applicable in any country to the *cases in which* the circumstances were the same as those for which the legislation was originally given although restricted to particular places?

The first opinion would circumscribe the usefulness of the canon considerably since few places in the world today have social circumstances that could be called the same as those which the sixteenth century missionaries found in their fields of labor. Particularly is this true of the circumstances of slavery in Africa and the New World which prompted Gregory XIII to issue the Constitution "*Populis.*"[1] As missionaries are well aware, polygamy is still common in what are called the pagan countries. And even in the more

[1] *Cf. supra,* pp. 63, 64.

Christian countries among peoples considered to have a highly developed civilization, successive polygamy is frequent enough to be a serious problem for priests working for the conversion of non-Catholics. Nevertheless, the circumstances in relatively few countries, or regions, could be called the *same* as those which existed in the particular places [2] to which the legislation was first directed. Some authors, however,[3] held the first opinion, that is, that *"in eisdem adiunctis"* had reference to countries or regions rather than to cases.

The second is the opinion almost universally held today. Vermeersch [4] argued for it, especially with reasons drawn from the condition of countries, the significance of the context, and from the mind of the legislator. Woods treated the question extensively,[5] citing numerous authors (not all of whose statements on the question, however, were without ambiguity) and concluding, among other reasons, from the changes that were made in the wording of the canon during the formation period of the Code, that it was the intention of the legislator to extend the provisions of the constitutions to cases *in eisdem adiunctis* in all parts of the world. Briefly, the arguments that make the second opinion the more acceptable are the following.[6]

Among the purposes in the codification of the canon law, as is clear from Cardinal Gasparri's Preface to the Code, was that of facilitating the safe application of the part of the great mass of previous legislation which was to continue in force. If the use of canon 1125 were to be subject to the discovery in a country, or even in a region within a country, of the same circumstances which existed

[2] *Cf. supra,* pp. 25-29.

[3] (Bachofen), Charles Augustine, *A Commentary on the New Code of Canon Law* (8 vols. Vol. V, 2 ed., St. Louis: Herder, 1920), p. 364; H. A. Ayrinhac, "Indissolubleness of Non-Catholic Marriages," *AER,* LXXII (1925), 408; Gregory, *The Pauline Privilege,* p. 87.

[4] "De Canone 1125 eiusque vi extensiva," *Periodica,* XX (1931), 1*-5*.

[5] *The Constitutions of Canon 1125,* pp. 73-82.

[6] *Cf.* Bouscaren, "An Inquiry Into the Practical Application of Canon 1125, etc.," *Miscellanea Vermeersch,* I, 283-286; Payen, *De Matrimonio* (2 ed., 3 vols. 1935-1936), II, n. 2404; Vromant, *De Matrimonio* (2 ed., 1938), n. 340; Léry, *La Privilège de la Foi,* nn. 84-86; Cappello, *De Sacramentis,* III (4. ed.), n. 787, § 7.

in the particular places centuries ago, the legislator's purpose would be frustrated. It is not reasonable to suppose that he would expect as a preliminary to the use of the canon such an historical study. The determination would be difficult if not impossible, and it is doubtful if the canon could be safely used in any but a very few places.

It can scarcely be presumed that the legislator intended to exclude from the use of the canon the territories for which the constitutions were originally given, yet today even they are not in the same circumstances which the missionaries found in the sixteenth century. And if, after the Code, because of the changed circumstances in those territories the constitutions could not be used in them, it may be asked whether there is any place in the world where they could be used. Even before the Code the concessions had been extended to other places certainly not in the same circumstances as the countries for which they were originally given. For example, Benedict XIV [7] gave to the Nuncio of Venice for use *in re* infidel, Jewish, and Turkish converts powers similar to those in the Constitution "*Populis.*" The word "*restringuntur,*" rather than the "*extenduntur*" of the canon, would be more fitted to the actual effect if the constitutions were meant to apply only to countries or regions where the same circumstances exist as were found in the original countries to which they applied.[8]

The universal extension of the law seems clear from the opposition between, "*quae pro peculiaribus regionibus scripta sunt,*" and "*ad alias quoque regiones.*" The canon makes the provisions of the constitutions applicable to "*alias quoque regiones*" which are not "*peculiaria loca,*" but if the same circumstances had to be present in them as were in the original countries then they too would be "*peculiaria loca.*" A local restriction could have been easily expressed in some such form as, "*ad alias regiones quarum adiuncta sint eadem,*" or "*quae in eisdem adiunctis versantur.*" [9] Since such

[7] Const., "*In suprema,*" 16 Jan., 1745—*Bullarium Benedicti XIV*, II, 183-184.

[8] Cf. Léry, *Le Privilège de la Foi*, n. 86.

[9] Vermeersch, "De Canone 1125 eiusque vi extensiva," *Periodica*, XX (1931), 2*.

an intention is not expressed, and because of the other reasons, there is little room to doubt that the phrase *"in eisdem adiunctis"* was meant by the legislator to refer not to countries or regions, but to cases wherever in the world they may occur.

Article 2. Treatment of Doubtful Matters in the Use of the *Privilegium Fidei*

The plan to be followed in the commentary is that of showing the employment of canon 1125 in the dissolution in favor of the Faith of the bond of marriage contracted in infidelity when there is an obstacle preventing the use of the Pauline privilege proper. The Code provides norms for the use of the Pauline privilege which set off the cases to which it applies in a fairly definite category of the *privilegium fidei*. Among the norms is that given in canon 1127 which governs the treatment of doubts that may arise concerning the conditions required for the use of the Pauline privilege. But the use of the principle enunciated, namely, *"in re dubia privilegium fidei gaudet favore iuris,"* is not limited to the Pauline privilege. The phrase *privilegium fidei* indicates the motive and end of the Pauline privilege, but it signifies also the use of the Papal power of dissolving, in favor of the true Faith, those marriages wherein the conditions necessary for the use of the Pauline privilege are not verified.[10] A consideration of the principle, *in re dubia, etc.*, will be an aid to a clear idea of the juridical use of the provisions of the constitutions.[11]

Privilegium fidei in its proper sense is the faculty granted to a convert, through power divinely bestowed, by which he may be freed from the bond of a marriage contracted in infidelity. By *favor iuris* here is meant the inclination of the law to admit the use of the

[10] G. Arendt, "Quomodo in favorem fidei solvatur a S. Pontifice matrimonium in infidelitate contractum, Nota theologico-canonica circa canonem 1127," *ETL*, I (1924), 184; Payen, *De Matrimonio* (2. ed.), II, n. 2415, *bis*, p. 758.

[11] Cappello: "Hoc principium (canon 1127) . . . respicit tum privilegium Paulinum tum usum potestatis vicariae R. Pontificis quatenus refertur ad omnes casus quibus nequit certo applicari illud privilegium, et qui subsunt potestati vicariae Papae."—*De Sacramentis*, III (4. ed.), n. 788.

privilegium fidei in a doubtful matter. Human and divine law are both involved, for no distinction should be made where the legislator has made none. The ecclesiastical law clearly favors the *privilegium fidei* in canon 1014, which establishes the general presumption of validity for marriage by granting it the favor of the law, *but excepts* the principle of canon 1127 in regard to the *privilegium fidei.* The nature of the matter involved, that is, the dissolution of the bond of marriage, requires divine power, for doubt is in the subjective order and does not change the objective validity that will exist in some doubtful cases which will be dissolved through the use of the principle. In its wider sense, then, in view of the principle of canon 1127 *privilegium fidei* includes or permits, in many doubtful matters connected with a marriage contracted or reputed to have been contracted in infidelity, that judgment which will pave the way for the Catholic baptism of the interested party.[12]

Doubt is the state of a mind hesitating to make a judgment between two or more opinions. Doubt may be of law, as when the requirements of the law cannot be determined with certainty, or of fact, as when the circumstances of a case cannot be certainly known. The doubt required in the principle here being considered is not that doubt which demands grave as well as probable reasons on both sides of the question.[13] A reason with some degree of probability inherent in it for following both opinions must, however, be present, for otherwise the mind would be in a state of mere ignorance or of simple negative doubt, which would not justify the use of the principle.[14] Yet, in this matter which concerns the favor of the Faith the doubt necessary may be so interpreted as not to require a strict opposition to ignorance. That doubt is sufficient which is present when, from an inquiry into the circumstances, moral certainty concerning the truth of one side or the other cannot be reached.[15] The

[12] *Cf.* A. Vermeersch, "Interpretatio canonis 1127, de favore iuris concesso privilegio Fidei," *Periodica,* X (1921), (25), (26).

[13] Vermeersch-Creusen, *Epitome,* II, n. 437.

[14] *Cf.* Cappello, *De Sacramentis,* III (4. ed.), n. 788, § 2; Payen, *De Matrimonio* (2. ed.), II, n. 2415 *bis.*

[15] Arendt, "Nota theologico-canonica circa canonem 1127," *ETL,* I (1924), 181, 182; Vromant: "Dubium non necessario intelligitur sensu ita stricto ut

very nature of the matter requires that a diligent and prudent examination according to the circumstances of the case be always made in order, if possible, to solve the doubt. Many responses of the Holy Office show its insistence upon the inquiry.[16]

For the use of the principle, the doubtful matter may concern the existence of a previous valid marriage, that is, after diligent inquiry and examination it may not be possible to arrive at moral certainty concerning the objective validity or invalidity of a previous marriage. In such case, when the conditions necessary for the use of the *privilegium fidei* are extant, the marriage may be assumed to be invalid in line with the principle of canon 1127, which is specifically safeguarded in canon 1014, which states the general norm that, in case of doubt, the validity of a marriage must be upheld until the contrary is proved. In addition to such doubt about the objective validity of a previous marriage, the principle of canon 1127 may be used when the doubtful point is any other matter essential to the *privilegium fidei* and which is subject to the ministerial power of the Pope.[17] The following are some specific matters that may remain doubtful after due examination:

1. The existence of a marriage reputed to have been entered in infidelity. For example, the man and woman may have begun cohabitation without performing the customary nuptial ceremonies, with the resulting doubt whether the union is not mere concubinage.

2. The validity of marriage contracted in infidelity. Among some pagans, due to evidence of a condition placed against an essen-

semper exigat rationes probabiles in utramque partem sed supponit certitudinis moralis exclusionem."—*De Matrimonio* (2. ed.), n. 368. Kelly take a stricter view: "It (the principle of canon 1127) can be used only when the doubt is positive and probable. A positive and probable doubt arises only when there are weighty and cogent reasons supporting two contradictory propositions, so that the mind is unable to choose which of the propositions is true."—"Recent Decree on Doubtful Baptisms and the Pauline Privilege," *AER*, XCVII (1937), 366.

[16] Instr. (ad Vic. Ap. Oceaniae Central.), 18 Dec. 1872, ad dub. 4—*Fontes*, n. 1024; resp. (Mongoliae), 29 Nov., 1882—*Fontes* (IV, p. 394), n. 1075; resp. (Siouxormen.), 18 Maii, 1892, ad 1, 2—*Fontes*, n. 1155; resp. (Niger), 17 Aug., 1898—*Fontes*, n. 1205.

[17] Vromant, *De Matrimonio* (2. ed.), n. 368, *in fine*.

tial quality of marriage, it may be seriously doubted that the ordinary marital union is founded upon a true marriage contract.[18] There may be doubt whether the marriage in question is not invalid because of a previous marriage bond or other diriment impediment of natural or civil law. The inability to arrive at the required moral certitude may be due to the refusal of one party to a marriage (not, of course, the party seeking to use the *privilegium fidei*) to give the information that is necessary to determine the validity of the marriage. Suppose, for example, that there is a probable doubt whether the first woman with whom a polygamist convert lived in a marital union was not bound by a previous valid marriage. She absolutely refuses to give any information on the point and after diligent inquiry the true state of affairs cannot be learned from other sources.

Doubt about validity may be of law or of fact: in either case the *privilegium fidei* enjoys the favor of divine and Church law.

3. The dissolution of a marriage contracted in infidelity. For example, a dissolution may be doubtful because it was considered to have been effected through the use of the Pauline privilege by a former infidel after he was validly baptized in an heretical or schismatical sect. Suppose that after having duly made the interpellations a validly baptized heretic entered a union with a woman also validly baptized in an heretical sect. Since the right to the use of the Pauline privilege by heretics has neither been clearly affirmed nor denied by the Holy See,[19] but is denied by some authors,[20] although admitted simply or as the far more probable opinion by

[18] *Cf.* the difficulties proposed in S. C. S. Off., instr. (ad Ep. S. Alberti), 9 Dec., 1874—*Fontes*, n. 1036; resp. (Siouxormen.), 18 Maii, 1892—*Fontes*, n. 1155.

[19] Gasparri reports that when the Holy Office took the matter before the Pope in 1859, the latter was unwilling to solve the question but answered *"Dilata,"* and the question *"adhuc perdurat."*—*Tract. Can. de Mat.* (ed. of 1932), II, n. 1136.

[20] Vlaming, *Praelect. Iuris. Mat.* II, n. 720, nota 3; Gasparri: " . . . nos certam habemus negativam sententiam."—*Tract. Can. de Mat.* (ed. of 1932), II, n. 1136; Vromant: "Haeretici et schismatici, etsi baptizati, privilegio Paulino probabiliter valide uti nequent."—*De Matrimonio* (2. ed.), n. 284.

most authors,[21] the dissolution of the first marriage could be a *res dubia* and hence also the status of the second marriage.[22]

4. The fulfillment of the requirements essential to the use of the Pauline privilege by a former infidel validly baptized in the Catholic faith (—to prescind from the controverted question concerning heretics and schismatics), for example:

a. The sufficiency of the cause for dispensing from interpellations, or for awaiting the infidel party's reply;
b. The interpretation or the significance of an ambiguous reply to the interpellations;
c. The sincerity of the infidel party's affirmative reply;
d. A question as to whether or not the infidel's departure was occasioned by a just cause.

5. The identity of the first wife of a polgygamist or first husband of a polyandrous woman.

6. With respect to one party only, the fact of baptism having been received in the Catholic Church or by a party converted to the Catholic faith from heresy or schism, that is, the doubt whether or not he actually went through a baptismal ceremony, or whether baptism actually administered was valid. Thus a marriage contracted between an infidel certainly not baptized and a doubtfully

[21] *Cf.* Wernz, *Ius Decretalium,* IV, n. 702, nota 59; Noldin, *De Matrimonio,* n. 32; Vermeersch, *De Casu Apostoli,* n. 42; De Becker, *De Matrimonio,* p. 242; Gregory, *The Pauline Privilege,* p. 50; De Smet, *De Spons. et Mat.,* n. 345; Cappello, *De Sacramentis,* III (4. ed.), n. 769; Vermeersch-Creusen, *Epitome,* II, n. 428; Payen, *De Matrimonio* (2. ed.), II, n. 2253; Léry, *Le Privilège de la Foi,* n. 40.

[22] Payen (*ibid.*) holds that in practice, a case involving a convert to the true Faith, who had previously conformed to the requirements of the Pauline privilege and entered a second union when he joined an heretical sect, should be referred to the Holy See. The elements of the case which Payen gives as an example are these: Cornelius, a Jew, married Iphigenia, an infidel. After a civil divorce Cornelius became an Episcopalian and, after having interpellated Iphigenia in vain on the question of cohabiting, entered a union with Lucy, an Episcopalian woman. After some years Iphigenia was converted to the Catholic Faith. Thereafter, both Cornelius and Lucy wished to be received into the Catholic Church. Payen advises that the question of whether or not they may be received into the Church without being made to separate should be referred to the Holy See.

baptized Catholic is by the *praesumptio iuris* of canon 1070, § 2,[23] to be considered valid (meaning that the existence of an impediment of disparity of cult is not to be presumed), but with the qualification of canon 1014. Canon 1014 ordains a presumption for the validity of doubtful marriage *"salvo praescripto can. 1127."* Therefore if the question of the baptism of the Catholic party remains doubtful after due inquiry, when the other party is an infidel, the status of the marriage may be considered to be that which will favor the use of the *privilegium fidei.*[24] Cappello, however,[25] applies to marriages between an infidel and a doubtfully baptized person, without distinction between Catholic and heretical baptism, the answer to the second question in the decree of the Holy Office, dated 10 June, 1937: [26]

1. Utrum in matrimonio contracto a duobus acatholicis dubie baptizatis, in casu dubii insolubilis circa Baptismum, possit permitti alterutri parti ad Fidem conversae usus Privilegii Paulini vi can. 1127 Codicis Iuris Canonici?

[23] It is agreed that canon 1070, § 2, has reference to the marriage referred to in canon 1070, § 1, that is, that the doubtful baptism in § 2 is that of a Catholic either baptized in the Catholic Church or converted to it. The presumption for the validity of the marriage in canon 1070, § 2, would be useless or absurd if applied to marriages between infidels and doubtfully baptized heretics or schismatics since by the law of the Code (canon 1070, § 1) such marriages are no longer subject to the impediment of disparity of cult. The later certain proof that one party was baptized in heresy or schism and the other party not baptized would not affect the status of the marriage. *Cf.* J. Creusen, "De dubio matrimonio ob dubium baptismum," *Periodica,* XVII (1928), 154*-155*; Cappello, *De Sacramentis,* III (4. ed.), n. 419, c.

[24] Vermeersch, "Interpretatio canonis 1127, de favore iuris, etc.," *Periodica,* X (1921), (27); De Smet: "Ita matrimonium inter unam partem certo infidelem et partem dubie baptizatam, quod matrimonium, juxta can. 1070, § 2, non est obnoxium impedimento disparitatis cultus ac censetur validum, potest, quousque dubium circa Baptismum perseverat, haberi uti legitimum, adeoque privilegio Paulino obnoxium."—*De Spons. et Mat.,* n. 355, nota 6; Arendt, "Nota theologico-canonica circa canonem 1127," *ETL,* I (1924), 182, 183; Léry, *Le Privilège de la Foi,* n. 114.

[25] *De Sacramentis,* III (4. ed.), n. 788, § 4, 2 °.

[26] *AAS,* XIX (1937), 305, 306. *Cf. AER,* XCVII (1937), 268; Bouscaren, *Canon Law Digest, Supplement—1938,* p. 29.

2. Utrum in matrimonio contracto inter partem non baptizatam et partem acatholicam dubie baptizatam, in casu dubii insolubilis de Baptismo, possint Ordinarii alterutri parti ad Fidem Catholicam conversae permittere usum Privilegii Paulini vi can. 1127?

Ad. 1. Negative.

Ad. 2. Recurrendum ad S. Officium in singulis casibus.

The decree definitely excludes the use of canon 1127 in order to arrive at a solution favorable to the use of the Pauline privilege if both parties are doubtfully baptized non-Catholics. If there is question of a marriage in which one party is certainly not baptized and the other is a doubtfully baptized non-Catholic, authorities inferior to the Holy See are restricted from applying the principle of the canon in order to permit the use of the Pauline privilege.[27] In view of the fact that disparity of cult is no longer an impediment to a valid marriage between an unbaptized person and a person who has received even certainly valid baptism outside the Catholic Church and has not thereafter been converted to the true Faith, the reason for the restriction is not obscure. The Pauline privilege applies only to a marriage entered between two infidels. If the doubtful baptism were in fact valid there would be no place for the Pauline privilege, but for due cause the Sovereign Pontiff could dispense in the natural bond of the marriage as was done in the Helena case.[28] The same difficulty does not beset a case which involves an unbaptized person and a person doubtfully baptized in the Catholic Church. If the baptism were in fact valid the marriage would be null by virtue of the diriment impediment of disparity of cult, provided, of course, that a dispensation from the impediment had not been obtained: if the baptism were in fact invalid then the marriage would be *legitimum* and hence subject to dissolution *servatis servandis* by the use of the Pauline privilege.[29]

In general it may be said of the force of canon 1127 that in the doubts of law or of fact to which the principle it enunciates validly

[27] *Cf.* Kelly, "Recent Decree on Doubtful Baptisms and the Pauline Privilege," *AER,* XCVII (1937), 366-372.

[28] *Cf.* Bouscaren, *Canon Law Digest,* I, 553, 554; *Periodica,* XIV (1925), 20.

[29] *Cf.* Vromant, *De Matrimonio* (2. ed.), n. 373.

applies, divine and canonical law permit that response to be given which favors the liberty of the converted party so that he may: enter a new marriage with a Catholic; or he may be permitted to remain in a new marriage already entered with a Catholic after his conversion.[80]

Article 3. Norms for Interpretation of the Constitutions

A. *Influence of Interpretation Before the Code*

Canon 6, which expresses the relation between the Code and the discipline formerly prevailing states that for the most part the Code retains the former discipline, but with opportune modifications. In extending to the whole world the provisions regarding marriage in the three constitutions canon 1125 makes a change in the previous discipline.

According to canon 6, 2°, the canons of the Code which restate former laws in their entirety are to be construed in accordance with the authority of the old law and the interpretation accepted by approved authors. The moot question of just who the approved authors may be is not of importance in regard to the present subject. It has been seen that a misunderstanding of the Papal power over the bond of marriage was responsible for the misconstruction of the force of the constitutions. The prevailing opinion as late as the middle of the eighteenth century was influential in causing so skilled a canonist as Benedict XIV to give a very unlikely and inadequate interpretation of the Constitution *"Populis"* [81] in order to avoid the conclusion that Gregory XIII was exercising the power of dissolving the bond of marriage contracted in infidelity that had become *ratum* through the baptism of both parties although not afterwards consummated.

Of more importance than the opinions of authors are the authentic declarations of the Holy See, but in considering such declarations

[80] *Cf.* Wernz-Vidal, *Ius Canonicum,* V, n. 631, p. 757 et nota 61; Vermeersch, "Interpretatio canonis 1127, de favore iuris, etc.," *Periodica,* X (1921), (28); Cappello, *De Sacramentis,* III (4. ed.), n. 788, § 3.

[81] *De Synodo Dioecesana,* lib. XIII, cap. XXI, nn. 4-6; *cf.* Gury-Ballerini, *Compendium Theologiae Moralis,* II, n. 759, nota 2, p. 517.

it is essential to be sure that the legislation to which they have reference is precisely that now being interpreted.[32] A declaration which concerns only a provision having some relation to the law is not an authentic declaration on the law itself. The legislator would first have to make known that the provision did in fact give the genuine sense of the law as such.

Before the middle of the century following that in which the constitutions were issued the Cong. for the Propagation of the Faith had included among its faculties for missionaries one that had a close relation to the constitutions:

> Dispensandi cum gentilibus et infidelibus plures uxores habentibus, ut post conversionem et baptismum, quam ex illis maluerint, si etiam ipsa fidelis fiat, retinere possint, nisi prima voluerit converti.

To the extent that this and certain other faculties conceded at various times [33] are evidently in conformity with the provisions of the constitutions, the declarations of the Sacred Congregations replying to questions concerning the use of those faculties will apply also to the same questions arising in connection with the use of the constitutions now that they have become a part of the common law, at least as giving a sense which will be within the limits of the broad interpretation to which it will be seen the constitutions are subject. It is clear, however, that the limits of the faculties are not to be taken arbitrarily as the limits of the powers granted in the constitutions. Unless such limitation were imposed by an authentic declaration of the Holy See it could stand only from the evidence of the constitutions themselves. The correction of laws is odious and derogation from them is not to be presumed.[34] The following examination into the declarations made before the Code indicates that they do not, in themselves, form a clear interpretation of the constitutions: this is particularly true in regard to the interpretation of the Constitution *"Romani Pontificis."*

The numerous declarations on the above faculty have not desig-

[32] *Cf.* Vermeersch-Creusen, *Epitome,* I, n. 76, § 2.

[33] *Cf. supra,* Chap. VI, Part II, Arts. 2, 3.

[34] *Cf.* c. 29, *de electione et electi potestate,* I, 6, in VI°.

nated specifically the concession of Paul III in his Constitution *"Altitudo"* as their subject. But the Constitutions *"Romani Pontificis"* of St. Pius V and *"Populis"* of Gregory XIII have been directly alluded to in decisions, in decrees of approved Synods and Councils, and in instructions and responses by being mentioned either in the statement of his problem by an Ordinary or in the solution of the problem by the respective Congregation. Rayanna [85] has given an extensive commentary on the jurisprudence of the Holy Office, the Congregation of the Council, and the Congregation for the Propagation of the Faith, in regard to the Constitution *"Romani Pontificis."*

Three declarations of the Holy Office offer particular difficulties. An Archbishop of Quebec in presenting his problem first mentioned his usual missionary faculty of dispensing polygamists so that they might choose to retain that one, from among their wives, who would be baptized with them unless the first desired to be converted. He asked for the further concession to dispense the polygamist converts from any obligation of choosing the first wife. The request was based on these words from the Constitution *"Romani Pontificis"*: *"Indi . . . in futurum baptizandi cum uxore quae cum ipsis fuerit baptizata remanere valeant, tamquam cum uxore legitima, aliis dimissis."* In its reply the Holy Office made no mention of St. Pius V's constitution, but said that if there was no question of the validity of the marriage, polygamists must retain the first wife if she would receive baptism or at least consent to cohabit without injury to the Creator.[86] Only when the validity of the marriage with the first wife could be seriously doubted was the polygamist convert to be allowed to choose one of the others provided that she be converted and also that consent be renewed. It is evident that the Sacred Congregation was only restating the usual requirements for the use of the Pauline privilege, and making no allowance either for the concession of the Constitution *"Romani Pontificis"* or the usual missionary faculty for polygamist converts.

A Vicar Apostolic of Siam inquiring whether a polygamist con-

[85] "De Constitutione S. Pii Papae V, etc.," *Periodica*, XXVIII (1939), 25-52, 129-134, q. v.

[86] 8 Jun., 1836—*Fontes*, n. 874.

vert might not omit interpellating his first wife suggested the constitution of St. Pius V as the basis for such an omission.[87] The Sacred Congregation gave no direct answer to this question but referred the Vicar Apostolic to cap. IX, § 8, of the prescriptions of the Synod of Su-tchuen, which requires that even in using the faculty to dispense polygamist converts the missionary follow the norm of Gregory XIII's Constitution *"Populis."* [88]

Later the Vicar Apostolic of Siam proposed a direct question in regard to the Constitution *"Romani Pontificis"* implicitly indicating his belief that the concession of St. Pius V gave wider powers than the usual missionary faculty for polygamist converts.[89] He first proposed the case of one Titius who as a pagan had married Lola a pagan woman. After some years Lola left him and began living with Brutus another pagan. Titius took to wife a second pagan woman, Flotilla, by whom he had children. Lola in the meantime had been sold into slavery by Brutus. Titius, Flotilla and the children became Christians. When Titius interpellated Lola she replied that she would return to him and become a Christian provided that he would free her from slavery. There were several difficulties in the way: due to his poverty it was impossible for Titius to free Lola; Brutus was unwilling to dismiss her and the civil law of the country held her to be his legitimate wife by reason of three years cohabitation; Titius was unwilling to dismiss Flotilla because she had been faithful and because after baptism they had renewed consent and cohabited. To the Vicar Apostolic's question concerning Titius: *"Potestne sic remanere coniunctus?"* The Holy Office replied:

[87] S. C. S., Off., resp. (Siam), 4 Jul., 1855, ad IV—*Fontes,* n. 931.

[88] Benedict XIV seemed to confuse the constitutions of St. Pius V and Gregory XIII since he referred the missionary faculty on dispensing polygamist converts to both the constitutions. *Cf. De Synodo Dioecesana,* lib. XIII, cap. XXI, n. 6. Gregory XIII's Constitution *"Populis"* made no reference to polygamists, yet the decree of the Synod of Su-tchuen, legislating the discipline for the use of the faculty, said in cap. IX, § 8, that missionaries "uti non debent tali facultate nisi ad normam supradicti Brevis Gregoriani [Constitutio *"Populis"*], scilicet ut non dispensetur ab interpellatione primae uxoris, nisi in casibus Brevi expressis; sufficit autem ut interpelletur num velit converti."—*Coll. Lac.* VI, col. 623; *Coll. S. C. P. F.,* II, p. 481, nota 1.

[89] S. C. S. Off., resp. (Siam), 22 Nov., 1871—*Fontes,* n. 1019.

"Iuxta exposita in casu de quo agitur, quatenus prima uxor adhuc in infidelitate permaneat, permitti posse Titio ut legitimo matrimonio cum secunda muliere coniungatur." "Quaesitum primum" which immediately follows need not necessarily be taken as connected with the case, that is, it may have been asked and may be considered independently of the case, yet an affirmative answer would obviate difficulties in the solution of cases similar to that of Titius. It is quite likely that the Vicar Apostolic purposely proposed the case and the *quaesitum* together.

> *Quaesitum primum*—An potestate a S. Pio V universe concessa per Breve quod incipit: *Romani Pontificis,* uti possint missionarii in tota sua latitudine.
>
> *Responsum.*—Breve s.m. Pii V spectare ad casum in quo prima uxor legitima nota non sit simulque sit difficillimum eam reperire; in eius vero usu servandum esse regulam ab eiusdem successore Gregorio XIII praescriptam, hoc est, ut, antequam neophytus cum alia muliere quae simul cum eo baptizata est matrimonio iungatur, per summarium et extraiudicialem processum constare debeat difficillimum reapse primam uxorem reperire.

Is this response to be taken as the authentic interpretation of *"Romani Pontificis"*? It posits as one of the conditions under which the concession of St. Pius V would apply to a case the circumstance that the first legitimate wife be not known. This is the same condition which Paul III required in the Constitution *"Altitudo,"* that is, that the polygamist be unable to remember his first wife, but no similar statement is found in St. Pius V's constitution. The Sacred Congregation required further that it be very difficult to find the unknown first wife, which is indeed a corollary to the first condition. If the identity of the first legitimate wife could not be determined after due inquiry (and this it may be supposed is the sense of the first condition), then it would not only be difficult but impossible to locate her person (*"eam reperire"*). Both conditions are thus reduced to that required for the use of Paul III's concession, and St. Pius V's Constitution *"Romani Pontificis"* would be superfluous. Yet the provisions regarding marriage in both constitutions are extended to the whole world by canon 1125. It can scarcely be presumed that the legislator would include both in the canon if one were sufficient.[40] The redundance would not serve to eliminate confusion in the laws of the Church as was intended in the codification.

It may be recalled here that in 1671 Clement X[41] decreed that the solution of doubts made by the Holy Office and the Cong. for the Propagation of the Faith were sent to missionaries and other ministers of the latter Congregation not as definitions but as simple instructions by which they could and ought to be governed in doubts which arose. Rayanna observes[42] that the response of the Holy Office could not have become generally known to the Ordinaries of the places for which the constitution was given before the first (1893) edition of the *Collectanea S. C. P. F.* was published. The response had previously appeared in the 1880 edition of the Paris Foreign Mission Society *Collectanea.* The preface, a letter of dedication, in the latter work called attention to the fact that particular replies oblige only those to whom they were given, although they are valuable for others also by indicating the opinion of the Holy See and a course to be followed in solving difficulties.[43]

Votum 12 of the First Council of China (1924)[44] is a further indication that the above response of the Holy Office does not consti-

[40] *Cf.* Rayanna, *op. cit., Periodica,* XXVIII (1939), 131.

[41] *Cf. Coll. Hong.*, n. 6; *cf.* also *supra,* p. 100.

[42] *Ibid.*

[43] "On a aussi regardé comme necessaire d'inquire tres—exactement à quelle contrée ou à quelle personne les pièces ont été adressées. Sur bien des points, en effet, la réglementation donnée à une Mission ou à un groupe de Missions ne s'etend pas au-delà des limites de ces Missions. C'est une remarque très-importante sur laquelle il est inutile d'insister, puisqu'elle est connue de tous nos chers Confrères. Il n'en est pas moins vrai qu'un grand nombre de rèponses donées a des consultations particulières sont applicables partout, et que les Instructions elles-mêmes qui ne regardent qu'une Mission, sont toujours précieuses pour les autres, puisqu'elles font connaître la pensée du Saint-Siege sur des points importants, et indiquent souvent la ligne de conduite à suivre dans les difficultés qui peuvent survenir."—*Coll. Hong.,* p. XIII. The preface of the first edition is reprinted on pp. XI-XV of this Hongkong edition, 1905.

[44] *Primum Concilium Sinense, Acta-Decreta et Normae-Vota, etc.* (Zi-Ka-Wei: Typographia Missionis Catholicae, 1929), p. 273.

tute an authentic general interpretation of the Constitution *"Romani Pontificis."* The *votum* will be considered more fully in the commentary on the constitution, but here it may be briefly noted that the Council of China petitioned the Holy See that, *"ad mentem Constitutionis S. Pii V (Romani Pontificis),"* Vicars and Prefects Apostolic of China might permit polygamist converts to remain with the second or further wife consenting to be baptized and from whom it would be very hard to separate them, and that this might be permitted without any interpellation of the first wife. In the petition there was no mention of the first wife not being known, nor of any difficulty in finding her, but only of the difficulty of breaking the union with the wife whom the polygamist convert wished to keep. The Holy See was asked whether or not it would be permitted to the Vicars and Prefects Apostolic to follow the procedure outlined; the answer was, *"Affirmative."*

A review of the various particular replies of the Sacred Congregations concerning the Constitution *"Romani Pontificis"* suggests the conclusion that its full force is to be determined, not from those replies, but from an interpretation of the constitution itself.[45] The pre-Code jurisprudence on the Constitution *"Populis"* of Gregory XIII is more definite and will be considered in the commentary on the constitution.

B. *Interpretation to be Governed by Canons 18 and 19*

The term "constitutions" applied in canon 1125 to the legislation of the three Popes is used in the strict sense denoting a law given by the Supreme Pontiff.[46] Bulls and briefs are among the forms of documents (*litterae Apostolicae*) by which Papal constitutions, *i. e.*, laws, are given. The bull is the more solemn form: it opens with

[45] *Cf.* Rayanna, *op. cit.*, *Periodica,* XXVIII (1939), 133, 134.

[46] *Cf.* Wernz, *Ius Decretalium*, I, n. 137, II; Wernz-Vidal, *Ius Canonicum,* I, n. 203, II. Van Hove, however, confines constitution in the strict sense to denote a pontifical act by which a *general* law is given for the Church.—*Commentarium Lovaniense in Codicem Iuris Canonici,* Vol. I, Tom. I, *Prolegomena ad Codicem Iuris Canonici* (Mechliniae et Romae: Dessain, 1928), nn. 58-59. The three constitutions as given were not general but special laws. The definition proposed by Wernz will be accepted here as being sufficiently clear.

the name of the Pope, omitting the numeral, followed by *Episcopus Servus Servorum Dei.* At its close the year of the pontificate is noted.[47] The brief, a less solemn form, opens with the name of the Pope *with* the numeral, and closes with "*Datum . . . sub annulo Piscatoris*" together with the date. In the usage of the Roman Curia the acts of the Supreme Pontiff are not designated according to their form as bulls or briefs, but bulls which contain laws are called *Constitutiones Apostolicae*; briefs are called *Litterae Apostolicae.* These are never signed by the Pope but by the Cardinal Secretary of State.[48]

The Constitution "*Altitudo*" is in the form of a bull: the Constitutions "*Romani Pontificis*" and "*Populis*" have the form of briefs. In view of their occasion all three are Decreta or Motus Proprii, but only the Constitution "*Romani Pontificis*" contains the clausula "*motu proprio*" in its body. When issued, the constitutions were particular legislation for determined districts; now by virtue of canon 1125 the legislator has extended to the whole world their provisions regarding marriage and consequently they are now three universal laws. Moreover, they are special laws as opposed to general, since they are made for a class of the faithful, namely, for converts who before baptism had married an unbaptized person; they are singular laws as opposed to common, since they contain exceptions to the ordinary rule. This last classification as singular laws calls for further discussion.

A law that establishes an exception to the ordinary rule is a *ius singulare,* and if the exception so established be favorable it is called a privilege,[49] but privilege in the wide sense of the term. A privilege in the strict sense, viewed from the point of its efficient cause (*objective*), is a provision of a superior granting a special favor to someone. Privilege in the wide sense, viewed from the point of its efficient cause, is a *ius singulare* which constitutes something favor-

[47] *Cf., v. g.,* the Constitution "*Altitudo,*" in the Appendix, *infra.*

[48] Vermeersch-Creusen, *Epitome,* I, n. 84.

[49] Philippus Maroto, *Institutiones Iuris Canonici ad Normam Novi Codicis* (2 vols.), Vol. I, *Tractatus Fundamentales* (3. ed., Romae; Apud "Commentarium Pro Religiosis," 1921), n. 24, D, c; Vermeersch-Creusen, *Epitome,* I, n. 24.

able for the benefit of a class of persons, things, or affairs.[50] To the extent that a *ius singulare* departs from a rule of law which ordinarily and commonly is to be observed, and grants a special benefit, it takes the name and mode of privilege.[51]

The concessions of the Popes in the three constitutions are laws containing favors to converts in the form of exceptions from a provision of the natural law which must be observed unless a relaxation be allowed through the exercise of power granted by its Author. As has been seen[52] the Vicar of Christ exercises such power in certain matters that are of obligation by natural law. Since a law that establishes an exception to the ordinary rule is a *ius singulare* and when the exception is favorable it is a *ius favorabile* and is called a privilege, the constitutions are *iura singularia favorabilia* and are privileges, but privileges in the wide sense of the term.[53] The distinction between privileges in the strict and in the wide sense must be considered in determining the norms for their interpretation. *Iura singularia favorabilia* as juridical institutes are laws, but with an accessory nature of privilege. They are governed by the norms applicable to ecclesiastical laws, but with a certain consideration of the accessory nature of privilege.[54] For example, general principles, such as the provision that in doubt the interpretation must not be so strict that the privilege confers no benefit,[55] would apply.

To specify further the character of the concessions in the Papal constitutions, prescinding from the fact that they are *iura singularia* and with reference to their accessory nature as privileges, it is to be

[50] Coronata, however, defines privilege both in the wide and in the strict sense as a *ius singulare favorabile*, the specific difference being placed in the passive subject.—*Institutiones Iuris Canonici* (5 vols., Taurini: Marietti, 1928-1936), I, nn. 84-85.

[51] Maroto, *op. cit.*, I, n. 291, A et B; *cf.* Van Hove, *De Priv.—De Disp.*, n. 11.

[52] *Cf. supra*, pp. 87-90.

[53] In the Constitution *"Populis"* of Gregory XIII there is an additional element of habitual faculties granted to certain ecclesiastical persons. According to canon 66, § 1, habitual faculties are to be considered as privileges *praeter ius.*

[54] *Cf.* Van Hove, *op. cit.*, n. 64.

[55] *Cf.* can. 68; Reg. 15, R. J., in VI°: "Odia restringi, et favores convenit ampliari."

noted that they are: privileges (in the wide sense) *contra ius*, that is, against the general provision of the natural law that the bond of marriage is permanent during the life of both parties; *personal* privileges in that they are directly and immediately granted to the person of the polygamist converts (in the Constitutions "*Altitudo*" and "*Romani Pontificis*"), in contradistinction to real privileges which only mediately grant a favor to a person because of his relation to a place, function, dignity, etc.; *affirmative* privileges granting a faculty to break the bond of marriage against the prohibition of the natural law; *common* privileges in that they directly and primarily regard the good of the community as aids to the spread of faith and the Catholic religion, rather than private privileges which primarily regard the good of the individual; *odious* or *unfavorable* privileges to the extent that their exercise may injure the right of another, namely, the spouse married in infidelity by the convert, as distinguished from favorable privileges which bring no prejudice to another.[56]

In determining the norms according to which the concessions are to be interpreted their status subjectively viewed as privileges granted by law, that is, that objectively they are *iura singularia favorabilia*, is the first consideration. Canon 68 provides that in doubt privileges must be interpreted according to the norm of canon 50. No distinction is made as between privileges in the wide or in the strict sense and so the norm would seem to apply indiscriminately to both types. Some authors [57] thus apply it. Van Hove,[58] however, and others [59] hold that privileges granted by law, that is, *iura singularia favorabilia*, since they are laws in a proper sense and only privileges in the wide sense, are to be interpreted according to the

[56] *Cf.* Maroto, *op. cit.*, n. 293; Cicognani, *Canon Law*, p. 782.

[57] *V. g.*, Maroto, *op. cit.*, n. 299; Coronata, *Institutiones Iuris Canonici*, I, n. 96; Cappello, *Summa Iuris Canonici* (3 vols., Romae: Apud Aedes Univ. Greg., Vols. I-II, 2 ed., 1932-1934; Vol. III, 1936), I, n. 172.

[58] *Op. cit.*, n. 201.

[59] *V. g.*, Vermeersch-Creusen, *Epitome*, I, n. 183, *in fine*; B. Ojetti, *Commentarium in Codicem Iuris Canonici* (4 vols., Romae: Pontificia Universita Gregoriana, 1927-1931), I, p. 146; Gommarus Michiels, *Normae Generales Iuris Canonici* (2 vols., Lublin: Universitas Catholica, 1929), I, 73, 450; II, 356.

norms for the interpretation of laws. The arguments are cogent. Law is stronger and more favorable than privilege; hence its juridical status prevails over the juridical status of privilege. In canons 18 and 19 the legislator made no distinction of the divers kinds of ecclesiastical law. These canons, then, seem to apply to all laws and therefore also to laws which grant privileges, which privileges when subjectively considered are the laws themselves. The interpretation of such privileges according to the norms for the interpretation of law rather than of privilege was commonly accepted before the Code; in doubt, that practice should not now be abandoned. The latter view will be accepted here. The concessions of the constitutions will be considered primarily as laws, but with an accessory nature of privilege, and the interpretation will follow the norms of canons 18 and 19.[60]

Canon 18. To the extent that the Holy See has not declared the meaning of the concessions the prime rule is that they are to be understood according to the proper sense of the formula of words by which they are expressed. The secondary rules require recourse to parallel places, to the end and circumstances of the law, and to the mind of the legislator, when doubts and obscurities remain after considering the proper sense of the law's formula of words. Michiels holds[61] that in order to arrive at the true sense of a law with certitude the first rule of interpretation should always be complemented with the use of the secondary rules. If the use of the first rule does not indicate a sense which is free from doubts and obscurities, the application of the other rules becomes of primary importance to arrive at the true sense. The purpose of interpretation of law is to discover the will of the legislator.[62]

[60] Reg. 42, R. J., in VI°: "Accessorium naturam sequi congruit principalis." *Cf.* Reiffenstuel: "Ratio regulae (42) est, tum, quia accessorium est connexum et adhaerens principali: connexorum autem eadem est ratio, idemque judicium . . . Tum quia magis dignum trahit ad se minus dignum . . . Principale autem regulariter loquendo est praecipuum, et magis dignum . . . Porro haec regula valde late patet, ita ut fere ubique procedat . . ."—*Tractatus de Regulis Juris*, Reg. XLII, n. 5.

[61] *Normae Generales*, I, 402, 403.

[62] A. Van Hove, *Commentarium Lovaniense in Codicem Iuris Canonici*, Vol. I, Tom. II, *De Legibus Ecclesiasticis* (Mechliniae-Romae: Dessain, 1930), n. 250; *cf. Wernz, Ius Decretalium*, I, n. 131.

The will of the legislator in the first instance to be discovered in the present matter is that of the Popes who issued the constitutions, since these have been brought into the Code intact from the old law. There can no longer be any question that the constitutions are not merely regulations modifying the discipline on interpellations in the use of the Pauline privilege. From what has been seen thus far it is evident their full force goes beyond the limits of the *Casus Apostoli,* yet from the very nature of the matter, namely, the breaking of the bond of marriage previously contracted in infidelity by a convert to the faith, their background and their milieu (if juridical relationships may be so expressed) is that of the Pauline privilege, the discipline of which is governed and has in the past been governed by ecclesiastical laws.

The parallel places to which recourse must be had in doubt of the sense of a law, according to the first (in the order given by canon 18) of the auxiliary or secondary rules of interpretation, are the various texts which treat of the same matter as the law which is being interpreted.[63] The parallel places may be in harmony with or in opposition to the law, but the comparison will be an aid to finding the law's true sense. The legislator is considered to have all laws enshrined *in pectore suo.* It is to be presumed that his intention is always the same [64] and that he does not multiply laws needlessly. The parallel places to which recourse should be had in doubt about the interpretation of the constitutions are those which govern the discipline of the Pauline privilege. Opposition between laws may result from the fact that one posits a principle or mode of action and the other an exception to it.[65] Such is found to be the case when the general provisions for interpellation in the use of the Pauline privilege are compared with the discipline of the constitutions. The opposition is recognized in the law of the Code by canon 1121, § 1, which requires the interpellations for validity of the new marriage, *"salvo praescripto can. 1125."* It is again to be stressed, however, that the relationship between the Pauline privi-

[63] Van Hove, *op. cit.*, n. 256; Michiels, *op. cit.*, I, 410.

[64] Cicognani, *Canon Law,* p. 611.

[65] *Cf.* Michiels, *op. cit.*, I, 412.

lege and the constitutions recognized in this paragraph, or elsewhere, is not to be taken in the sense that they are coterminous.

The second of the auxiliary rules of interpretation when doubts and obscurities remain after the primary rule is applied, is that recourse is to be had to the end (*"finis" seu ratio*) and circumstances of the law. The *intrinsic* end of a law is that purpose to which it is ordained by its nature. A law must always be interpreted according to this end with due regard, of course, to the proper sense of the formula of words which express it. The *extrinsic* end is the motive which induced the legislator to make the law and is called the *ratio legis*. *"Ratio legis est anima legis."* [66] Yet care is to be taken in the use of the rule to avoid extending it to imply, for example, that the *ratio legis* is *per se* the intrinsically determinative cause of the law or of the determined will of the legislator. Law is imposed by act of the reasonable will of the legislator; hence the *ratio legis*, even though it is expressed in the law, *per se* is not a sufficient and still less an adequate sign of that will. The expressed *ratio* is only a sign of the fitness or utility which the legislator sees in the matter so that he may introduce necessity into it by law.[67] Nor is the rule an independent basis for extension or restriction of the proper sense of the words of the law. It may be used to extend or to restrict when obscurities are present and when otherwise the law would require something disadvantageous, but it may never be used in violation of the clear sense of the formula of words or in such a way as to put in second place the first rule of interpretation.[68]

Laws given before the Code usually contained a *pars motiva* which gave the end or *ratio* of the law proper, which was expressed in the dispositive part. The constitutions are thus divided. Their primary extrinsic end, their *ratio*, is to promote the salvation of souls by eliminating obstacles which, in the absence of the constitu-

[66] Van Hove, *op. cit.*, n. 260; *cf.* Cicognani, *op. cit.*, p. 611.

[67] Suarez, *De Legibus*, lib. VI, cap. III, n. 12.

[68] *Cf.* Michiels, *op. cit.*, I, 421-423; D'Annibale, *Summula Theologiae Moralis*, I, n. 188.

tions, would be physically or morally insurmountable barriers to the conversion of many infidels. Subsidiary ends may be discovered as, for example, the desire expressed by St. Pius V in his Constitution "*Romani Pontificis*" to free the missionaries from scruples.

Recourse to the circumstances in which a law was given in order to discover its true meaning is of no small value. "To have known the historical circumstances under which a law was made is practically the same as knowing its cause," [69] and a knowledge of the cause is an aid, in the obscurities of a law, to understand the effect intended by the legislator. A law is to be understood according to the will of the legislator at the time at which it was given.[70] The circumstances of time and place connected with the constitutions are undoubtedly of a nature to be of considerable help in arriving at the supreme norm to which all rules of interpretation are directed, namely, the intention or will of the legislator,—the *mens legislatoris*.[71]

CANON 19. According to canon 19 laws which contain an exception from the (common) law are to receive a strict interpretation. At first sight it might seem that the constitutions are affected by the prescription in so far as they derogate from the common law requiring interpellations and dispensation from disparity of cult (the latter *in re "Altitudo"*). But, as was seen above, the constitutions are *iura singularia* providing concessions for a certain class of persons. They contain only a material exception from other law and were constituted because of necessity or utility. The necessity or utility has motivated the legislator to provide the *iura singularia*—parallel laws "*alteri pleno iure coordinatae*." They are not subject to the strict interpretation imposed by canon 19, but are under wide interpretation.[72] Laws which favor religion—and the constitutions

[69] Cicognani, *op. cit.*, p. 612.

[70] Van Hove, *op. cit.*, n. 265.

[71] *Cf.* Van Hove, *op. cit.*, n. 266; Vermeersch-Creusen, *Epitome*, I, n. 124. "Verba sunt intelligenda, non secundum quod sonant, sed secundum mentem proferentis."—*cf.* cc. 6, 15, X, *de verborum significatione*, V, 40. Reg. 88, R. J., in VI°: "Certum est, quod is committit in legem, qui verba legis complectens contra legis nititur voluntatem."

[72] Michiels, *op. cit.*, I, 450; Van Hove, *op. cit.*, n. 307; Vermeersch-Creusen, *Epitome*, I, n. 126, § 3.

are of this order—are to be considered as favorable laws and are not to be strictly interpreted.[73]

Strict interpretation is that which understands the words of the law in the strictest or least extended signification of the proper sense which is discovered by the use of the rules of interpretation. Wide interpretation also understands the words of the law in their proper sense according to the rules of interpretation, but gives that sense the widest extension possible.[74]

[73] Cicognani, *op. cit.*, pp. 617, 618; S. C. de Prop. Fide, resp. (C. P. pro Sin.—Cochinchin.), 2 Jul., 1827—*Fontes*, n. 4738, *in fine*.

[74] Michiels, *op. cit.*, I, 380, 381.

CHAPTER VIII

PROVISIONS FOR POLYGAMIST CONVERTS

I. THE CONSTITUTION *"ALTITUDO"*

For convenient reference, but not for interpretation, an English translation will be given for each constitution in the respective chapter which treats of it. The interpretation must be made according to Documents VI, VII, and VIII in the Code. The translations will follow the Latin originals as given previously in the historical part of the dissertation, therefore the notes on sources will be the same as before and need not be repeated.

The section which makes provisions regarding marriage in the Constitution "*Altitudo*" given by Pope Paul III, 1 June, 1537, is contained in Document VI of the Code:

> . . . Since, as we have learned with great joy, many inhabitants of West and South India, ignorant though they are of divine law, through the enlightenment of the Holy Spirit have utterly rejected from their minds and hearts the errors to which they have hitherto been subject, and having embraced the truth of the Catholic faith and the unity of Holy Church desire and intend to live according to the manner of the Roman Church . . . We decree that this is to be observed in the matter of their marriages: that those who before their conversion had, according to their customs, several wives and are unable to recall whom they married first shall, on their conversion, take from among them the one whom they wish and contract marriage with her, wording the contract in the present tense, as is the custom; those, however, who do remember whom they married first shall retain her and dismiss the others. To them we also grant that until the Holy See decides otherwise they shall not be excluded from marriage, even though they be related in the third degree whether of consanguinity or affinity . . . [1]

[1] Translation by the author of this dissertation. For the Latin text of the complete constitution, *cf.* Appendix, *infra.*

ARTICLE 1. INTERPRETATION OF "THOSE WHO . . . HAD . . . SEVERAL WIVES"

The constitution of Pope Paul III (*"Altitudo"*) and that of Pope St. Pius V (*"Romani Pontificis"*) both directly concern only those converts from infidelity who before their conversion had several wives. According to the rule of law: *"Pluralis locutio duorum numero est contenta,"* [2] the provisions of the constitutions will apply to those who had two wives or more.

The terms "polygamy" or "polygamist" do not appear in the Papal documents themselves, but they have been used here thus far and will be used to denote the marital status in infidelity of the converts to whom the constitutions apply. In present day usage the generic term "polygamy" includes the conditions denominated by the specific terms "polygyny," meaning the marital union of one man with more than one woman, and "polyandry," meaning the marital union of one woman more than one man.

The disposition of law is considered to be the same wherever the same reason is present. *"Casu expresso (a lege), similis non censetur amissus."* The Code recognizes the rule in canon 20 by directing recourse to parallel places, except in the matter of applying punishments, when an express prescription concerning a particular matter is lacking. Especially is the rule true in regard to correlatives such as husband and wife. Correlatives are to be considered equal, and equity requires that the same rules apply to both where no disparity of reason can be assigned and there is no provision to the contrary in a contract.[3] By equity of law, therefore, the concessions of the constitutions apply to women converts who have lived in polyandry as well as to men who have lived in polygyny. The Roman Congregations have thus interpreted the missionary faculty [4] in regard to

[2] Reg. 40, R. J., in VI°.

[3] *Cf.* Zephyrinus Zitelli, *De Dispensationibus Matrimonialibus* (Romae, 1884), p. 16.

[4] Now F III, 24, or *FTM* 24 as it will hereafter be referred to in these pages. *Cf. supra*, p. 108. The declarations of the Sacred Congregations on questions which arose in the use of the missionary faculties are of value in answering the same questions which may arise in the use of the constitutions, at least as giving a sense within the limits of their broad interpretation, but

dispensing infidels who had many wives.[5] Whatever, therefore, is declared as applying to men who before their conversion had many wives, is to be considered *servatis servandis*, as of equal force for women converts who had many husbands.

The Popes, moreover, made no distinction in the constitutions between converts who in paganism had lived with more than one wife at the same time in simultaneous polygamy and those who lived first with one wife and then with another or others in successive polygamy. Both types of polygamy were found among the peoples for whom the concessions were granted,[6] hence both types were "according to their customs." The phrase, *"iuxta eorum mores,"* which Paul III inserted in the text of the Constitution *"Altitudo,"* would seem to indicate that the concession was meant to extend to every convert polygamist whatever may have been the peculiarities in the polygamous customs or practices of his particular people. Its parenthetical character and relation to the rest of the sentence strengthens the probability that such may be the correct interpretation.

The Cong. for the Propagation of the Faith[7] answered in the affirmative a question as to whether or not the faculty *FTM* 24 applied in cases of successive polygamy. A decree of divorce in a valid marriage given by a civil court does not, before God or the Church,[8] exempt from the nature of successive polygamy a subsequent marriage of either party with a third person during the life of the first valid spouse.[9] The matter is of importance for the use of the concessions in

only to the extent that the faculties and the constitutions are in agreement, as was pointed out above, p. 124.

[5] S. C. de Prop. Fide, resp. (C. P. pro Sin.), 14 Jan., 1793—*Coll. S. C. P. F.*, n. 611; S. C. S. Off., resp. (Cochin. Occident.), 12 Jun., 1850, ad 2—*Fontes*, n. 910; S. C. S. Off., resp. (Praefectus Ap. Thibet.), 5 Sept., 1855—*Fontes*, n. 933. *Cf.* Payen, *De Matrimonio*, II, n. 2405; Vromant, *Facultates Apostolicae Quas Sacra Congregatio De Propaganda Fide Delegare Solet Ordinariis Missionum* (2. ed., Bruxelles et Paris: Museum Lessianum, 1938), n. 78; Vromant, *De Matrimonio* (2. ed.), n. 341.

[6] *Cf. supra*, Chap. II, Art. 3.

[7] Resp. (C. P. pro Sin.—Tunkin. Orient.), 14 Jan., 1806, ad 1—*Fontes*, n. 4686.

[8] *Cf.* Pius XI, ency. *"Casti connubii,"* 31 Dec., 1930—*AAS*, XXII (1930), 552.

[9] *Cf.*, in regard to the use of faculty *FTM* 24 for successive polygamists of this kind—Konings-Putzer, *Commentarium in Facultates Apostolicas*, n. 127,

the Constitutions *"Altitudo"* and *"Romani Pontificis"* in countries where civil divorce is common. The divorce statistics for the United States, for example, give an evidence of the possible need for the use of the concessions for converts who have been successive polygamists in this country. In 1925 the number of civil divorces obtained was approximately 14.6% of the number of marriages contracted in the same year: in 1932, the latest year for which statistics are available, the numerical relation of divorces to marriages had risen to approximately 16%: and an estimate for the year 1937 placed the relation at approximately 18%, or nearly one divorce granted for every five marriages contracted.[10]

It has been doubted[11] whether the phrase *"iuxta eorum mores"* may not exclude the use of the Constitution *"Altitudo"* from regions where polygamy is a very rare exception. The above interpretation[12] together with the fact that grammatically the expression is parenthetical[13] weakens the likelihood that it implies such a restric-

b; Vromant, *Facultates Apostolicae* (2. ed.), n. 79; in regard to the application of the Constitutions *"Altitudo"* and *"Romani Pontificis"* to the same type of polygamists—G. Vromant, "De Dispensatione ab interpellationibus in ordine ad privilegium fidei," *Periodica*, XX (1931), 109*, 112*; Vromant, *De Matrimonio* (2. ed.), nn. 341, 344.

[10] 1925—marriages, 1,199,334; divorces, 175,449: 1932—marriages, 981,903; divorces, 160,338: 1937—(estimates) marriages, 1,426,000; divorces, 250,000. The figures for 1925 and 1932 are actual statistics collected by the Census Bureau of the U. S. Government. The Federal inquiry on marriage and divorce was discontinued in 1933. Estimates for the nation for the years 1933-1937, based on the available marriage and divorce statistics of the individual states, were prepared by Prof. S. A. Stouffer of the University of Chicago and published in an article entitled, "Recent Increases in Marriage and Divorce," by Samuel A. Stouffer and Lyle M. Spenser, *American Journal of Sociology*, 1939, pp. 551-554.—From the Bulletin, "Marriage and Divorce Statistics," March 11, 1939, Department of Commerce, Bureau of the Census, Washington.

[11] Payen, *De Matrimonio*, II, n. 2405.

[12] *Cf.* also, Woods (*The Constitutions of Canon 1125*, pp. 40, 41), who explains the phrase as having been intended to preclude the impression that it was possible for the natives to have several legitimate wives—"If the pope had not included these words, the Constitution would have read in such a manner that the impression would prevail that these infidels had had several legitimate wives—a thing which is repugnant to the natural and the Divine positive law."

[13] *Cf.* Léry, *Le Privilège de la Foi*, n. 77.

tion. The lack of probability in the doubt of law involved, and the norms of interpretation to which the constitution is now subject, exclude the restriction until there is an authentic declaration to the contrary.

Article 2. The Concessions Granted in the Constitution *"Altitudo"*

In the Constitution *"Altitudo"* no choice among his marital partners in paganism is granted to the polygamist convert who can recall which of them was his first wife.[14] In this case he is to retain her and dismiss the others, *salvo privilegio Paulino.*[15] When the circumstances of any particular case will permit the application of the Pauline privilege the clause guarding the convert's right to use it is to be understood, whatever is found to be the special privileges for polygamist converts. It cannot be presumed that the legislator either in the constitutions or in the Code intended to derogate from the *Casus Apostoli.*

If the convert cannot recall which of the women was his first wife, or if the identity of the first wife or the validity of the first marriage is doubtful according to the norms for the use of canon 1127,[16] the convert's case and its disposition is subject to the principle enunciated in that canon. The question then remains as to what particular force the Constitution *"Altitudo"* now has to account for its inclusion in canon 1125.

The force of the constitution and the special favor it grants concerns the valid and licit marriage which a polygamist convert may

[14] The first relationship of a marital nature which the convert had as a pagan, even though it involved cohabitation for some time, may have been only concubinage and not true marriage. Obviously, from the nature of the matter, the legitimate first wife is the woman with whom the convert first contracted a marriage that was valid according to divine law and it is she who is referred to in the constitution. The term "first wife" will be used in that sense in these pages. *Cf.* Vermeersch, "Commentaria de Formulis Facultatum, etc." *Periodica,* XI (1922), (138): Payen, *De Matrimonio* (2. ed.), II, n. 2405, § 1. If that first wife had died then the term would apply to the woman who succeeded her in a valid marriage with the polygamist convert.

[15] Vermeersch-Creusen, *Epitome,* II, n. 436.

[16] *Cf. supra,* Chap. VII, Art. 2; Payen, *De Matrimonio* (2. ed.), n. 2405, § 1.

contract with a woman chosen from among those with whom he lived in a marital relationship before his conversion. The essential condition for the use of the favor is that the convert be not able to recall the identity of his first wife.

Interpretation of the favor may conveniently be divided into points concerning: (A.) a possible impediment of affinity or consanguinity; (B.) the person whom the convert polygamist may choose; (C.) the juridical requirements for validity and licitness of the marriage with the person chosen. It may be noted again that a woman who before her conversion lived with more than one man and is not able to recall which of them was her first and legitimate husband enjoys the same favor granted to a man convert who before conversion lived with more than one woman.

A. Consanguinity in the Third Degree of the Collateral Line is Not an Impediment

According to the constitution the convert may choose and validly and licitly contract marriage with one of his former partners even though she be related to him in the third degree of consanguinity or affinity.[17] The provision in regard to affinity is no longer of consequence since by the general law (canon 1077, § 1) affinity in the collateral line is an impediment only up to the second degree inclusive. By virtue of the constitution the impediment of consanguinity in the collateral line *ipso iure* is reduced to the second degree inclusive for the convert who is permitted to make a choice among his former partners. A dispensation, therefore, from the impediment of consanguinity in the third degree of the collateral line (canon 1076, § 2) which otherwise would be present if the woman chosen were thus related to the convert is not required under the constitution for the validity or licitness of the marriage. As was seen above,[18] Paul III was considered to have reduced the impediments of consanguinity and affinity to the second degree for the natives in the places for which the constitution was issued. It was a *ius singulare* with the accessory nature of a local privilege. The provision now is a *ius*

[17] Vermeersch-Creusen, *Epitome,* II, n. 436.

[18] *Cf.* pp. 40, 41.

singulare with the nature of a personal privilege for those polygamist converts who do not recall which of their former partners was first taken. It does not apply to all polygamists.[19]

B. The Persons Among Whom the Choice May Be Made

The force of the constitution and the special favor which it grants, aside from the provision in regard to the impediment of consanguinity, is that of allowing the polygamist convert who does not recall who was his first wife to choose one of his former partners and validly and licitly contract marriage with her even though she remains an infidel.[20]

Paul III placed no restriction upon the choice other than that it be among the wives the convert had in his paganism. Those wives who have been dismissed previous to the time of the conversion of the polygamist, even if the dismissal has been effected by a divorce decree of a civil court, are not excluded from the number of those among whom the choice may be made.[21] The concession was originally given for peoples who "according to their customs" had many wives.

[19] Payen, *De Matrimonio* (2. ed.), n. 2405, § 2; *cf.* Vermeersch-Creusen, *ibid.;* Vromant, *De Matrimonio* (2. ed.), n. 341.

[20] Vermeersch-Creusen, *ibid.;* Woods, *The Constitutions of Canon 1125,* p. 44; Vromant, *op. cit.,* n. 342. Payen: "At non videtur necessarium ut haec mulier quam, e suis uxoribus eligunt, convertatur et baptismum recipiat."—*De Matrimonio* (2. ed.), n. 2405, § 1.

[21] S. C. de Prop. Fide, resp. (C. P. pro Sin.—Tunkin. Orient.), 14 Jan., 1806, ad 1—*Fontes,* n. 4686; Woods, *op. cit.,* pp. 42, 43; Vromant, *op. cit.,* nn. 341, 344; *cf.* Payen, *ibid.;* Léry, *Le Privilège de la Foi,* p. 102.

In the first edition of his *De Matrimonio,* II, n. 2405, Payen considered to be *satis certa* the opposite opinion, as held by some authors, that is, that the choice was to be made only among those wives retained by the convert up to the time of his conversion. Vromant (*Facultates Apostolicae* [1. ed.], n. 79, ad 4), was the only author cited. The place cited has direct reference to *FTM* 24 rather than to the Constitution *"Altitudo."* In the second (1938) edition of *Facultates Apostolicae,* n. 79, ad 2, Vromant changed his commentary on *FTM* 24 to permit the choice from among those wives who had been dismissed. In direct reference to the concession made in the constitution, which is the matter here being considered, in *both* editions of *Facultates Apostolicae,* n. 77, Vromant gives this commentary:

Successive polygamy was a custom among some of them. Probability would favor the first woman lived with, or one of the earlier ones, as being the man's legitimate wife. In the absence of a clear statement it would be gratuitous and questionable to interpret the Pope as intending to exclude the dismissed women, among whom the legitimate wife, if the convert had one, would more probably be found.

Obviously the concession does not extend to the point of allowing the convert to choose one of his dismissed partners who has since entered a valid marriage with a third person. The situation could arise, for example, if the dismissed woman had herself become converted and by virtue of her preceding polyandry had made use of the concession.

The privilege of making a choice is not withheld even if one of the concubines or uncertain wives also desires to become a convert [22] or if a dismissed former partner has already been baptized. The circumstances under which the present concession may be used are distinct from those to which the Pauline privilege applies. The essential condition for the use of the provisions of the Constitution *"Altitudo"* is that the convert be not able to remember the identity of the first wife. The conversion of one of the uncertain wives makes no fundamental change in the case which would restrict the broad interpretation of the choice.

In a particular case it could happen that the question of which was the first wife would be limited to only a few, perhaps to three or four, of the many women with whom the polygamist convert had

> Unica condicio hic essentialis est dicenda, nempe: *ut non recordentur* polygami quamnam uxorem *primo* acceperint. Qua condicione impleta, missionarii possunt permittere ut eligant ex uxoribus quamcumque voluerint, dummodo hanc apud se adhuc retinuerint; licet haec non convertatur . . .

Therefore Vromant's opinion on the matter is not clear if reference is made only to the two editions of his *Facultates Apostolicae.* Elsewhere, however, as in his *De Matrimonio* (1 ed.), nn. 355, 358; (2. ed.), nn. 341, 344, and in the article "De Dispensatione ab interpellationibus in ordine ad privilegium fidei," *Periodica,* XX (1931), 112*, he clearly states that a choice is allowed among the wives had before conversion, whether the convert had retained them up to the time of his conversion or had previously dismissed them, and that the dismissal by decree of a civil court had no influence upon the nature of the matter.

[22] Vromant, *De Matrimonio* (2. ed.), n. 342.

lived. Vromant [23] holds that in that case, when the convert cannot remember which of these few was the first wife the choice allowed according to the Constitution *"Altitudo"* is confined to their number. Thus to restrict the choice reduces the probability of the convert not keeping the first wife, whoever she may have been. But is there any basis for assuming that it was, or is, the legislator's intention when the wife who is undoubtedly the first cannot be known, to insist upon the choice among the others which will be more likely to hit upon the first, but at best must be doubtful? The principle in canon 1127 seems opposed to the assumption. The constitution does not distinguish and there seems to be nothing in it, or in the circumstances of the converts in the places for which it was originally given, to indicate that Paul III intended thus to circumscribe the choice.

C. *Requirements for the Marriage With the Person Chosen*

The constitution requires that the convert contract marriage *per verba de praesenti* with the woman chosen. The exchange of matrimonial consent is necessary, at least *ad cautelam,* since there is doubt whether the parties were previously united in a valid marriage. When the woman chosen is not a Catholic, canons 1102 and 1109, § 3, are to observed in the ceremony.

In the constitution Paul III made no requirement that the woman chosen become a Christian nor did he make mention of the impediment that would exist if she remained an infidel. The impediment of disparity of cult through custom had become diriment in the twelfth or thirteenth century,[24] but up to the opening of the sixteenth century there was no precedent for granting a dispensation from it. The Christians of the late Middle Ages did not even consider entering marriage with the unbaptized. The question of dispensation from the impediment "was altogether foreign to the mind of an age bent on the extermination of heresy and infidelity." [25]

[23] *Ibid.*

[24] Francis J. Schenk, *The Matrimonial Impediments of Mixed Religion and Disparity of Cult* (The Catholic University of America, Canon Law Studies, n. 51, Washington: The Catholic University of America, 1929), pp. 41, 42.

[25] Schenk, *op. cit.,* p. 44.

The circumstances of converts in the missions were far different from those of Catholics where the Church was long established. When a question was raised in the latter part of the sixteenth century whether the impediment of disparity of cult was binding in the missions of Japan and China since it had no foundation in custom in those parts as it had in the non-pagan world, the Holy See by its practice approved the affirmative opinion, but Gregory XIII provided the missionaries of Japan and China with wide faculties to dispense from the impediment.[26] It is possible that Paul III had in mind that the woman chosen according to his grant would become a Christian before marriage or before the renewal of consent with the polygamist convert. But the Constitution *"Altitudo"* gives no hint of a requirement that the woman be baptized and with solid reasons it is interpreted as allowing the marriage of the convert with a woman chosen from among his former partners but who remains an infidel. The diriment impediment of disparity of cult exists in that case. In view of the status of the impediment in the Church's matrimonial discipline of the time, if the Pope intended that an individual dispensation was to be granted in each case, there should be an indication to that effect. As late as 1637 the formula of faculties granted to the Bishops of Asia, Africa and America did not contain a faculty for dispensing in the impediment of disparity of cult.[27] The only indication that they had it at the time of the Constitution *"Altitudo,"* is found in the general power of missionaries to do whatever was advantageous for the conversion of the infidels.[28] The clergy of the time were unaccustomed to dealing with the impediment, and so it seems a safe conclusion that in the circumstances the force of the constitution itself included the dispensation.

Payen [29] accepted the conclusion in his first edition, but in the second he requires that a dispensation be given from the impediment

[26] Gasparri, *Tract. Can. de Matr.* (3. ed. 1904), I, n. 696; Wernz, *Ius Decretalium*, IV, n. 504.

[27] *Cf.* Vermeersch, "Commentaria de Formulis Facultatum, etc.," *Periodica*, XI (1922), (47)-(51).

[28] Raymond Caron, *Apostolatus Evangelicus*, pp. 135 sq., apud Grentrup, *Ius Missionarium*, I, 23. *Cf. supra*, pp. 34, 35, note 13.

[29] *De Matrimonio*, II, n. 2405, § 1; (2. ed.), II, n. 2405 *bis*.

of disparity of cult if the wife chosen refuses to be converted and to receive baptism.

In 1931 it was Vromant's opinion [80] that a dispensation from the impediment seemed necessary. His supporting argument was that the faculty in canon 1125 is to be considered as granted according to the norm of the common law unless the contrary is manifest. Later authors [81] have been in agreement with this first opinion of Vromant's. But the juridical status of the constitution as a *ius singulare* sets it off from the *ius commune:* it is a true derogation from the common law, for the special utility of a determined class.[82] Therefore the argument proposed for requiring the dispensation does not apply.

The conclusion that follows from a consideration of the constitution itself is that the granting of a dispensation from the impediment of disparity of cult is not necessary for the validity or the licitness of the marriage contract when a polygamist convert chooses a woman from among his former partners in order to make her his wife even though she remains unbaptized.[83]

A further question remains as to the necessity of the *cautiones* which are required in the marriage of a Catholic with a non-Catholic.[84] The canon law requires that these be obtained, regularly in writing, before a dispensation from the impediment of disparity of cult be granted. The Supreme Pontiff himself cannot dispense in the natural law prohibiting a marriage if the infidel will not live without

[80] "De Dispensatione ab interpellationibus, etc.," *Periodica,* XX (1931), 110*, 111*; *De Matrimonio,* n. 357.

[81] Woods, *The Constitutions of Canon 1125,* p. 44; Léry: ". . . il vaut mieux, dans la pratique, obtenir une dispense de disparite de culte."—*Le Privilège de la Foi,* p. 102.

[82] *Cf.* Van Hove, *De Legibus,* n. 306.

[83] Vromant adopted this opinion in the second edition of his *De Matrimonio* (n. 343): "Si non convertatur uxor electa, *dispensatio super impedimento disparitatis cultus non est necessaria.*" *Cf.* Vermeersch-Creusen, *Epitome,* II, n. 436. To the contrary, De Smet: "Si uxor, vi privilegii electa, est infidelis, opus est dispensatione, super disparitate cultus."—*De Spons. et Matr.* (4. ed.), n. 353, nota 2, p. 300.

[84] Canons 1061, 1071.

insult to the Creator,[35] and the Holy See has more than once declared that in marriages of a Catholic with a non-Catholic the necessity for opportune precautions guarding against the perversion of the Catholic party and providing for the rearing of all the children in the Catholic religion is founded in the natural and the divine law.[36]

The *cautiones* are the usual means by which the precautions (*cautelae*) are to be provided for more safely. The Church can never dispense from the *cautelae*,[37] but it may for a just cause dispense from the *cautiones*, which it has established by its own law, when there is moral certainty that the requirements of the divine and natural law will be observed. The position taken here is that the Constitution *"Altitudo"* grants to the polygamist convert the dispensation from the impediment of disparity of cult, but that the use of the dispensation in the individual case is predicated upon the moral assurance of the reality of the required precautions or *cautelae*. The more definite way of assuring the presence of the *cautelae* is to obtain the formal *cautiones*, but it is at least uncertain that these *cautiones* must be demanded when a polygamist convert makes use of the concession granted him by the Constitution *"Altitudo,"* and exchanges matrimonial consent with one of his former partners who does not also become a Catholic.[38]

The duty of the Ordinary or priest before the required explicit exchange or renewal of consent will be to make sure that the circumstances of the case bring it within the scope of the concession, and that, if the woman (man) chosen by the polygamist convert is not also converted, there be moral certainty that the Catholic party will not be in danger of being perverted from the Faith, and that all the children resulting from the marriage will be both baptized and educated in the Catholic religion. Since the fundamental condition

[35] Wernz, *Ius Decretalium*, IV, n. 510, nota 40; *cf.* Payen: *"Necesse est* ut mulier electa velit pacifice et sine contumelia Creatoris cohabitare."—*De Matrimonio* (2. ed.), II, n. 2405.

[36] Secret. Stat. iussu Pii PP. IX, instr. (ad Omnes Episcopos), 15 Nov., 1858—*Coll. S. C. P. F.*, n. 1169; S. C. S. Off., instr. (ad Omnes Epp. Ritus Orient.), 12 Dec., 1888, ad 5—*Coll. S. C. P. F.*, n. 1696. *Cf.* Gasparri, *Tract. Can. de Matr.* (3. ed., 1904), I, nn. 496-498.

[37] *Cf.* Vromant, *De Matrimonio* (2. ed.), n. 163.

[38] *Cf.* Vromant, *ibid.*, n. 343.

for the use of the concession by the polygamist convert is that he (she) does not know whom he (she) married first, the interpellations of the validly married wife (husband) whom he (she) possessed in any earlier matrimonial union is, of course, morally impossible, and *ipso iure* no dispensation from the interpellations is required.[39]

When there is danger of scandal arising from the marriage because of a misunderstanding of the Church's marriage laws prudence requires that due care be used, according to the judgment of the Ordinary, to avoid the scandal. Also, as a matter of record, a reference to the use of canon 1125 should be made with the entry in the marriage register.

[39] Wernz-Vidal, *Ius Canonicum,* V, n. 633; Vromant, *ibid.*

CHAPTER IX

PROVISIONS FOR POLYGAMIST CONVERTS

II. THE CONSTITUTION *"ROMANI PONTIFICIS"*

POPE PIUS V

FOR the future.

It has been the custom for the Roman Pontiff, in his equitable and circumspect providence, to see to it by declarations and other opportune means that hesitation or doubt does not impede the working out of measures that must be provided for the salutary guidance of the Indians newly converted to the Faith. Therefore since, as we have learned, infidel Indians are permitted to have several wives whom they repudiate for the least reason, it has resulted that they are permitted after their conversion to remain with that wife who received baptism at the same time as her husband; and since very often it happens that because she is not the first wife both priests and Bishops are torn by grave doubts that that is not a true marriage; but because it is most severe (*durissimum esset*) to separate them from the wives with whom they received baptism, especially because it is most difficult to find (*maxime quia difficillimum foret . . . reperire*) the first wife, We, desiring in Our paternal affection to consult the best interests of the Indians themselves and to free the Bishops and priests from their anxiety, on Our own initiative (*motu proprio*) and with certain knowledge and the fullness of Our apostolic power, by these presents declare in virtue of Our apostolic authority that Indians both baptized and to be baptized may remain with the wife who has been or will be baptized with them, and affirm that such a marriage between them is legitimate and must be so pronounced by all judges and commissioners of whatever authority they may be, there being removed from them singly and collectively (*sublata eis et eorum*) all authority and right of deciding otherwise; and We declare null and void whatever decision may have been knowingly or in ignorance made by anyone whatsoever in virtue of any authority whatsoever, notwithstanding any general or special

Constitution or Ordination, whether it be of Apostolic origin or given by provincial or synodal decree or any other decision to the contrary.

Given at Rome at St. Peter's, under the ring of the Fisherman, 2 August, 1571.[1]

The concession granted by St. Pius V in the Constitution "*Romani Pontificis*," like that granted by Paul III in the Constitution "*Altitudo*," applies only to polygamist converts. By polygamist is meant both the man who before his baptism lived with more than one woman, in either simultaneous or successive polygyny, and the woman who before her baptism lived with more than one man, in either simultaneous or successive polyandry. The concession applies with equal force to a polygynist or to a polyandrist, and whatever is said of the polygynist is true also of the polyandrist in the same circumstances. Dismissal of a spouse through decree of a civil court does not change the nature of the successive polygamy which attaches to a subsequent marriage with a third person while the valid spouse still lives.[2]

In order to distinguish the circumstances of the particular cases to which the concession of the Constitution "*Romani Pontificis*" applies under the law of the Code, the principle of canon 1127 is to be kept in mind.[3] The canon states, "*In re dubia privilegium fidei gaudet favore iuris.*" If after a prudent and diligent inquiry there remains a morally insoluble doubt concerning the status of all the unions of the polygamist before his conversion, that is, if it cannot be determined with moral certainty that any one of them was a valid marriage, it is permitted to determine according to the norm of canon 1127 the scope of his freedom to marry after conversion.[4]

It scarcely needs to be mentioned that when the unbaptized legitimate first wife is certainly known and can be interpellated the polygamist convert may use the Pauline privilege. When he receives a negative answer to the interpellations, *ceteris paribus* he

[1] Translation by the author of this dissertation. *Cf. supra*, p. 48 for sources; Document VII of the Code for the official text according to which interpretation must be made.

[2] *Cf.* discussion of these points in Chap. VIII, Art. 1.

[3] *Cf.* Léry, *Le Privilège de la Foi*, n. 79.

[4] *Cf. supra*, Chap. VII, Art. 2.

may marry any Catholic woman. If one of his former concubines is baptized he may make her his wife,[5] but his choice, when he uses the Pauline privilege, is not restricted to those of his former partners who, like him, have also become Catholic.

Article 1. The Force of the Constitution

The previous Constitution of Paul III had permitted the polygamist after his conversion to make any one of his former partners his valid wife when he did not remember which of them was the first. There would have been no cause for the anxieties and doubts which St. Pius V desired to remove from the Bishops and priests if they had been conforming to the provisions of that constitution. When the first wife was certainly known, but there was difficulty in finding her, there would have been some basis for the troubles of conscience if the Bishops and priests on their own authority were considering the difficulty to be a sufficient cause to dispense from the interpellations. But aside from that, when the first wife was certainly known, neither would there have been cause for anxieties if they had been insisting upon the regular requirements for the use of the Pauline privilege. The constitution itself, as will be seen, indicates that there was a reason other than the difficulty of finding the first wife inducing the Bishops and priests to allow the polygamist convert to remain with a partner who was baptized with him, and hence the doubts. The dispensation from interpellating an absent wife was provided for later by Gregory XIII in the Constitution *"Populis"* which is now a part of canon 1125 and will be considered in the next chapter.

The particular force of the Constitution *"Romani Pontificis"* in the law of the Code is to be found in its application to the case of a polygamist convert whose first wife is certainly known and could be interpellated if the Pauline privilege were to be used. In such a case, if it will be very harsh or severe (*durissimum*) to separate the convert from one of the concubines with whom he has lived and who

[5] In regard to the matter of the impediment of *publica honestas* not being binding, or being only doubtfully binding, after baptism upon those who lived in concubinage before baptism but not after, *cf.* Vermeersch-Creusen, *Epitome,* II, n. 361; Payen, *De Matrimonio,* I, n. 1545; Cappello, *De Sacramentis,* III (4. ed.), n. 552, § 6; Vromant, *De Matrimonio* (2. ed.), n. 58.

will be baptized with him, there is no necessity to make any interpellation of the first wife.[6]

It has already been seen[7] how inconclusive are the results of examining the pre-Code declarations of the Roman Congregations in order to arrive at a clear idea either of the force of the constitution or of the circumstances of a case to which it applies. Authors since the Code have not been in agreement about the latter point. Some have thought that the interpellations could be omitted only when it would be very difficult to find the first wife.[8] Such a conclusion does not follow from the text of the constitution itself.

Like most laws given before the Code[9] the constitution contains a *pars motiva* followed by the *pars dispositiva* which expresses the will of the legislator. In the first part the *causae motivae,* which give the reasons why the legislator makes this particular provision or grants this particular favor, are to be prudently distinguished from the *causae impulsivae* which are concerned rather with the opportuneness of the law. Subsequent change or disappearance of the *causae impulsivae* will have no effect on the law since it is already in existence, but its application remains dependent upon the same *causae motivae.*[10]

[6] Vermeersch, "Commentaria de Formulis Facultatum, etc.," *Periodica,* XI (1922), (139); Wernz-Vidal, *Ius Canonicum,* V. n. 633, *in fine;* Gregory, *The Pauline Privilege,* p. 39; Vromant, *De Matrimonio* (2. ed.), n. 344, § 3; Cappello, *De Sacramentis,* III (4. ed.), n. 787, § 5; Rayanna, "De Constitutione S. Pii Papae V, etc.," *Periodica,* XXVIII (1939), 205. Woods: " . . . It appears that no interpellation . . . need be made. . . . By force of the Constitution he is dispensed from both interpellations."—*The Constitutions of Canon 1125,* p. 55. The following hold that according to St. Pius V the convert is under no obligation to interpellate the first wife on the question of cohabiting and *probably* there is no obligation to interpellate on either point: Vermeersch-Creusen, *Epitome,* II, n. 436, § 2; Payen, *De Matrimonio* (2. ed.), II, n. 2406, *in fine;* Léry, *La Privilège de la Foi,* p. 107.

[7] *Cf. supra,* pp. 126-129.

[8] De Smet: " . . . Ad normam Constit. Pii V, declaratur neutram interpellationem esse faciendam, sed tunc quando nonnisi difficillime reperire potest prima uxor."—*De Spons. et Matr.* (4. ed.), n. 353, p. 301, nota 2; Vromant, *De Matrimonio* (1. ed.), n. 359. Vromant changed his opinion in the second edition, n. 344, § 3.

[9] *Cf.* Michiels, *Normae Generales,* p. 420, nota 2.

[10] *Cf.* Vermeersch, "De Canone 1125 eiusque vi extensiva," *Periodica,* XX (1931), 3*.

In giving the constitution St. Pius V was concerned with providing for the best interests of the Indians, and with removing from the Bishops and priests the anxieties they suffered from allowing the convert polygamist to remain with the woman who would be baptized with him. The latter cause has disappeared but the Pope will always be interested in aiding the conversion of souls. The reasons for this particular grant are expressed thus: "*quia durissimum esset separare eos ab uxoribus, cum quibus ipsi Indi baptismum susceperunt, maxime quia difficillimum foret primam coniugem reperire.*"

To restrict the concession to cases in which it is very difficult to find the first wife is to interpret the above phrases as meaning that *only then* is there sufficient cause to use the concession *when* the severity or harshness of separating the polygamist from the woman who will be baptized with him arises from the difficulty of finding the first wife. Clearly such is not the meaning of the text. Even the strictest interpretation must find that the "*maxime*" leaves room for other reasons which would make the separation of the convert couple a severe hardship. So that usually there are two reasons given for the concession, namely, either the difficulty of finding the first wife, or the severity of separating a polygamist convert from the woman who will be baptized with him.[11]

The true sense of the phrases, as Rayanna has well pointed out,[12] seems to be that the fundamental cause for granting the concession, and therefore the one necessary condition for its use, is the hardship that would result from separating the couple. There could be many reasons why the separation would be a severe requirement. The difficulty of finding the first wife calls for special consideration among the reasons, because if the first wife could not be found the convert who is required to separate from the woman who will be baptized with him would be forced to lead a celibate life. Other reasons that would make the separation a hardship will be an especial love between the converts, or considerations for children begotten of the

[11] Payen, *De Matrimonio* (2. ed.), II, n. 2406, § 1; Cappello, *De Sacramentis,* III (4. ed.), n. 787, § 5; Léry, *Le Privilège de la Foi,* n. 79.

[12] "De Constitutione S. Pii Papae V, etc.," *Periodica,* XXVIII (1939), 199-202.

woman who will be baptized whereas the first wife had none, or even so great an abhorrence for the first wife that being forced to cohabit with her would deter the polygamist from embracing the means of salvation.

In the dispositive part of the constitution St. Pius V made provision for the previously mentioned Indians, that is, for the polygamists whose conversion put them in the matrimonial difficulty he had outlined. He therefore intended the concession to apply to the convert for whom it would be a hardship to separate from the woman who would be baptized with him. "*Motu proprio et ex certa scientia Nostra, ac apostolicae potestatis plenitudine,*" he decreed that marriages of this sort which had been allowed in the past or would be allowed in the future were legitimate. The women other than the one who would be baptized and kept were, of course, to be dismissed ("*aliis dimissis*").

Clearly, in order that a marriage with a woman other than the first wife be legitimate the natural bond of the first marriage had to be dissolved. There is no question now about the Pope's power in this regard.[18]

The Cong. for the Propagation of the Faith has given a declaration which is of particular value in support of the opinion that no interpellation whatsoever of the first wife need be made when the privilege granted by St. Pius V in the Constitution "*Romani Pontificis*" is used. The declaration is a response to a *dubium* or *votum* of the First Council of China (1924). The *votum* is number 12 in the "*Vota et Postulata*" of the Council, and is inscribed:

> De facultate Ordinariorum circa Matrimonia catechumenorum plures uxores habentium.
> Votum—"Facultatem habent Ordinarii Sinenses 'dispensandi cum gentilibus et infidelibus plures uxores habentibus, ut, post conversionem et baptismum, quam ex illis maluerint, si etiam ipsa fidelis fiat, retinere possint, nisi prima voluerit converti.'
>
> "Unde deduci videtur, in omni casu polygamiae etiam successivae, virum polygamum non posse secum retinere tanquam propriam uxorem mulierem secum baptizatam, nisi interpellationibus praemissis, ut sciatur num prima uxor converti voluerit.

[18] *Cf. supra,* Chap. V, Art. 4.

"Aliunde, in Constitutione S. Pii V *'Romani Pontificis,'* can. 1125, absolute dici videtur ut in casu polygamiae successivae possit neophytus secum retinere tanquam propriam uxorem mulierem quae cum ipso baptizata fuerit, nulla facta quaestione praemittendae interpellationis.

"Primum Concilium Sinense videns frequenter inter nostros catechumenos reperire tales qui cum secunda vel ulteriore successive uxore, in baptismum consentiente, baptismum petant, quibus durissimum est et fere impossibile tale matrimonium dissolvere, humillime Sedem Apostolicam orat utrum, ad mentem Constitutionis S. Pii V supra citatae, liceat Vicariis Apostolicis et Praefectis Apostolicis tales catechumenos cum tali in baptismum consentiente uxore simul baptizare, data eis insuper facultate ut in eodem matrimonio tanquam legitimo permanere valeant, absolute et sine ulla interpellatione primae uxoris an non."

Responsum: *"Affirmative."* [14]

As is clear, the Fathers of the Council made a distinction in the *votum* between *FTM* 24 which was among the faculties for the Ordinaries of China, and the constitution of St. Pius V contained in canon 1125. The faculty requires interpellation of the first wife on one point since that is the means of knowing whether or not she desires to be converted. But often it is most severe to dissolve an existing union between a catechumen and a woman consenting to be baptized with him but who is not his first wife. The doubt presented for solution to the Sacred Congregation was whether or not, *according to the mind of the Constitution "Romani Pontificis,"* Vicars and Prefects Apostolic could baptize the couple, allow them to remain in the marriage, and do that without any interpellation of the first wife. To which the answer was, *"Affirmative."*

It has been stated [15] that the Cong. for the Propagation of the Faith here gave an *interpretatio extensiva* of *FTM* 24 for China, and therefore it is not to be transferred to other places. The direct reference of the *votum* was to the constitution and not to the faculty. Seemingly, *FTM* 24 was mentioned to show its limitations

[14] *Primum Concilium Sinense, Anno 1924 . . . Celebratum: Acta-Decreta et Normae-Vota, etc.* (Zi-Ka-Wei: Typographia Missionis Catholicae, 1929), p. 273.

[15] Vromant, *De Matrimonio* (1. ed.), n. 370, p. 293, et nota 4.

in regard to the difficulties found in individual cases. The safe use of the grant in the constitution was the matter at issue. The manner in which it was given, as well as a comparison of the circumstances of the cases outlined in the *votum* with those dealt with in the constitution, reveals no basis for thinking the reply of the Sacred Congregation to be an *interpretatio extensiva* of the constitution.[16]

The reply at least gives a sense of the grant which is within the limits of the broad interpretation to which the constitution is subject.

Article 2. Probable Restriction When the First Wife Expresses Desire to Be Baptized

It can easily happen, especially in pagan countries where simultaneous polygamy is common, that without being interpellated the first wife upon learning that her husband is a catechumen will also ask for baptism. The constitution does not explicitly consider the situation. A broad interpretation of the grant would seem to indicate that even in this contingency the polygamist could remain with the other woman if it would be *durissimum* to separate them and she too would receive baptism.[17]

The question here is one of interpretation of the will of the legislator in the circumstances and not of the Papal power to dissolve the first marriage even though one party be unwilling. The fundamental motive behind the Constitution *"Romani Pontificis"* is that of removing obstacles to the conversion of the pagans. *Per se,* as a *ius singulare favorabile* and as contributing to the good of religion, it is subject to broad interpretation, but *per accidens* a strict interpretation may be called for.

Rights acquired by the parties through a valid matrimonial contract are founded in the natural law and when the application of any positive human law is clearly prejudicial to such rights that

[16] *Cf.* Payen: "Arbitramur eam non esse certam."—*De Matrimonio* (2. ed.), II, n. 2407 *bis,* § 2; Cappello, *De Sacramentis,* III (4. ed.), n. 787, § 5.

[17] Thus: Cappello, *ibid.;* Rayanna, "De Constitutione S. Pii Papae V, etc.," *Periodica,* XXVIII (1939), pp. 51, 52.

law is to receive a strict interpretation. Canon 19 requires a strict interpretation of ecclesiastical laws which restrict the free exercise of rights, and canon 68 refers the interpretation of privileges to canon 50, which demands a strict interpretation when acquired rights are subject to injury.

The whole Church discipline on the dissolution of the natural bond of marriage is founded upon the desire to aid in the salvation of souls. Is there any reason to suppose that St. Pius V favored the conversion of one of the parties over the other? The basis for a hatred of religion, and hence the detriment of religion rather than its advantage, as well as the detriment of souls, could be increased by the refusal to recognize the rights of a legitimate wife even after she had made clear her desire to do what was necessary for her conversion.

When it is no longer beyond doubt that the first wife is willing to receive baptism it seems rash, in a doubt of law, to interpret the legislator as being prepared to deprive her of acquired rights. It is an established principle that in all cases equity enjoys a stronger position than strict law.[18] The juridical background of the concession was the Pauline privilege which requires that even a pagan spouse is to be retained who will live peacefully and without insult to the Creator. The preceding constitution of Paul III likewise required that the pagan first wife be kept if she were known. Granted that preceding legislation does not limit the basic Papal power which was given by God, it can be an aid to the discovery of the mind of the legislator.[19]

[18] "Quoties verborum proprietas induceret injustitiam, vel similem absurditatem circa mentem legislatoris, trahenda sunt verba ad sensum etiam improprium in quo lex sit justa et rationabilis, quia haec praesumitur esse mens legislatoris . . . Ergo si necessaria sit etiam impropria interpretatio ut voluntas sit vel praesumatur justa, in eo sensu accipienda est lex, quia alias non conservabitur voluntas legislatoris cum lex injusta non sit lex."—Suarez, *De Legibus,* lib. VI, cap. I, n. 17.

[19] "Ex comparatione ad alia jura potest indagari mens legislatoris in aliqua lege, etiam praeter vim et proprietatem verborum eius, idque dupliciter: primo, ex repugnantia et contrarietate aliarum legum quae oriretur in uno verborum sensu, et vitatur in alio; tunc enim interpretamur mentem legislatoris non fuisse derogare superioribus legibus aut illas corrigere, et ideo usum fuisse verbis in ea significatione quae cum aliis juribus stare possit; quia non

In the doubt of law which exists in the matter the foregoing considerations lead the author to adopt the opinion that the concession of St. Pius V is not to be interpreted as allowing the polygamist convert to make another his valid wife when his first wife has expressed her desire to be baptized.[20]

Article 3. The Concession in Practice

Those who before their conversion, that is, before baptism, were polygamists in the sense of the term outlined above in Article 1 of Chapter VIII are the subjects of the concession. Women who before conversion have lived in polyandry may use it as well as men who have loved in polygyny. The particular circumstances in which it applies are these:

(a.) the marriage with the first wife (husband) was contracted when both parties were unbaptized;

(b.) the first wife (husband) is certainly known and has not yet been baptized nor expressed her (his) desire to be baptized;

(c.) one of the parties other than the first wife (husband) will be baptized with the convert polygamist;

(d.) it would be *durissimum* to separate the convert polygamist from the partner who will be baptized with him (her).

(a.) The concession was originally given for conditions which existed among the pagans in mission countries. The first marriages were between pagans. It is clear from the present discipline of the Church that if a first valid marriage had been contracted between an unbaptized person and a person baptized in an heretical sect the concession would not apply even though the convert had lived in

receditur a jure antiquo, nisi quatenus in novo exprimitur. . . . Altera via colligendi mentem legislatoris per comparationem ad alia jura est per concordiam."—Suarez, *De Legibus*, lib. VI, cap. I, n. 18. *Cf.* Canon 18: " . . . quae si dubia et obscura manserit, ad locos Codicis parallelos . . . est recurrendum."

[20] Thus: Woods, *The Constitutions of Canon 1125*, pp. 54, 55; Payen, *De Matrimonio* (2. ed.), II, n. 2407, § 3, et n. 2407 *ter*, Tertius casus; Léry, *Le Privilège de la Foi*, n. 83; Vromant, *De Matrimonio* (2. ed.), n. 344, § 3.

concubinage with others after the first marriage and hence could be called a polygamist. A special act of the Holy See, as in the Helena case, would be required to dissolve the bond of such a marriage in favor of the Faith.

(b.) (If the validity of the first marriage is doubtful, even when the persistence of the doubt is due to the refusal of the first wife [husband] to give the information necessary for its solution, the case may be handled according to the principle enunciated in canon 1127 [*cf. supra,* Chapter VII, Article 2]; if the polygamist convert does not recall the identity of the first wife [husband] Paul III's concession [*cf. supra,* Chapter VIII] may be used.)

The first wife (husband) must still be unbaptized. If the first wife (husband) has expressed the desire to be baptized, then according to the opinion accepted here the concession may not be used. The point, however, is controverted; *cf.* Article 2 of the present Chapter.

(c.) The baptism of the former partner who is to be a party to the new valid marriage must precede the marriage, but it does not seem that the two need be baptized at the same time, for example, on the same day. After baptism, the polygamist convert may not, of course, be permitted to cohabit *maritaliter* with the other party until their position is regularized, but some interval could separate their respective baptisms without prejudice to the concession.[21]

(d.) The judgment of the harshness or severity of separating the convert couple will necessarily be based upon the remarks of the polygamist convert and prudent attention to the adjuncts of of the case.[22] In general, it may be said, *favores ampliandi sunt.* A case accompanied with the difficulty of finding the woman (man) who is known for certain as the partner of the first and valid mar-

[21] *In re* (a.), (b.), (c.), *cf.* Payen, *De Matrimonio* (2. ed.), II, n. 2407 *quater.* Rather than referring directly to the Constitution *"Romani Pontificis,"* Payen circumspectly refers to the conditions requisite for missionaries in China to use the affirmative response of the Cong. for the Propagation of the Faith to *Votum* 12 of the First Council of China which in turn, as seen above, inquired into the *"mens Constitutionis 'Romani Pontificis.'"*

[22] *Cf.* Rayanna, "De Constitutione S. Pii Papae V, etc.," *Periodica* XXVIII (1939), pp. 199-202.

riage is to be handled in accordance with the norm established by Gregory XIII in his Constitution "*Populis*" and now enacted as universal law in canon 1125.

The concept of "separating" seemingly is not limited to the idea of causing a physical separation of two people who are actually living together at the time of conversion of the polygamist. That is, it is not to be taken in so strict a sense as to exclude a previously dismissed partner with whom the polygamist after conversion would wish to lead a married life. If one so dismissed, even by divorce decree of a civil court, will be baptized with the polygamist they may be allowed to marry. This opinion is based upon a response of the Cong. for the Propagation of the Faith to a doubt that arose about a similar question in the use of *FTM* 24.[23]

If some of the intermediate partners or concubines were baptized persons the nature of the case is not changed since the continuance of the valid first marriage precludes a subsequent valid marriage until the first is dissolved by the death of one party or by divine power. If the woman from whom it would be difficult to separate the polygamist convert is among these intermediate baptized partners, it is probable that the concession of the constitution can be invoked and they may be allowed to marry. It is true that the woman would not then be being baptized *with* the polygamist convert, but in view of the broad interpretation to which the constitution is subject, and in view of the principle *favores ampliandi sunt*, the opinion seems probable. If the circumstances requisite for incurring the impediment of *crimen*[24] by the baptized party have been verified, indirectly the unbaptized party would also be bound by the impediment.[25] A dispensation from the impediment would then be necessary, for there is no basis for thinking that by virtue of the constitution a dispensation would be given *ipso iure* from such an impediment.

[23] Resp. (C. P. pro Sin.—Tunkin. Orient.), 14 Jan., 1806, ad 1—*Fontes*, n. 4686. *Cf.* Vromant, *De Matrimonio* (2. ed.), n. 344, § 2; Woods, *The Constitutions of Canon 1125*, pp. 54, 55. To the contrary, Cappello: ". . . si durissimum sit eum separare a muliere quam nunc habet et quae cum eo baptizatur." —*De Sacramentis*, III (4. ed.), n. 787, § 5, *in fine*.

[24] Canon 1075.

[25] *Cf.* Vromant, *De Matrimonio* (2. ed.), n. 55.

Interpellations of the first wife are omitted *ipso iure.* Matrimonial consent is to be exchanged between the baptized parties according to the form required by canon law.

The concession is granted directly to the polygamist convert, yet Ordinaries may establish rules to assure its prudent use. In general the Ordinary, or the priest who assists at the marriage, should see to it that the above conditions are verified, that precautions are taken to guard against the marriage being an occasion for scandal, and that some record of the use of canon 1125 be included with the entry in the marriage register.

CHAPTER X

THE PROVISIONS OF THE CONSTITUTION *"POPULIS"* POPE GREGORY XIII

For the future.

It is advisable to be lenient (*expedit indulgere*), in the matter of freedom to contract marriage, toward the peoples and nations recently converted from paganism to the Catholic Faith, lest men, unaccustomed to continence, might less willingly persevere in the Faith and deter others from receiving it by their example. Now, since it often happens that many infidels of both sexes, especially men, who have contracted marriage in pagan rites have been captured and taken from Angola, Ethiopia, Brazil and other countries of the Indies and exiled in distant lands far from their own country and their spouses, so that both they and those who remain captive in their own country cannot, as is required when they are converted, ask their infidel spouses, who are separated from them by such wide expanses of land, whether they are willing to cohabit with them without insult to the Creator, either because sometimes access even by messenger to hostile and barbarous regions is impossible, or because they do not know whither they have been transported, or because the length of journey presents great difficulties; therefore, aware that marriages of this kind contracted among infidels, although they are true marriages, are not so stable (*rata*) that they cannot be dissolved in cases of necessity, and compassionating in Our paternal love the weakness of these peoples, We by Our Apostolic authority, by these presents grant to each and every Ordinary and to pastors of these regions, and to the priests of the Society of Jesus approved for hearing confessions by the superiors of that Society and sent for a time to the aforesaid regions or admitted therein, full faculty of dispensing the Christian inhabitants, of both sexes, natives of the aforesaid lands who have in serious mind embraced the Faith and have contracted marriage before their baptism, so that all of them, despite the survival of the infidel spouse and without asking his or her consent or awaiting his or her reply, may licitly contract marriage with any Christian even of another rite, and solemnize it before the Church, and after its consummation remain in it as long as they live: provided that it be evident even from a summary and extrajudicial investigation that the aforesaid absent spouse cannot be admonished according to law, or has not, within the time fixed in the monition, signified his or her intention; moreover, these marriages are never to be rescinded even though it become known afterwards that the infidel was prevented by just cause from declaring his or her intention and had even become a convert at the time of the second marriage, but in virtue of Our decree shall remain valid and firm, and the offspring shall be legitimate. All Apostolic constitutions and decrees and those emanating even from general Councils and all else to the contrary notwithstanding. And because it would be difficult for this letter to be shown and published in every place where it will have effect, We will that the same credence be placed in its printed copies, when signed by the hand of a Notary Public or the Secretary of the aforesaid Society and stamped by the seal of an ecclesiastical dignitary or of the Superior General of the said Society then in office, as would be placed in this letter itself if it could be exhibited and shown.

Granted at Rome at St. Peters, under the ring of the Fisherman, the 25th day of January, 1585, in the thirteenth year of Our pontificate. Jo. Baptist Canobius.[1]

Whereas the preceding constitutions of Paul III and St. Pius V were concerned entirely with converts who before their conversion had many wives, the constitution of Gregory XIII made no distinction between polygamist and monogamist. The favor granted could be used for the benefit of either type of convert.

The inhuman treatment forced upon the victims of the flourishing slave trade of the latter sixteenth century [2] was the occasion for the Pope's grant. An African husband might be captured and carried across the sea far from his wife, or both husband and wife

[1] Translation by the author of this dissertation. *Cf. supra*, pp. 68, 69, for sources; Document VIII of the Code for the official text according to which interpretation must be made.

[2] *Cf. supra*, pp. 63, 64.

might be captured and taken each to a different place. The difficulties arising from this separation of spouses was a *causa impulsiva* disposing the Pope to act, but the fundamental motive was that of fostering the conversion of pagans [3] as the preamble makes clear. The immediate motive of the grant was the impossibility or the difficulty of making the interpellations required for the use of the Pauline privilege, but its full force extends beyond the limits of that privilege.

When Gregory XIII ordained that the new marriage of the convert, contracted after a dispensation granted when the due conditions were present, must be considered valid, even though it should afterwards become known that the absent first wife had also become a Christian by the time of her husband's new marriage,[4] he was legislating for a case not comprehended by the Pauline privilege. The new marriage could be valid only if the bond of the first marriage were dissolved. That Gregory intended precisely this is shown by his clear statement: " . . . *Nos attendentes huiusmodi connubia inter infideles contracta, vera quidem, non tamen adeo rata censeri, ut necessitate suadente dissolvi non possint. . . .*" To effect the dissolution, for the benefit of converts from paganism and *in favorem fidei* the Pope exercised the power over the bond of marriage granted by Christ to His Vicar on earth. When the absent wife remained pagan the marriage bond affected was still natural; [5] but when the absent wife had also become a Christian the bond was that of a *ratum* marriage.[6] In the latter case there is a dissolution of a *consummatum et ratum* marriage, presuming that the infidels had consummated their marriage before the separation, but not of a *ratum et consummatum* marriage since the conversion of the parties took place after their separation.[7]

[3] Payen, *De Matrimonio* (2. ed.), n. 2408, § 1, nota 1.

[4] The constitution permits the dispensation to be granted for either sex. For convenient treatment of the subject the wife will be considered as the absent party.

[5] *Cf.* statement of the Helena Case: S. C. S. Off., decr., 5 Nov., 1924—*AER*, LXXII (1925), 188; *Periodica*, XIV (1925), 19, 20; Bouscaren, *Canon Law Digest*, I, 553, 554.

[6] De Smet, *De Spons. et Matr.*, n. 178.

[7] *Cf. supra*, pp. 65 and 72.

Another difference between the two previous constitutions and the present one, *"Populis,"* is that the latter delegated to certain ecclesiastics the power to dispense in the interests of converts from paganism, whereas the provisions of the former constitutions directly affected the polygamist converts without any necessary intervention of others. Gregory XIII made the exercise of the power he delegated essential to the use of his grant. The immediate object of the power exercised is that of granting a dispensation from the interpellations which the Church always requires for the use of the Pauline privilege [8] unless a dispensation from them be granted. Hence the procedure contemplated by the constitution is that ordained for the use of the Pauline privilege, but it may in fact be true and afterwards appear that the ultimate effect of the use of the power in granting the dispensation was to dissolve the bond of a *ratum* marriage to which the Pauline privilege does not apply.[9]

Article 1. Circumstances of a Case to Which the Constitution Applies

The constitution provides two faculties of dispensing for use when it is evident from a summary and extrajudicial investigation that the absent spouse cannot be admonished according to law, or has not signified his or her intention within the time fixed in the monition.[10]

The first faculty has in view cases in which it is impossible to make the interpellations, but here the important question arises as to what circumstance or circumstances can safely be interpreted as grounds for the conclusion that the absent party cannot be admonished according to law.

In the *pars motiva* of the constitution Gregory XIII described the particular difficulties of the captured natives. At times it was impossible to make the interpellations because a messenger could

[8] *Cf. supra*, Chap. VI, Art. 1.

[9] *Cf.* Bouscaren, "An Inquiry into the Practical Application of Canon 1125, etc.," *Miscellanea Vermeersch*, I, 292.

[10] ". . . dummodo constet etiam summarie et extrajudicialiter, coniugem, ut praefertur, absentem moneri non posse, aut monitum intra tempus in eadem monitione praefixum suam voluntatem non significasse."

not be sent into a hostile country where the absent spouse was to be found; sometimes the length of the journey was the difficulty; and sometimes it was not known where the other party had been taken.[11] These examples are representative of cases in which the absent spouse cannot be interpellated. They were the results of a separation of the parties made by force, but the *dummodo* clause in the dispositive part of the constitution does not require this as the cause of absence. With less reason can capture or a forced separation be considered a necessary cause of the absence now that the provisions of the constitution have been extended to the whole world. The legislator is not to be presumed to have made a general provision of the Code for circumstances that would occur in only a few isolated places in modern times.[12]

If the interpellations can be made, but only after a long journey, the difficulty of making them cannot be called more than a moral impossibility. When asked whether the words *"moneri legitime non posse"* could be understood to include a moral as well as a physical impossibility of making the interpellations. The Holy Office passed over the direct question without answer.[13] Later in reply to an inquiry on what distance and circumstances of the journey were to be considered as a sufficient criterion of the impossibility of making the interpellations the Sacred Congregation answered that, in accordance with paragraph eight of Chapter IX of the Synod of Su-tchuen statutes, that distance suffices which, when all the circumstances are considered, causes a great difficulty.[14] A great difficulty is not synonomous with physical impossibility, but it may constitute moral impossibility.

[11] It was a feature of the slave trade that the stronger and more warlike tribes captured members of the weaker and sold them to the foreign slavers for shipment to the New World.

[12] *Cf.* Chelodi, *Ius Matrimoniale,* n. 160; De Becker, *De Matrimonio,* p. 257; Vermeersch, "De Canone 1125 eiusque vi extensiva," *Periodica,* XX (1931), 4*; Woods, *The Constitutions of Canon 1125,* pp. 65, 66; Bouscaren, *op. cit.,* p. 288; Léry, *Le Privilège de la Foi,* n. 89.

[13] Resp. (Ind. Orient.), 13 Jan., 1757—*Fontes,* n. 807.

[14] "Iuxta statuta Synodi Sutchuensis, Cap. IX, n. VIII, illam longitudinem sufficere, quae perpensis omnibus locorum et rerum adiunctis magnam affert difficultatem."—S. C. S. Off. (Mongoliae), 29 Nov., 1882, ad 1—*Fontes,* n. 1075.

From Pope Gregory's inclusion of the case when the long journey was necessary it seems clear that he intended to authorize a dispensation from the interpellations in at least one type of moral impossibility. The more common opinion of authors is that a moral impossibility of making the interpellations is sufficient [15] The nature of the matter and the spirit of the discipline of the common law on interpellations obviously require caution against a too easy persuasion that it is impossible to make them. Nevertheless, circumstances are as various as cases and places, and the gravity of the difficulty or danger which may be accounted a moral impossibility must be left to the prudent judgment of the Ordinary or priest using the faculty after the summary and extrajudicial inquiry.

A further question that may be asked is whether circumstances which make the interpellations useless, but not impossible, are sufficient grounds for using the faculty granted by the constitution. Bouscaren [16] is of the opinion that they are and gives as an example the case in which the infidel party, after a civil divorce, is civilly married to another partner.

On at least two occasions the Holy Office has given responses permitting Ordinaries to dispense from interpellations when it would be useless to make them. The first response was in answer to the specific question about interpellating a divorced infidel who had subsequently remarried.[17] The Constitution *"Populis"* is not named,

[15] Payen, *De Matrimonio* (1. et 2. ed.), II, n. 2409, § 3; Bouscaren, *op. cit.*, p. 294; Léry, *op. cit.*, n. 89; Cappello, *De Matrimonio* (4. ed.), n. 787, § 6; Vromant, "De Dispensatione ab interpellationibus, etc.," *Periodica*, XX (1931), 116*.

[16] *Ibid.*

[17] "R. Ad mentem. La mente è che nè il divorzio, nè il secundo matrimonio civile sono sufficienti per esimere dall' obbligo dell' interpellazione—Quatenus vero saltem summarie et extraiudicialiter constet interpellationem vel impossibilem vel inutilem fore, utetur (Episcopus) facultate dispensandi, si ea polleat: sin minus supplicandum SSmo pro facultate pro decem casibus."—S. C. S. Off., resp. (Portland), 18 Jun., 1884—*Coll. S. C. P. F.*, n. 1620. ". . . A qua interpellatione, si iustae rationabilesque causae adsint, dispensabitur. Iustae autem huiusmodi causae tunc aderunt cum ex processu saltem summario et extraiudiciali moraliter constet coniugem infidelem interpellari non posse, aut interpellationem vel inutilem vel graviter periculosam futuram esse. . ."—S. C. S. Off., resp. (ad Vic. Ap. Iaponiae Merid.), 4 Feb., 1891, *in fine*—*Fontes*, n. 1130.

but reference to the summary and extrajudicial process suggests the constitution. The responses clearly are concerned with the use of the Apostolic faculties granted to Ordinaries. There does not seem to be justification for extending the phrase "*moneri legitime non posse*" of the constitution to cases in which the inutility of making the interpellations is the *only* reason for the dispensation.[18] The declarations of the Roman Congregations have several times [19] referred the inquirer to Chap. IX, § VIII, of the Synod of Su-tchuen, where it is directed that the faculty to dispense from interpellations is to be used according to the norm established in the Brief of Gregory XIII, namely, that a dispensation be not given except when the converted party cannot admonish the absent infidel spouse. In other cases interpellation must be made even if it seems useless or likely to prove very injurious.[20]

In the response to the Bishop of Portland cited above the Holy Office expressed its mind as being that neither divorce nor the second civil marriage is sufficient to exempt from the obligation of interpellation. No doubt often when an infidel party who has been separated by virtue of a civil divorce decree is living in another union there will be a moral impossibility of making the interpellations, and hence due reason for giving the dispensation on this ground. As to other cases when it is certainly useless, but not physically or morally impossible, to make the interpellations the following disposition of the Holy Office is not abrogated by the Code: [21]

> Quoties coniugem infidelem nec Christi fidem amplecti, nec sine contumelia Creatoris cum coniuge converso velle cohabitare

[18] *Cf.* Vromant: "Condicio essentialis dispensationis impertiendae est *impossibilitas* partem infidelem interpellandi . . . Certo requiritur ut impossibilitas oriatur ex absentia partis infidelis. . ."—*De Matrimonio* (2. ed.), n. 348.

[19] *V. g.*, S. C. de Prop. Fide, instr. (ad Vic. Ap. Siam), 20 Mar., 1836—*Fontes*, n. 4762; S. C. S. Off., instr. (Siam), 4 Jul., 1855—*Coll. S. C. P. F.*, n. 1114; S. C. S. Off. (Mongoliae), 29 Nov., 1882, ad 1—*Fontes*, n. 1075.

[20] ". . . ut non dispensetur nisi quando fidelis coniugem infidelem absentem . . . monere nequit. . . Extra hos casus omnino fieri debet interpellatio, etiamsi inutilis aut perniciosa videatur. . ." *Cf. Coll. S. C. P. F.*, II, p. 481, nota 1.

[21] De Becker, A Recension, *ETL*, II (1925), 445, 446; De Smet, *De Spons. et Matr.*, n. 353, p. 300.

> certo constet, Episcopi tamquam Apostolicae Sedis delegati, et Vicarii Apostolici dispensare potuerunt super interpellatione, dummodo urgeat necessitas, nec tempus suppetat recurrendi ad S. Sedem.[22]

The second faculty granted by the constitution provides for a dispensation to be given when the infidel party, whether absent or present,[23] after having been duly interpellated does not signify his (her) intention within the time given him (her) to reply. According to the norm of canon 1122, § 1, the dispensation in this case amounts to a declaration that the failure to reply is to be considered a negative response.[24] The appropriate period of time which should be allowed the infidel to make reply will vary with circumstances: a period of a month is suggested[25] with extensions or restrictions according to charity and justice. The party is to be informed that failure to answer within the time set will be construed as a negative answer.

The use of the faculties is subject to the condition expressed in the *dummodo* clause, namely, that it appear from a summary and extrajudicial investigation that the infidel cannot be interpellated or if interpellated has failed to answer within the prescribed time. Even when the Ordinary or priest is convinced that there is a moral or physical impossibility of making the interpellations there must be an extrajudicial process and a written statement of the necessity for the dispensation.[26] After due investigation the matter is to be written up in a short statement for the ecclesiastical records, but the process is not required for *validity* of the dispensation when the

[22] S. C. S. Off., resp., 11 Aug., 1859—*Fontes*, n. 954. *Cf.* canon 81.

[23] Payen, *De Matrimonio* (2. ed.), II, n. 2409, § 3.

[24] Vromant, *De Matrimonio* (2. ed.), n. 349.

[25] Vermeersch, *De Casu Apostoli*, n. 59; Gregory, *The Pauline Privilege*, pp. 92, 93.

[26] S. C. S. Off., instr. (ad Superior. Mission. Peguan.), 11 Jun., 1760—*Fontes*, n. 811; S. C. S. Off., resp. (Vicar Apost. N.), 24 Sept., 1896, ad 2: "Non sufficere ut Vicarius apost. vel Missionarii omnino sint persuasi de impossibilitate aut difficultate interpellationem exsequendi; sed omnino faciendum esse in singulis casibus, et in scriptis, processum saltem summarium et extrajudicialem, in Formulis facultatum praescriptum."—*Coll. Hong.*, n. 1490.

impossibility of making the interpellations is evident or when it is certain that no answer was received within the time set.[27]

Article 2. Those to Whom the Power Is Granted

In answer to a doubt proposed by the Vicar Apostolic of Cambodia as to whether the faculties contained in the constitutions of canon 1125 were to be understood as granted only to Ordinaries, or in fact to all priests exercising the care of souls, the President of the Pontifical Commission for the authentic interpretation of the canons of the Code replied that these faculties of dispensing are to be understood according to the tenor of the constitutions mentioned in canon 1125.[28] The Constitution "*Populis*" grants the power of dispensing to Ordinaries of places, to pastors, and to priests of the Society of Jesus approved for hearing confessions by the Superiors of that Society.

A further doubt arose as to whether or not the faculty of dispensing granted to *parochi* by Gregory XIII also applied to *quasi-parochi*. The President of the Pontifical Commission for the interpretation of the canons of the Code answered this doubt in the affirmative.[29] According to the norm of canon 216, § 3, therefore, the rectors of divisions of Vicariates and Prefectures Apostolic as *quasi-parochi* enjoy the power equally with *parochi*. Likewise, since in the law of the Code according to canon 451, § 2, 2°, those parochial vicars who are possessed of full parochial power are, like *quasi-parochi*, equivalent to *parochi* with all parochial rights and obligations, they too may exercise the power granted by the constitution.[30]

[27] *Cf.* Veermeersch, *op. cit.*, n. 79; Payen, *De Matrimonio* (2. ed.), II, n. 2409, § 4; Vromant, *De Matrimonio* (2. ed.), n. 350.

[28] Dubium: "Utrum facultates dispensandi, quae continentur in constitutionibus relatis in canon 1125, intelligantur concessae tantum Ordinariis, an vero omnibus sacerdotibus curam animarum exercentibus." Responsum: "Dictae facultates dispensandi aestimandae sunt ex tenore constitutionum, de quibus in canone 1125." Pont. Comm. resp., 26 Jan., 1919—*Sylloge*, n. 66.

[29] Resp., 3 Aug., 1919: "Al dubbio proposto 'Utrum vi canonis 1125 *iure* concessa sit facultas dispensandi, de qua in Constitutione *Populis* Gregorii XIII, etiam quasi-parochis,' il sottoscritto Emo Cardinale Presidente della Commissione risponde: *Affirmative*. Pietro Card. Gasparri."—*Sylloge*, n. 72.

[30] *Cf.* Vromant, *De Matrimonio* (2. ed.), n. 351.

The essential point in regard to the use of the power by the various parochial vicars is that it is permitted to them only when they are endowed with the full powers of a *parochus*. (*Cf.* canons 471-475 for norms.)

The juridical basis for the opinion that all missionaries who exercise the entire care of souls *ipso iure* have the faculty even though they are not *parochi* or *quasi-parochi* [31] is not so clear. The constitution was given for use in missionary countries, yet the Pope singled out particular officials to exercise the power. The completeness of his statement in regard to Jesuit confessors would suggest a more general terminology in regard to missionaries if it were his intention to give the power to others than Ordinaries of places, pastors, and Jesuit confessors. *Per se* a law is not to be extended because of identity or similarity of reason.[32] In view of these reasons and the response of the Pontifical Commission dated 26 January, 1919, cited above, it is at least doubtful that the faculty is enjoyed *ipso iure* by others than those named in the constitution and those who, according to canon 451, § 2, come under the name and right of *parochi*.

The power of dispensing given by the constitution is connected with the office of Ordinaries of places [33] and of *parochi*,[34] in any part of the world. The power is therefore ordinary [35] and may be delegated,[36] and it may be used in both fora.[37] Moreover, Ordinaries of places and *parochi* may use the power to dispense their own

[31] *Cf.* Payen, *De Matrimonio* (1. et 2 ed.), II, n. 2409; Woods, *The Constitutions of Canon 1125*, p. 68; Léry, *Le Privilège de la Foi*, n. 91.

[32] Van Hove: "Lex per se non est extendenda ob similitudinem aut identitatem rationis. Nam in iis quae pendent a libera voluntate legislatoris, non concluditur *a pari aut a minori ad minus.* Ratio enim legis non est ipsa lex et silentium legislatoris facile importat exclusionem illorum quae sub silentio premuntur, nec absque ratione cogente est recedendum a proprio sensu verborum."—*De Legibus Ecclesiasticis*, n. 263.

[33] Cf. Canon 198, § 1, et § 2.

[34] Canon 451, § 1, et § 2.

[35] Canon 197. *Cf.* Vermeersch-Creusen, *Epitome*, II, n. 435, § 1; Bouscaren, "An Inquiry into the Practical Application of Canon 1125," *Misc. Ver.* I, 295-296; Vromant, *De Matrimonio* (2. ed.), n. 351.

[36] Canon 199, § 1.

[37] *Cf.* Canon 202, § 3.

subjects wherever the subjects may be, and to dispense anyone actually living in their territory: [38] the same is true of those priests to whom either the Ordinaries of places or *parochi* have delegated the power without restriction. Those who have the power by delegation may subdelegate it, but only in individual cases, that is, *ad actum*, not *habitualiter*.[39]

Priests of the Society of Jesus approved by their Superiors for hearing confessions and sent into or admitted into the regions for which the constitution was given were also granted the power of dispensing. As has been seen,[40] there was a wide communication of favors and privileges among the Religious Orders in the missions in the sixteenth century, and especially among the Mendicant Orders. St. Pius V had proclaimed the Society of Jesus a Mendicant Order [41] so that it participated in the communication.

Veracruz [42] under the heading, *"Communicatio privilegiorum,"* listed six Orders as Mendicant *"pro declaratione huius materiae,"* namely,

> "Ordo fratrum praedicatorum, ordo fratrum minorum, ordo S. Augustini, ordo carmelitarum. . . Et per Paul. 4. etiam minimi sunt mendicantes. . . Et modo per grego. 13. fratres de societate sunt mendicantes. [In fact, it was St. Pius V who proclaimed the Society of Jesus to be a Mendicant Order.]
> "Secundo est sciendum, quod omnes isti ordines per communicationem privilegiorum gaudent omnibus privilegiis, indultis, gratiis, in temporalibus, et spiritualibus concessis, et concedendis cuilibet ipsorum ordinum, ac si essent unus ordo, ut patet per Sixtum quartum anno 1474. qui omnia privilegia concessa, et concedenda fratribus praedicatoribus communicavit, et concessit perpetuo in omnibus, et per omnia, et sine ulla differentia, perinde ac si quae uni sunt concessa omnibus simul nominatim concessa fuissent, aut in posterum concederentur. . ."

[38] This according to the norm of Canon 1043. *Cf.* Vermeersch-Creusen, *ibid.*

[39] Canon 199, § 3.

[40] *Cf.* supra, pp. 70, 71, note 29.

[41] Const., *"Dum indefessae,"* 7 Jul., 1571—*Bull. Rom.*, VII, 923.

[42] *Omnium previlegiorum* [*sic*] *compendium, illorum maxime concessorum ordinibus mendicantium pro conversione infidelium* (Mss., 1581 ?), folio 34, recto. *Cf. supra*, pp. 41, 42, note 32, for information on the Mss.

The Pontifical Commission for the interpretation of the canons of the Code was asked whether canon 613, § 1, is to be understood in the sense that privileges which were acquired by religious Institutes by communication according to law and were peacefully enjoyed before the Code, are revoked. The Commission replied in the negative.[43]

No doubt religious other than those listed by Veracruz[44] may, by communication of privileges, have acquired and thereupon have been in "*pacifica possessione*" of the power of dispensation granted by the Constitution "*Populis*" to the priests of the Society of Jesus, and so may still exercise it now that the constitution is a part of the universal law, but there does not seem to be any reason to hold that inclusion of the constitution in the Code extends the power to *all* confessors.[45]

Under the present law[46] general jurisdiction for hearing confessions must be obtained, even by exempt religious, from the Ordinary of the place. The approval of their subjects for hearing confessions by the Superior General of the Society of Jesus and the corresponding Superior for other religious who are entitled to use the power is not sufficient for its exercise. The grant of diocesan faculties to the aforesaid confessors by the Ordinary of the place does not confer an "*officium*" in the sense of canon 145.[47] The jurisdiction of the confessors, therefore, is not "ordinary," but the power of dispensing granted by the Constitution "*Populis*" and canon 1125 to the approved confessors may be subdelegated according to canon 199, § 2.[48] The approval (now the granting of faculties by the Ordinary

[43] 30 Dec., 1937—*AAS,* XXX (1938), 73; Bouscaren, *Canon Law Digest, Supplement—1938,* pp. 22, 23.

[44] *Cf.* Bernardus a Vasto, *De Communicatione Privilegiorum Praesertim Inter Religiones,* n. 28; Tatjer, "De Communicatione privilegiorum inter Religiones," *Apollinaris,* V (1932), 460 sq.

[45] *Cf.* Vermeersch-Creusen, *Epitome,* II, n. 435; Woods, *The Constitutions of Canon 1125,* pp. 68, 69; Payen, *De Matrimonio* (2. ed.), II, n. 2409, § 2; Cappello, *De Sacramentis,* III (4. ed.), n. 787, § 6, nota 69.

[46] Canon 874, § 1.

[47] Vermeersch-Creusen: "Munus autem confessarii (qua talis) . . . non est officium, nisi lato sensu,"—*Epitome,* I, n. 263.

[48] *Cf.* Bouscaren, "An Inquiry into the Practical Application of Canon 1125, etc.," *Misc. Ver.,* I, 297, 298.

of the place) of the privileged confessors is a *condicio sine qua non* for the use and subdelegation of the power granted by the legislator. The confessors' use of the power is not limited to the internal forum.[49]

Article 3. The Power in Practice

In practice the provisions of the Constitution *"Populis,"* now extended by canon 1125 to cases in any part of the world, contemplate the procedure for the use of the Pauline privilege when there are difficulties in the matter of the interpellations.

(a.) The marriage of the convert in whose interest the power of the constitution is being used must have been contracted in infidelity, that is, when both parties were unbaptized. If the convert was a polygamist it is the first legitimate marriage which is in question, presuming the other party to be still living, but the use of the provisions of the Constitution *"Populis"* is not limited to, nor primarily concerned with, polygamists.

(b.) From a summary and extrajudicial inquiry it should appear that it is at least morally impossible to interpellate the absent party,[50] or if interpellated that he or she has not answered within the time allotted. The results of the inquiry are to be written up in a short report showing the sufficient cause for the dispensation. This statement is not required for validity, but is rather a regulation which the Ordinary may require, both from *parochi* and from the privileged confessors even though they be exempt religious, together with a testimonial that the dispensation has been granted, when the dispensation is given in the external forum or internal non-sacramental forum.[51]

(c.) Upon verification of (a.) and (b.) the priests who have the power granted by the Constitution *"Populis"* may grant the dispensation, either in the external or in the internal forum, which prepares the way for marriage of the convert with a Catholic person and without further concern about interpellations.

[49] *Cf.* Canon 202, § 3; Bouscaren, *op. cit.*, I, 298.

[50] But *cf. supra*, pp. 169, 170, in regard to the question of useless interpellations.

[51] *Cf.* Bouscaren, *op. cit.*, I, 297, 298; Cappello, *De Sacramentis*, III (4. ed.), n. 787, § 6.

(d.) The effect of the dispensation is to make the new marriage certainly valid even though it should afterwards become known that the absent party of the first marriage had also become a baptized convert prior to the new marriage of the other party, or a just cause had prevented him (her) from answering the interpellations in due time.

Article 4. Time at Which the Bond of the First Marriage Is Dissolved

From the twelfth or thirteenth century the principle has been accepted in the use of the Pauline privilege that the bond of the prior marriage contracted in infidelity is dissolved only when the converted party has contracted the new marriage. Opinions differ on whether or not the same is true when a dispensation has been given in accordance with the provisions of the three constitutions of canon 1125.

Prat[52] in comparing the Pauline privilege with the constitutions of St. Pius V and Gregory XIII holds: " . . . as to *time,* the dispensation of the Pope breaks the old marriage bond from the moment it is applied or announced, while the Pauline privilege allows it to continue until the contract of a new marriage."

Benedict XIV, after treating of the Constitution *"Populis"* in which, indeed, he mistakenly thought that the Pope did nothing more than take away the rigor of judicial interpellation, explained that the effect of the dispensation from the interpellations thus provided for, is to dissolve irrevocably the first marriage at the moment when the convert party entered a second marriage with a baptized person.[53] When the power granted by the Constitution *"Populis"* is used for a case which, in fact, could be simply a case within the limits of the Pauline privilege and hence the use of the power affects

[52] *The Theology of St. Paul,* translated from XIth French Edition by John L. Stoddard (2 vols., London: Burns, Oates and Washbourne, 1926), I, 115.

[53] "Primum enim matrimonium eo ipso momento, et quidem irrevocabiliter, solutum remanet, quo conjux conversus ad alias nuptias cum fideli transivit . . . quia peculiares rerum circumstantiae viam aperuerunt Indulto Apostolico, quo sublata fuit interpellandi necessitas. . ."—*De Synodo Dioecesana,* lib. XIII, cap. XXI, n. 5.

only a dispensation from the interpellations, the bond of the first marriage is dissolved only when the second marriage is contracted.[54] The same would seem to be true in regard to a marriage dissolved by the use of the power granted in the constitution when the case is one would could not come within the limits of the Pauline privilege.[55]

Gasparri [56] gives the following reasons why the general principle enunciated in canon 1126, that the bond of a prior marriage contracted in infidelity is dissolved only when the converted party has validly contracted a new marriage, should apply also to cases of dissolution of the bond of marriage effected through Papal dispensation:

(a.) The words of the canon are general and not limited to the use of the Pauline privilege, therefore it seems to comprehend also the cases of Papal dispensation in the bond;

(b.) The principle is placed in the canon immediately following that which treats of the Papal constitutions providing for a dispensation of the natural bond of marriage;

(c.) The relationship between the two cases (use of the Pauline privilege, and exercise of the Papal power to dispense in the bond) is admittedly of an analogous character. Thus, as in the use of the Pauline privilege God desired the bond of the first marriage to continue up to the moment when the second valid marriage begins, so in the case of Papal dispensation the same must be said to be His will until the contrary is established for certain.

The arguments give strong support to the opinion, yet Gasparri admits that they are not conclusive and says that the individual case must be submitted to the Holy Office if the solution of a question concerning the validity or invalidity of a marriage depends upon whether or not the principle of canon 1126 applies to the dissolution of the natural bond through Papal dispensation.

Article 5. General Conclusion

Since, by virtue of canon 1125, the privileges and faculties granted in the three constitutions treated therein are now applicable any

[54] *Cf.* Bouscaren, *op. cit.*, I, 298.

[55] *Cf.* Augustinus Lehmkuhl, *Theologia Moralis* (11. ed., 2 vols., Friburgi Brisgoviae, 1910), II, n. 930.

[56] *Tract. Can. de Matr.* (ed. 1932), II, n. 1167.

place in the world to cases in which the required conditions are verified, a question may be raised about the utility of certain of the Apostolic faculties still being provided by the Cong. for the Propagation of the Faith.[57] In reference to *FTM* 24 and *FTM* 25 Vermeersch in 1922[58] said that the advantage of the faculties was to prescribe norms for the prudent application of the constitutions.[59] In 1931 the same author[60] added that the faculties provided by the Cong. for the Propagation of the Faith were not yet completely accommodated to the Code and that new formulas of faculties were then being prepared.[61]

A further question concerns the possibility that the privileges and faculties provided in the constitutions might be used to the detriment of the established matrimonial discipline of the Church.[62] It is to be remembered that the constitutions were originally issued, and are now included in the general law of the Church, as an aid to the conversion of unbaptized persons to the Faith. The conditions for the use of the privileges and faculties granted in the constitutions must be verified before they can be employed with valid effect. The fundamental condition required in every case is that the first marriage, the bond of which is being dissolved by virtue of one or other of the constitutions, must have been contracted when both parties were unbaptized.

Ordinaries may establish rules for the prudent use of the powers granted in the constitutions, in order to assure their correct applica-

[57] *Cf. supra*, p. 108, *FTM* 24, *FTM* 25, *FTM* 26.

[58] "Commentaria de Formulis Facultatum Quas S. Congr. De Propaganda Fide Concedere solet," *Periodica*, XI (1922), (139), nota 1.

[59] It may be noted here, with special reference to the Constitution *"Romani Pontificis,"* that this statement was made before the reply of the Cong. for the Propagation of the Faith to *Votum 12* of the First Council of China held in 1924. *Cf. supra*, pp. 156, 157.

[60] "De Canone 1125 eiusque vi extensiva," *Periodica*, XX (1931), 4*, 5*.

[61] Rayanna ("De Constitutione S. Pii Papae V, etc.," *Periodica*, XXVIII [1939], 206) notes that Vermeersch himself had been engaged in helping to adapt the formulas to the Code and that this work, having been interrupted after the death of Cardinal Van Rossum, had not yet (1939) been resumed.

[62] Bouscaren ("An Inquiry into the Practical Application of Canon 1125, etc.," *Misc. Ver.*, I, 299, 300) treats this question with special reference to the Constitution *"Populis."*

tion and to preclude scandal that might arise from a misunderstanding of Church law. It must be said, however, that such rules cannot affect the validity, according to the law of the Code, of the employment of the privileges and faculties when they have been used in cases in which the required conditions are verified.

In order that the record may show the circumstances under which marriages entered in virtue of canon 1125 were entered, it would seem that Ordinaries should in all cases require [63] that a notation of the use of the privileges or faculties granted in the constitutions should be included with the entry in the marriage register.

[63] *Cf.* canon 1103, § 1; *cf.* also, Instructio de Iudiciis Ecclesiasticis circa Causas Matrimoniales, § 45, in the Appendix of *Acta et Decreta Concilii Plenarii Baltimorensis Tertii,* p. 278, where it is required that the fact of interpellations having been made or a dispensation from them having been granted should always be accurately indicated in the matrimonial register. This ruling, given in regard to the use of the Pauline privilege, through the analogy of circumstances seems a prudent one also when canon 1125 is used.

CONCLUSIONS

1. The investigation into the marriage customs among the natives of the places for which the Constitutions *"Altitudo"* of Paul III and *"Romani Pontificis"* of St. Pius V were originally issued reveals that almost every conceivable variation of the two general types of polygamy (simultaneous and successive) existed in one place or another.

2. By virtue of canon 1125, since the promulgation of the Code, the provisions regarding marriage in the three constitutions mentioned in the canon, are applicable in any part of the world to cases in which the required conditions are verified. Therefore, for example, the provisions of the constitutions are applicable to such cases in the United States and Canada, as well as to cases in countries which are still under the jurisdiction of the Congregation for the Propagation of the Faith.

3. When the concession granted by the Constitution *"Altitudo"* is used, namely, when a convert polygamist who does not remember which was his (her) first and legitimate wife (husband) and chooses one of them with whom to exchange matrimonial consent, a dispensation from the impediment of disparity of worship is granted *ipso iure* if the party chosen by the polygamist convert is not also baptized. The constitution also includes an *ipso iure* dispensation from making any interpellation.

4. In the use of the Constitution *"Romani Pontificis," ipso iure* the polygamist convert is granted a dispensation from interpellating the wife (husband) who is known to be the validly married spouse and whom it is morally possible to interpellate, but if that spouse spontaneously asks to be baptized before the polygamist convert has made use of the concession granted by the constitution, that is, if he (she) has not yet entered a second valid marriage, then the concession may not be used.

5. The Constitution *"Populis"* of Gregory XIII *ipso iure* grants to Ordinaries of places, to pastors and to those who according to the norm of canon 451, § 2, are comparable to pastors, and to approved

confessors of the Society of Jesus (and to approved confessors of certain other religious Institutes who by communication of privileges enjoy the same status in this matter as confessors of the Society of Jesus), the power to dispense from interpellations in cases in which certain conditions are verified. The dispensation thus granted has the especial effect that if afterwards it become known that the absent party to the first marriage, who by virtue of the dispensation was not interpellated, had also become a Catholic before the second marriage of the other party that second marriage is nevertheless valid.

APPENDIX

The Constitution *"Altitudo"*

Paulus Episcopus

Servus Servorum Dei

Venerabilibus Fratribus universis Episcopis Occidentalis et Meridionalis Indiae Salutem et Apostolicam Benedictionem.[1]

Altitudo divini concilii quod humana nequit ratio comprehendere ex suae immensae bonitatis essentia, aliquid semper ad salutem humani generis pullulans, tempore congruo, et soli suo secreto ministerio quod ipse Deus novit opportuno producit, et manifestat, ut cognoscant mortales ex suis meritis tamquam ab ipsis, nihil proficere posse, sed eorum salutem, et omne donum gratiae ab ipso summo Deo, et Patre luminum provenire. **Sane cum sicut non sine grandi, et spirituali mentis nostrae laetitia accepimus, quam plures incolae Occidentalis et Meridionalis Indiae, licet divinae sint legis expertes, Sancto Spiritu tamen cooperante illustrati, errores, quos hactenus observarunt, penitus ab eorum mentibus, et cordibus abjecerint, ac Fidei Catholicae veritatem, et Sanctae Ecclesiae unitatem amplecti, et secundum ritum eiusdem Romanae Ecclesiae vivere desiderent et proponant;**[2] Nos, quibus omnes oves divinitus sunt commissae, cupientes eas, quae extra verum ovile, quod est Christus, sunt, ad ipsum ovile, ut fiat ex illis unus pastor, et unum ovile, perducere, ac sanctissimorum Apostolorum, qui nobis verbo, et exemplo pastoralis officii formam tradentes, nascentis Ecclesiae infantiam lacte, provectam vero eius aetatem solido cibo nutrierunt, vestigiis inhaerendo, novellas plantationes ipsius Ecclesiae, quas in dicta Occidentali, et Meridionali India, Altissimus plantare dignatus est, sic donec coalescant, ut non omnia, quae per orbem Ecclesia iam firmata custodit, illis custodienda mandemus, sed tanquam parvulis in Christo aliqua paterno affectu indulgeamus, confovere. Ac circa eorum regenerationes nonnulla, ut etiam accepimus, suborta dubia primitus forte, submovere volentes, matura sub hoc deliberatione praehabita authoritate Apostolica nobis ab ipso Domino Nostro Jesu Christo per beatum Petrum, cui, et suc-

[1] *Appendix ad Bullarium S. C. P. F.*, I, 25.

[2] Document VI of the Code of Canon Law is composed of the two parts of the Constitution *"Altitudo"* which are here printed in bold face type.

cessoribus suis, apostolatus ministerii dispensationem commissit, tradita, tenore praesentium decernimus, et declaramus illos, qui Indos ad Fidem Christi venientes, non adhibitis caeremonii, et solemnitatibus ab Ecclesia observatis, in Nomine tamen Sanctissimae Trinitatis baptizaverunt, non peccasse, cum, consideratis tunc occurrentibus, sic illis bona ex causa putamus visum fuisse expedire.[3] Et ut huiusmodi novellae plantationes, quantae dignitatis sit lavacrum regenerationis, quantumcumque ab illis lavacris, quibus antea in sua infidelitate utebantur, differt, non ignorent; statuimus, ut qui in posterum extra urgentem necessitatem Sacrum Baptisma ministrabunt, ea observent, quae a dicta Ecclesia observantur, oneratis super hac tali necessitate conscientiis eorum, extra quam quidem necessitatem in Sacro Baptismo haec quatuor observentur. Primum, aqua sacris actionibus sanctificetur. Secundum, catechismus et exorcismus fiat singulis. Tertium, sal, saliva, capella, et candela ponatur duobus vel tribus pro omnibus utriusque sexus tunc baptizandis. Quartum, chrisma ponatur singulis in vertice capitis, et oleum catechumenorum ponatur super cor viri adulti, puerorum et puellarum, adultis vero mulieribus ponatur in illa parte, quam ratio pudicitiae demonstrabit. **Super eorum vero matrimonium hoc observandum decernimus, ut qui ante conversionem plures iuxta eorum mores habebant uxores, et non recordantur, quam primo acceperint, conversi ad Fidem, unam ex illis accipiant, quam voluerint, et cum ea matrimonium contrahant per verba de praesenti, ut moris est; qui vero recordantur, quam primo acceperint, aliis dimissis, eam retineant. Ac eis concedimus, ut conjuncti etiam in tertio gradu tam consanguinitatis, quam affinitatis non excludantur a matrimoniis contrahendis donec huic S. Sedi super hoc aliud visum fuerit statuendum.** Et circa abstinentiam ab illis suscipiendam etiam statuimus, quod in Vigilia Nativitatis, et Resurrectionis Domini Nostri, et omnibus sextis feriis Quadragesimae jejunare teneantur, ceteros vero jejuniorum dies eorum beneplacito propter novam ad Fidem eorum conversionem,[4] et ipsius gentis infirmitatem permittimus, ita quod jejunium repugnans, vel non bene quadrans officio vel exercitio alicuius non censeatur illi ab Ecclesia praeceptum. Eisque etiam concedimus, quod quadragesimalibus et aliis temporibus anni prohibitis lacticiniis, ovis et carnibus tunc temporibus dumtaxat vesci possint, cum

[3] *Concilios Provinciales Primero y Segundo* (Mexico), pp. 29, 30.

[4] The phrase, "propter novam ad Fidem eorum conversionem," as here given is found in the constitution as it appears in *Concilios Provinciales Primero y Segundo* (Mexico), p. 31. The *Appendix ad Bullarium S. C. P. F.*, I, 25, has this phrase in an unlikely form, namely, "propter eorum ad novam ad Fidem conversionem."

caeteris christianis ob aliquod sanctum opus obeundum similibus cibis vesci posse a Sede Apostolica pro tempore fuerit concessum. Dies autem in quibus volumus eos ab operibus servilibus cessare, declaramus esse omnes dies Dominicos, ac Nativitatis, Circumcisionis, et Epiphaniae, Ressurectionis, et Ascensionis, ac Corporis eiusdem Domini Jesu Christi, et Pentecostes, nec non Nativitatis, Annunciationis, Purificationis, et Assumptionis gloriosae Dei Genitricis Virginis Mariae, ac BB. Petri et Pauli eius Coapostoli. Ceteros vero dies festos ex causis supradictis illis indulgemus. Et insuper considerantes maximam ipsius Indiae Occidentalis, et Meridionalis a Sede Apostolica distantiam, tam vobis, qui in partem Apostolicae solicitudinis assumpti estis quam iis, quibus super hoc vices vestras, auctoritate per nos super hoc concessa, specialiter duxeritis committendas, omnes noviter conversos praedictos in quibuscumque Sedi Apostolicae reservatis casibus, etiam in Literis in die Caenae Domini legi consuetis, nihil nobis de illorum absolutionibus reservantes, auctoritate Apostolica injuncta eis poenitentia salutari in forma Ecclesiae consueta, prout prudentiae vestrae videbitur expedire, absolvendi plenam et liberam ad dictae Sedis beneplacitum facultatem concedimus. Et postremo ne isti in Christo parvuli malis exemplis corrumpantur, quod aliquis apostata in illas partes se conferre non praesumat, sub excommunicationis latae sententiae poena, a qua nisi post suum istinc decessum absolvi nequeat decernimus.

Datum Romae apud Sanctum Petrum Anno Incarnationis Dominicae 1537.[5] Kalend. Junii, Pontificatus nostri anno tertio. Blosius B. Motta.[6]

[5] *Appendix ad Bullarium S. C. P. F.*, I, 25, 26.

[6] *Concilios Provinciales Primero y Segundo* (Mexico), p. 33. *Cf. Annales Minorum seu Trium Ordinum a S. Francisco Institutorum* (3. ed., 17 vols., Ad Claras Aquas [Quaracchi], 1931-1935), XVI, nn. 416, 417, pp. 480-482, for the complete constitution.

BIBLIOGRAPHY

Sources

Acta Apostolicae Sedis, Commentarium Officiale, Romae, 1909—

Acta et Decreta Concilii Plenarii Baltimorensis Tertii (1884), Baltimorae: Typis Joannis Murphy et Sociorum, 1886.

Acta et Decreta Sacrorum Conciliorum Recentiorum, Collectio Lacensis, 7 vols., Friburgi, Brisgoviae, 1870-1890.

Acta Sanctae Sedis, 41 vols., Romae, 1865-1908.

Aguirre, Josephus Saenz de, *Collectio Maxima Conciliorum Omnium Hispaniae et Novi Orbis,* 4 vols., Romae, 1693-1694.

Annuario Pontificio per L'Anno 1939, Citta del Vaticano: Tipografia Poliglotta Vaticana, 1939.

Appendix ad Bullarium Pontificium Sacrae Congregationis de Propaganda Fide, 2 vols., Romae, Typis Collegii Urbani. (No date given on title page.)

Bullarium Diplomatum et Privilegiorum Sanctorum Romanorum Pontificum, Taurinensis Editio, 24 vols. et Appendix, Augustae Taurinorum-Neapoli, 1857-1872.

Bullarium Ordinis Fratrum Minorum Capucinorum, 10 vols., Vols. I-VII ed. a Michaele a Tugio in Helvetia, Romae, 1740-1752; Vols. VIII-X ed. a Petro Damiani a Münster, Oeniponte, 1844.

Bullarium Sanctissimi Domini Nostri Benedicti Papae XIV, 4 vols. in 10, Venetiis, 1777-1784.

Codex Iuris Canonici Pii X Pontificis Maximi iussu digestus, Benedicti Papae XV auctoritate promulgatus, Romae: Typis Polyglottis Vaticanis, 1917.

Codicis Iuris Canonici Fontes cura Emi Petri Card. Gasparri editi, 9 vols., Romae (later Civitate Vaticana): Typis Polyglottis Vaticanis, 1923-1939. (Vol. VII-IX *ed. cura et studio Emi Iustiniani Card. Serédi.*)

Collectanea Constitutionum, Decretorum, Indultorum ac Instructionum S. Sedis ad usum Societatis Missionum ad exteros, 2. ed., Hongkong, 1905.

Collectanea S. Congregationis de Propaganda Fide, Romae, 1893.

Collectanea S. Congregationis de Propaganda Fide, 2 vols., Romae, 1907.

Corpus Iuris Canonici, ed. Lipsiensis 2., Aemilius Ludovicus Richter-Aemilius Friedberg, 2 vols., Lipsiae, 1879-1881.

Corpus Scriptorum Ecclesiasticorum Latinorum, Vindobonae, 1866—

Denziger, Henr., et Bannwart, Clem., *Enchiridion Symbolorum Definitionum et Declarationum de Rebus Fidei et Morum,* 16. et 17. ed., Friburgi Brisgoviae: Herder, 1928.

Friedberg, Aemilius, *Quinque Compilationes Antiquae,* Lipsiae, 1882.

Haroldus, Franciscus, *Lima Limata Conciliis, Constitutionibus Synodalibus et aliis Monumentis Quibus Venerab. Servus Dei Toribius Alphonsus Mogroveius, Archiepisc. Limanus Provinciam Limensem seu Peruanem Imperium Elimavit et ad Normam SS. Canonum Composuit*, Romae, 1673.

Laderchio, Jacobo de, *Annales Ecclesiastici, ab anno 1556 ubi Odericus Raynaldus desinit*, Tom. XXII, Romae, 1728.

Lorenzana, Francisco Antonio, *Concilios Provinciales Primero Y Segundo*, Mexico, 1769.

———, *Concilium Mexicanum Provinciale III*, Mexici, 1770.

Mansi, Joannes, *Sacrorum Conciliorum Nova et Amplissima Collectio*, 53 vols., Parisiis, 1901-1927.

Migne, Jacques Paul, *Patrologiae Cursus Completus, Series Latina*, 221 vols., Parisiis, 1844-1864.

———, *Patrologiae Cursus Completus, Series Graeca*, 53 vols., Parisiis, 1856-1866.

Primum Concilium Sinense, Anno 1924 . . . Celebratum: Acta—Decreta et Normae—Vota, etc., Zi-Ka-Wei: Typographia Missionis Catholicae (T'OU-SÊ-WÊ), 1929.

Waddingus Hibernus, Luca, *Annales Minorum seu Trium Ordinum a S. Francisco Institutorum*, 3. ed., 17 vols., Ad Claras Aquas (Quaracchi), 1931-1935.

Authors

Acosta, Josephus, *De Natura Novi Orbis et de Promulgatione Evangelii apud Barbaros sive De Procuranda Indorum Saluti Libri Sex*, Salmanticae, 1589.

———, *De Natura Novi Orbis Libri Duo et De Promulgatione Evangelii apud Barbaros, sive De Procuranda Indorum Salute, Libri Sex*, Coloniae Agrippinae, 1596.

Aquinas, Thomas, *Divi Thomae Aquinatis Opera*, 2. ed. Veneta, 28 vols., Venetiis, 1775-1788.

Avendano, Didacus de, *Thesaurus Indicus*, 2 tomus et Additiones ad tomum posteriorum, in 1 vol., Antverpiae, 1668.

Azpilcueta, Martinus (Navarrus), *Consilia seu Responsa in Quinque Libros iuxta Numerum et Titulos Decretalium Distributa*, 2 vols., Venetiis, 1621.

(Bachofen), Charles Augustine, *A Commentary on the New Code of Canon Law*, 8 vols., Vol. V, 2. ed., St. Louis: Herder, 1920.

Bardenhewer, Otto, *Patrology*, translated from 2. ed. by Thomas J. Shahan, Freiburg in Breisgau and St. Louis, 1908.

Baptista, Ioan, *Advertencias Para Los Confessores de los Naturales*, Mexico, 1600.

Benedictus XIV, *De Synodo Dioecesana*, 2 vols., Romae, 1767.

———, *Opera Omnia*, 17 vols. in 18, Prati, 1839-1847.

Billot, Ludovicus, *De Ecclesiae Sacramentis Commentarius in Tertiam Partem S. Thomae*, 6. ed., 2 vols., Romae, 1922.

Cajetan, Cardinal, *Opuscula Omni D. Thomae de Vio in Tres Distincta Tomos*, in 1 vol., Lugdini, 1585.

Cappello, Felix M., *Summa Iuris Canonici*, 3 vols., Romae: Apud Aedes Univ. Greg., Vols. I-II, 2. ed., 1932-1934; Vol. III, 1936.

———, *Tractatus Canonico-Moralis de Sacramentis*, Vol. III, *De Matrimonio*, 3. ed., Taurinorum Augustae: Marietti, 1933.

———, *Tractatus Canonico-Moralis de Sacramentis*, Vol. III, *De Matrimonio*, 4. ed., Taurinorum Augustae: Marietti, 1939.

Cardenas, Joannes de, *Crisis Theologica*, Venetiis, 1696.

Catholic Encyclopedia, 15 vols., New York, 1907-1912.

Cerato, Prosdocimus *Matrimonium a Codice Iuris Canonici Integre Desumptum*, 4 ed., Patavii: Typis Seminarii Patavini, 1929.

Chelodi, Joannes, *Ius Matrimoniale iuxta Codicem Iuris Canonici*, 3. ed., Tridenti: Libr. Edit. Tridentum, 1921.

Cicognani, Amleto G., *Canon Law*, 2. revised edition, authorized English version, translated by J. M. O'Hara and F. Brennan, Philadelphia: Dolphin Press, 1935.

Clericatus, Joannes, *Decisiones Sacramentales*, 2 vols., *Decisiones de Matrimonio*, Augustae Vindelicorum, 1730.

Cornelius a Lapide, *Commentaria in Scripturam Sacram*, ed. A. Crampon, Vol. XVIII, *In Epistolas Divi Pauli*, Parisiis, 1866.

Cornely, Rudolphus, *Commentarius in S. Pauli Apostoli Epistolas, II, Prior Epistola ad Corinthios*, 2. ed., Parisiis, 1909.

Coronata, Matthaeus Conte a, *Institutiones Iuris Canonici*, 5 vols., Taurini: Marietti, 1928-1936.

D'Annibale, Josephus, *Summula Theologiae Moralis*, 3. ed., 3 vols., Romae, 1892.

De Becker, Iulius, *De Matrimonio Praelectiones Canonicae*, ed. nova ad tramites Codicis Iuris Canonici accomodata, Louvain: Fr. Ceuterick, 1931.

De Smet, A., *Betrothment and Marriage*, 2. ed., 2 vols., translated from 3rd Latin edition of 1920, by W. Dobell and A. Owens, Bruges: Beyaert, 1923-1925.

———, *Tractatus Theologico-Canonicus De Sponsalibus et Matrimonio*, 4. ed., Brugis: Beyaert, 1927.

Dobrizhoffer, Martin, *An Account of the Abipones, an Equestrian People of Paraquay*, 3 vols., translated from the Latin, London, 1822.

Feije, Henricus Ioannes, *De Impedimentibus et Dispensationibus Matrimonialibus*, 3. ed. Lovanii, 1885.

Gasparri, Petrus, *Tractatus Canonicus de Matrimonio*, 2 vols., Paris, 1891.

———, *Tractatus Canonicus de Matrimonio*, 2. ed., 2 vols., Parisiis-Lugduni, 1900.

———, *Tractatus Canonicus de Matrimonio*, 3. ed., 2 vols., Parisiis, 1904.

———, *Tractatus Canonicus de Matrimonio*, ed. nova, ad mentem Codicis I. C., 2 vols., Romae: Typis Polyglottis Vaticanis, 1932.

Geiger, Maynard, *The Franciscan Conquest of Florida (1573-1618)*, The Catholic University of America, Studies in Hispanic-American History, Vol. I, Washington: The Catholic University of America, 1937.

Gigot, Francis E., *Christ's Teaching Concerning Divorce*, New York, 1912.

Giovine, Petrus, *Consultationes Canonicae De Dispensationibus Matrimonialibus*, 2 vols., Neopoli, 1863.

Gómara, López de, *Hispania Victrix, Segunda Parta de la Cronica de Las Indias*, in Vol. XXII *Biblioteca de Autores Espanoles*, 71 vols., ed. by Manuel Rivadeneyra, Madrid, 1846-1880.

Gregory, Donald J., *The Pauline Privilege*, The Catholic University of America, Canon Law Studies, n. 68, Washington: The Catholic University of America, 1931.

Grentrup, Theodorus, *Jus Missionarium Quod in Formam Compendii Redactum*, Tom. I, Steyl Hollandiae: Typographia Domus Missionum, 1925.

Gury, Joannes Petrus—Ballerini, Antonius, *Compendium Theologiae Moralis*, 2. ed., Romae—Taurini, 1869.

Harisse, Henry, *The Diplomatic History of America—Its First Chapter, 1452, 1493, 1494*, London, 1897.

Hobhouse, L. T., Wheeler, G. C., and Ginsberg, M., *The Material Culture and Institutions of the Simpler Peoples: An Essay in Correlation*, London: Chapman and Hall, 1930.

Hostiensis (Henricus de Segusio), *Commentaria in Libros V. Decretalium*, 3. vols., Venetiis, 1581.

Huarte, Gabrielis, *Tractatus de Ordine et Matrimonio*, 3. ed., Romae: Apud Aedes Universitatis Gregorianae, 1931.

Johnston, Harry H., *The Negro in the New World*, London, 1910.

Joyce, George Hayward, *Christian Marriage*, London and New York: Sheed and Ward, 1932.

Konings, Antonius—Putzer, Joseph, *Commentarium in Facultates Apostolicas*, 4. ed., New York, 1897.

Lehmkuhl, Augustinus, *Theologia Moralis*, 5. ed., 2 vols., Friburgi Brisgoviae, 1888.

———, *Theologia Moralis*, 11 ed., 2 vols., Friburgi Brisgoviae, 1910.

Léry, Louis Chaussegros de, *Le Privilège de la Foi*, Montreal: Collection des Studia, 1938.

Liguori, Alphonsus, *Theologia Moralis*, 9 vols., Vesuntione, 1828.

Lugo, Joannes de, *Opera Omnia*, 7 vols. in 4, Venetiis, 1718.

Mac Nutt, Francis Augustus, *Bartholomew De Las Casas*, New York, 1909.

Maroto, Philippus, *Institutiones Iuris Canonici ad Norman Novi Codicis*, 2 vols., Vol. I, *Tractatus Fundamentales*, 3. ed., Romae: Apud Commentarium pro Religiosis, 1921.

Means, Philip Ainsworth, *Ancient Civilization of the Andes*, New York: Scribner's, 1931.

Michiels, Gommarus, *Normae Generales Iuris Canonici*, 2 vols., Lublin: Universitas Catholica, 1929.

Morelli, Cyriacus, *Fasti Novi Orbis et Ordinationum Apostolicarum ad Indias Pertinentium Brevarium,* Venetiis, 1776.

Noldin, H., *De Matrimonio,* 5. ed., Oeniponte, 1904.

Noldin, H. et Schmitt, A., *Summa Theologiae Moralis iuxta Codicem Iuris Canonici,* 32. ed., 3 vols., Oeniponte: Rauch, 1932.

Ojetti, B., *Commentarium in Codicem Iuris Canonici,* 4 vols., Romae: Apud Aedes Univ. Greg., 1927-1931.

Ottaviani, Alaphridus, *Institutiones Iuris Publici Ecclesiastici,* 2 ed., 2 vols., Romae: Typis Polyglottis Vaticanis, 1936.

Palmieri, Dominicus, *Tractatus De Matrimonio Christiano,* Romae, 1880.

Pastor, Ludwig Freiherr von, *The History of the Popes From the Close of the Middle Ages,* 29 vols., translation, Vols. I-VI ed. by Frederick I. Antrobus; Vols. VII-XXIV, ed. by Ralph F. Kerr; Vols. XXV-XXIX, ed. by Dom Ernest Graf, St. Louis: Herder, 1906-1938.

Payen, G., *De Matrimonio in Missionibus ac Potissimum in Sinis Tractatus Practicus et Casus,* 3 vols., Zi-ka-wei: Typographia T'OU-SÉ-WÉ, 1928-1929.

———, *De Matrimonio in Missionibus ac Potissimum in Sinis Tractatus Practicus et Casus,* 2. ed., 3 vols., Zi-ka-wei: Typographia T'OU-SÉ-WÉ, 1935-1936.

Perrone, Joannes, *De Matrimonio Christiano Libri Tres,* 3 vols., Romae, 1858.

———, *Praelectiones Theologicae,* 32. ed., Taurini, 1868.

Pesch, Christianus, *Praelectiones Dogmaticae,* 3. ed., Vol. VII, *De Sacramentis,* Pars II, Friburgi Brisgoviae, 1909.

Pontius, Basilius, *De Sacramento Matrimonii Tractatus,* 2. ed., Bruxelles, 1627.

Prat, Ferdinand, *The Theology of St. Paul,* translated from the 11th French ed. by John L. Stoddard, 2 vols., London: Burns, Oates, and Washbourne, 1926.

Prescott, William H., *History of the Conquest of Mexico,* 2 vols., New York, 1843.

———, *History of the Conquest of Peru,* 2 vols., New York, 1890.

Reiffenstuel, Anacletus, *Ius Canonicum Universum,* 7 vols., Parisiis, 1864-1870.

Sanchez, Thomas, *De Sancto Matrimonii Sacramento Disputationum Libri Decem, in Tres Tomos Distributi,* Venetiis, 1712.

Schenk, Francis J., *The Matrimonial Impediments of Mixed Religion and Disparity of Cult,* The Catholic University of America, Canon Law Studies, n. 51, Washington: The Catholic University of America, 1929.

Schmidlin, Joseph, *Catholic Mission Theory,* a translation, Techny: Mission Press S.V.D., 1931.

———, *Catholic Mission History,* a translation, edited by Matthias Braun, Techny: Mission Press S.V.D., 1933.

Solorzano Pereira, Joannes de, *De Indiarum Jure,* 2 vols., Matriti, 1777.

Suarez, Franciscus, *Opera Omnia,* ed. C. Berton, 28 vols., Parisiis, 1856-1878; Vols. V et VI, *Tractatus De Legibus.*

Techo, Nicolaus del, *Historia Provinciae Paraquariae Societatis Jesu,* Leodii, 1673.

———, *Relatio Triplex De Rebus Indicis,* Antverpiae, 1654.

Triebs, Franz, *Praktisches Handbuch des geltenden kanonischen Eherechts im Vergleichung mit dem deutschen staatlichen Eherecht,* Breslau: Ostdeutsche Verglagansantalt, 1933.

Van Hove, A., *Commentarium Lovaniense in Codicem Iuris Canonici,* Vol. I, Tom. I, *Prolegomena ad Codicem Iuris Canonici,* Mechliniae-Romae: Dessain, 1928.

Vol. I, Tom. II, *De Legibus Ecclesiasticis,* Mechliniae-Romae: Dessain, 1930.

Vol. I, Tom. V, *De Privilegiis—De Dispensationibus,* Mechliniae-Romae: Dessain, 1939.

Vasquez, Gabriel, *Commentariorum ac Disputationum in Primam Secundae Sancti Thomae Tomus Primus,* Lugdini, 1620.

Vasto, Bernardus a, *De Communicatione Privilegiorum, Praesertim inter Religiones,* Aquilae in Vestinis: Auctor, 1936.

Veracruce, Ill[d?]ephonsus a, *Speculum Coniugiorum,* Mexici, 1556.

Veracruce, Alphonsus a, *Omnium previlegiorum compendium, illorum maxime concessorum ordinibus mendicantium pro conversione infidelium,* (1581 ?), Manuscript n. 26 in John Carter Brown Library, Brown University, Providence, R. I.

Vermeersch, A., *De Matrimoniali Casu Quem Apostoli Vocant, Seu de Fidei Privilegio,* Brugis, 1911.

Vermeersch, A., et Creusen, J., *Epitome Iuris Canonici,* 3 vols., Vol. I, 6. ed., Vols. II et III, 5. ed., Mechliniae et Romae: Dessain, 1934-1937.

Vlaming, Th. M., *Praelectiones Iuris Matrimonii ad Normam Codicis Iuris Canonici,* 3. ed., 2 vols., Bussum in Hollandia: Sumptibus Societatis Editricis Anonymae, 1919-1921.

Vromant, G., *Facultates Apostolicae Quas Sacra Congregatio de Propaganda Fide Delegare Solet Ordinariis Missionum, Commentaria in Formulam Tertiam,* Louvain: Museum Lessianum, 1926.

———, *Facultates Apostolicae Quas Sacra Congregatio de Propaganda Fide Delegare Solet Ordinariis Missionum, Commentaria in Formulam Tertiam,* 2. ed., Bruxelles et Paris: Museum Lessianum, 1938.

———, *Ius Missionariorum,* Vol. V., *De Matrimonio,* Louvain; Museum Lessianum, 1931.

———, *Ius Missionariorum, De Matrimonio,* 2. ed., Bruxelles et Paris: Museum Lessianum, 1938.

Wernz, Franciscus X., *Ius Decretalium,* 2. ed., 6 vols., Romae et Prati, 1905-1913.

Wernz, Franciscus et Vidal, Petrus, *Ius Canonicum,* 7 toms. in 9 vols., Romae: Apud Aedes Universitatis Gregorianae, 1923-1938; *Ius Matrimoniale,* Vol. V., 2. ed., 1928.

Westermarck, Edward, *The History of Human Marriage*, 5. ed., 3 vols., New York: Allerton, 1922.

Woods, Francis F., *The Constitutions of Canon 1125 and Their Application in the United States*, Milwaukee: Bruce, 1935.

Zitelli, Zephyrinus, *De Dispensationibus Matrimonialibus*, Romae, 1884.

Periodicals

Analecta Ecclesiastica, Romae, 1893-1911.

Apollinaris, Romae, 1928—

Archiv für katholisches Kirchenrecht, Innsbruck, 1857-1861; Mainz, 1862—

Ecclesiastical Review, The (originally *The American Ecclesiastical Review*), Philadelphia, 1889—

Ephemerides Theologicae Lovanienses, Brugis, 1924—

Hispanic American Historical Review, Baltimore, Vols. 1-5, 1918-1922; Durham, N. C., Vols. 6—, 1926—

Jus Pontificium, Romae, 1921—

Periodica de Re Canonica et Morali utili praesertim Religiosis et Missionariis, Brugis, 1905—; ab anno 1927: *Periodica de Re Morali, Canonica, Liturgica*.

Articles

Arendt, G., "Quomodo in favorem fidei solvatur a S. Pontifice matrimonium in infidelitate contractum, Nota theologico-canonica circa canonem 1127," *ETL*, I (1914), 174-184.

Bouscaren, T. Lincoln, "An Inquiry Into the Practical Application of Canon 1125 Outside of Mission Territories," *Miscellanea Vermeersch*, I, 279-302. *Miscellanea Vermeersch*, 2 vols., Romae; Pontificia Università Gregoriana, 1935.

Braun, Karl Ludwig, "Zur Lehre von der Natur des paulinischen Privilegiums. I Cor. VII," *AKKR*, LI (1884), 209-227.

Creusen, J., "De dubio matrimonio ob dubium baptismum," *Periodica*, XVII (1928), 153*-159*.

De Becker, Julius, Recensions in *ETL*, II (1925), 271-275, 444-447.

Kelly, James P., "Recent Decree on Doubtful Baptisms and the Pauline Privilege," *AER*, XCVII (1937), 366-372.

Loughran, E. Ward, "First Episcopal Sees in Spanish America," *Hispanic American Historical Review*, X (1930), 167-187.

O'Connor, William R., "The Indissolubility of a Ratified Consummated Marriage," *ETL*, XIII (1936), 692-722.

Rayanna, Puthota, "De Constitutione S. Pii Papae V, *Romani Pontificis*, (3 [2?] Augusti, 1571)," *Periodica*, XXVII (1938), 295-331; XXVIII (1939), 24-52, 112-134, 190-209.

Staedler, E., "Die Donatio Alexandrina und die 'Divisio Mundi' von 1493," *AKKR*, CXVII (1937), 363-402.

Tatjer, Honestus, "De Communicatione privilegiorum inter Religiones," *Apollinaris,* V (1932), 458-486.

Vermeersch, A., "Interpretatio canonis 1127, de favore iuris concesso privilegio Fidei," *Periodica,* X (1921), (25)-(28).

———, "Commentaria de Formulis Facultatum Quas S. Congr. de Propaganda Fide Concedere Solet," *Periodica,* XI (1922), (33)-(144).

———, "De Canone 1125 eiusque vi extensiva," *Periodica,* XX (1931), 1*-5*.

Vromant, G., "De Applicatione Canonis 1127," *Ius Pontificium,* XII (1932), 115-121.

———, "De Dispensatione ab Interpellationibus in Ordine ad Privilegium Fidei: Applicationes Practicae Canonis 1125," *Periodica,* XX (1931), 108*-117*.

LIST OF ABBREVIATIONS

AAS—Acta Apostolicae Sedis.

AER—The Ecclesiastical Review.

ASS—Acta Sanctae Sedis.

AKKR—Archiv für katholisches Kirchenrecht.

Coll. Hong.—Collectanea Constitutionum, Indultorum ac Instructionum ad usum Societatis Missionum ad exteros, 2. ed.

Coll. Lac.—Acta et Decreta Sacrorum Conciliorum Recentiorum, Collectio Lacensis.

Coll. S.C.P.F.—Collectanea S. Congregationis de Propaganda Fide, ed. 1907.

ETL—Ephemerides Theologicae Lovanienses.

Fontes—Codicis Iuris Canonici Fontes.

FTM—Facultatum Apostolicarum Formula Tertia Maior.

Misc. Ver.—Miscellanea Vermeersch.

MPG—Migne, Patrologia Series Graeca.

MPL—Migne, *Patrologia Series Latina.*

Sylloge—Sylloge Praecipuorum Documentorum Recentium Summorum Pontificum et S. Congregationis de Propaganda Fide necnon aliarum SS. Congregationum Romanarum.

ALPHABETICAL INDEX

BIOGRAPHICAL NOTE

Francis James Burton was born May 11, 1902, at Saginaw, Mich. His primary and secondary education were received at St. Mary's School, Saginaw, Mich. He entered the novitiate of the Congregation of Holy Cross at Notre Dame, Ind., in 1928, where he was professed on August 2, 1929. The same year he entered the University of Notre Dame from which he received the A.B. degree in 1933. After the four year Theological course pursued at Holy Cross College, Washington, D. C., he was ordained to the priesthood June 24, 1937. In preparation for work in the missionary diocese of Dacca, Bengal, India, he was sent to the Catholic University of America from which he received the Baccalaureate in Canon Law in June, 1938, and the Licentiate in Canon Law in June, 1939.

CANON LAW STUDIES

1. Freriks, Rev. Celestine A., C.PP.S., J.C.D., Religious Congregations in Their External Relations, 121 pp., 1916.
2. Gallizer, Rev. Daniel M., O.P., J.C.D., Canonical Elections, 117 pp., 1917.
3. Borkowski, Rev. Aurelius L., O.F.M., J.C.D., De Confraternitatibus Ecclesiasticis, 136 pp., 1918.
4. Castillo, Rev. Cayo, J.C.D., Disertacion Historico-Canonica sobre la Potestad del Cabildo en Sede Vacante o Impedida del Vicario Capitular, 99 pp., 1919 (1918).
5. Kubelbeck, Rev. William J., S.T.B., J.C.D., The Sacred Penitentiaria and Its Relation to Faculties of Ordinaries and Priests, 129 pp., 1918.
6. Petrovits, Rev. Joseph, J.C., S.T.D., J.C.D., The New Church Law on Matrimony, X-461 pp., 1919.
7. Hickey, Rev. John J., S.T.B., J.C.D., Irregularities and Simple Impediments in the New Code of Canon Law, 100 pp., 1920.
8. Klekotka, Rev. Peter J., S.T.B., J.C.D., Diocesan Consultors, 179 pp., 1920.
9. Wanenmacher, Rev. Francis, J.C.D., The Evidence in Ecclesiastical Procedure Affecting the Marriage Bond, 1920 (Printed 1935).
10. Golden, Rev. Henry Francis, J.C.D., Parochial Benefices in the New Code, IV-119 pp., 1921 (Printed 1925).
11. Koudelka, Rev. Charles J., J.C.D., Pastors, Their Rights and Duties According to the New Code of Canon Law, 211 pp., 1921.
12. Melo, Rev. Antonius, O.F.M., J.C.D., De Exemptione Regularium, X-188 pp., 1921.
13. Schaaf, Rev. Valentine Theodore, O.F.M., S.T.B., J.C.D., The Cloister, X-180 pp., 1921.
14. Burke, Rev. Thomas Joseph, S.T.D., J.C.D., Competence in Ecclesiastical Tribunals, IV-117 pp., 1922.
15. Leech, Rev. George Leo, J.C.D., A Comparative Study of the Constitution "Apostolicae Sedis" and the "Codex Juris Canonici," 179 pp., 1922.
16. Motry, Rev. Hubert Louis, S.T.D., J.C.D., Diocesan Faculties According to the Code of Canon Law, II-167 pp., 1922.
17. Murphy, Rev. George Lawrence, J.C.D., Delinquencies and Penalties in the Administration and the Reception of the Sacraments, IV-121 pp., 1923.
18. O'Reilly, Rev. John Anthony, S.T.B., J.C.D., Ecclesiastical Sepulture in the New Code of Canon Law, II-129 pp., 1923.
19. Michalicka, Rev. Wenceslas Cyrill, O.S.B., J.C.D., Judicial Procedure in Dismissal of Clerical Exempt Religious, 107 pp. 1923.

20. Dargin, Rev. Edward Vincent, S.T.B., J.C.D., Reserved Cases According to the Code of Canon Law, IV-103 pp., 1924.

21. Godfrey, Rev. John A., S.T.B., J.C.D., The Right of Patronage According to the Code of Canon Law, 153 pp., 1924.

22. Hagedorn, Rev. Francis Edward, J.C.D., General Legislation on Indulgences, II-154 pp., 1924.

23. King, Rev. James Ignatius, J.C.D., The Administration of the Sacraments to Dying Non-Catholics, V-141 pp., 1924.

24. Winslow, Rev. Francis Joseph, M.M., J.C.D., Vicars and Prefects Apostolic, IV-149 pp., 1924.

25. Correa, Rev. Jose Servelion, S.T.L., J.C.D., La Potestad Legislativa de la Iglesia Catolica, IV-127 pp., 1925.

26. Dugan, Rev. Henry Francis, A.M., J.C.D., The Judiciary Department of the Diocesan Curia, 87 pp., 1925.

27. Keller, Rev. Charles Frederick, S.T.B., J.C.D., Mass Stipends, 167 pp., 1925.

28. Paschang, Rev. John Linus, J.C.D., The Sacramentals According to the Code of Canon Law, 129 pp., 1925.

29. Pointek, Rev. Cyrillus, O.F.M., S.T.B., J.C.D., De Indulto Exclaustrationis necnon Saecularizationis, XIII-289 pp., 1925.

30. Kearney, Rev. Richard Joseph, S.T.B., J.C.D., Sponsors at Baptism According to the Code of Canon Law, IV-127 pp., 1925.

31. Bartlett, Rev. Chester Joseph, A.M., LL.B., J.C.D., The Tenure of Parochial Property in the United States of America, V-108 pp., 1926.

32. Kilker, Rev. Adrian Jerome, J.C.D., Extreme Unction, V-425 pp., 1926.

33. McCormick, Rev. Robert Emmett, J.C.D., Confessors of Religious, VIII-266 pp., 1926.

34. Miller, Rev. Newton Thomas, J.C.D., Founded Masses According to the Code of Canon Law, VII-93 pp., 1926.

35. Roelker, Rev. Edward G., S.T.D., J.C.D., Principles of Privilege According to the Code of Canon Law, XI-166 pp., 1926.

36. Bakalarczyk, Rev. Richardus, M.I.C., J.U.D., De Novitiatu, VIII-208 pp., 1927.

37. Pizzuti, Rev. Lawrence, O.F.M., J.U.L., De Parochis Religiosis, 1927. (Not Printed.)

38. Bliley, Rev. Nicholas Martin, O.S.B., J.C.D., Altars According to the Code of Canon Law, XIX-132 pp., 1927.

39. Brown, Mr. Brendan Francis, A.B., LL.M., J.U.D., The Canonical Juristic Personality with Special Reference to its Status in the United States of America, V-212 pp., 1927.

40. Cavanaugh, Rev. William Thomas, C.P., J.U.D., The Reservation of the Blessed Sacrament, VIII-101 pp., 1927.

41. Doheny, Rev. William J., C.S.C., A.B., J.U.D., Church Property: Modes of Acquisition, X-118 pp., 1927.

42. Feldhaus, Rev. Aloysius H., C.PP.S., J.C.D., Oratories, IX-141 pp., 1927.
43. Kelly, Rev. James Patrick, A.B., J.C.D., The Jurisdiction of the Simple Confessor, X-208 pp., 1927.
44. Neuberger, Rev. Nicholas J., J.C.D., Canon 6 or the Relation of the Codex Juris Canonici to the Preceding Legislation, V-95 pp., 1927.
45. O'Keefe, Rev. Gerald Michael, J.C.D., Matrimonial Dispensations, Powers of Bishops, Priests, and Confessors, VIII-232 pp., 1927.
46. Quigley, Rev. Joseph A. M., A.B., J.C.D., Condemned Societies, 139 pp., 1927.
47. Zaplotnik, Rev. Johannes Leo, J.C.D., De Vicariis Foraneis, X-142 pp. 1927.
48. Duskie, Rev. John Aloysius, A.B., J.C.D., The Canonical Status of the Orientals in the United States, VIII-196 pp., 1928.
49. Hyland, Rev. Francis Edward, J.C.D., Excommunciation, Its Nature, Historical Development and Effects, VIII-181 pp., 1928.
50. Reinmann, Rev. Gerald Joseph, O.M.C., J.C.D., The Third Order Secular of Saint Francis, 201 pp., 1928.
51. Schenk, Rev. Francis J., J.C.D., The Matrimonial Impediments of Mixed Religion and Disparity of Cult, XVI-318 pp., 1929.
52. Coady, Rev. John Joseph, S.T.D., J.U.D., A.M., The appointment of Pastors, VIII-150 pp., 1929.
53. Kay, Rev. Thomas Henry, J.C.D., Competence in Matrimonial Procedure, VIII-164 pp., 1929.
54. Turner, Rev. Sidney Joseph, C.P., J.U.D., The Vow of Poverty, XLIX-217 pp., 1929.
55. Kearney, Rev. Raymond A., A.B., S.T.D., J.C.D., The Principles of Delegation, VII-149 pp., 1929.
56. Conran, Rev. Edward James, A.B., J.C.D., The Interdict, V-163 pp., 1930.
57. O'Neill, Rev. William H., J.C.D., Papal Rescripts of Favor, VII-218 pp., 1930.
58. Bastnagel, Rev. Clement Vincent, J.U.D., The Appointment of Parochial Adjutants and Assistants, XV-257 pp., 1940.
59. Ferry, Rev. William A., A.B., J.C.D., Stole Fees, V-136 pp., 1930.
60. Costello, Rev. John Michael, A.B., J.C.D., Domicile and Quasi-Domicile, VII-201 pp., 1930.
61. Kremer, Rev. Michael Nicholas, A.B., S.T.B., J.C.D., Church Support in the United States, VI-136 pp., 1930.
62. Angulo, Rev. Luis, C.M., J.C.D., Legislation de la Iglesia sobre la intencion en la application de la Santa Misa, VII-104 pp., 1931.
63. Frey, Rev. Wolfgang Norbert, O.S.B., A.B., J.C.D., The Act of Religious Profession, VIII-174 pp., 1931.
64. Roberts, Rev. James Brendan, A.B., J.C.D., The Banns of Marriage, XIV-140 pp., 1931.
65. Ryder, Rev. Raymond Aloysius, A.B., J.C.D., Simony, IX-151 pp., 1931.

66. Campagna, Rev. Angelo, PhD., J.U.D., Il Vicario Generale del Vescovo, VII-205 pp., 1931.
67. Cox, Rev. Joseph Godfrey, A.B., J.C.D., The Administration of Seminaries, VI-124 pp., 1931.
68. Gregory, Rev. Donald J., J.U.D., The Pauline Privilege, XV-165 pp., 1931.
69. Donohue, Rev. John F., J.C.D., The Impediment of Crime, VII-110 pp., 1931.
70. Dooley, Rev. Eugene A., O.M.I., J.C.D., Church Law on Sacred Relics, IX-143 pp., 1931.
71. Orth, Rev. Clement Raymond, O.M.C., J.C.D., The Approbation of Religious Institutes, 171 pp., 1931.
72. Pernicone, Rev. Joseph M., A.B., J.C.D., The Ecclesiastical Prohibition of Books, XII-267 pp., 1932.
73. Clinton, Rev. Connell, A.B., J.C.D., The Paschal Precept, IX-108 pp., 1932.
74. Donnelly, Rev. Francis B., A.M., S.T.L., J.C.D., The Diocesan Synod, VIII-125 pp., 1932.
75. Torrente, Rev. Camilo, C.M.F., J.C.D., Las Processiones Sagradas, V-145 pp., 1932.
76. Murphy, Rev. Edwin J., C.PP.S., J.C.D., Suspension Ex Informata Conscientia, XI-122 pp., 1932.
77. MacKenzie, Rev. Eric F., A.M., S.T.L., J.C.D., The Delicit of Heresy in Its Commission, Penalization, Absolution, VII-124 pp., 1932.
78. Lyons, Rev. Avitus E., S.T.B., J.C.D., The Collegiate Tribunal of First Instance, XI-147 pp., 1932.
79. Connolly, Rev. Thomas A., J.C.D., Appeals, XI-195 pp., 1932.
80. Sangmeister, Rev. Joseph V., A.B., J.C.D., Force and Fear as Precluding Matrimonial Consent, V-211 pp., 1932.
81. Jaeger, Rev. Leo A., A.B., J.C.D., The Administration of Vacant and Quasi-Vacant Episcopal Sees in the United States, IX-229 pp., 1932.
82. Rimlinger, Rev. Herbert T., J.C.D., Error Invalidating Matrimonial Consent, VII-79 pp., 1932.
83. Barrett, Rev. John D. M., S.S., J.C.D., A Comparative Study of the Third Plenary Council of Baltimore and the Code, IX-221 pp., 1932.
84. Carberry, Rev. John J., Ph.D., S.T.D., J.C.D., The Juridical Form of Marriage, X-177 pp., 1934.
85. Dolan, Rev. John L., A.B., J.C.D., The Defensor Vinculi, XII-157 pp., 1934.
86. Hannan, Rev. Jerome D., A.M., S.T.D., LL.B., J.C.D., The Canon Law of Wills, IX-517 pp., 1934.
87. Lemieux, Rev. Delise A., A.M., J.C.D., The Sentence in Ecclesiastical Procedure, IX-131 pp., 1934.
88. O'Rourke, Rev. James J., A.B., J.C.D., Parish Registers, VII-109 pp., 1934.

89. TIMLIN, REV. BARTHOLOMEW, O.F.M., A.M., J.C.D., Conditional Matrimonial Consent, X-381 pp., 1934.

90. WAHL, REV. FRANCIS X., A.B., J.C.D., The Matrimonial Impediments of Consanguinity and Affinity, VI-125 pp., 1934.

91. WHITE, REV. ROBERT J., A.B., LL.B., S.T.B., J.C.D., Canonical Ante-Nuptial Promises and the Civil Law, VI-152 pp., 1934.

92. HERRERA, REV. ANTONIO PARRA, O.C.D., J.C.D., Legislacion Ecclesiastica sobra el Ayuno y la Abstinencia, XI-191 pp., 1935.

93. KENNEDY, REV. EDWIN J., J.C.D., The Special Matrimonial Process in Cases of Evident Nullity, X-165 pp., 1935.

94. MANNING, REV. JOHN J., A.B., J.C.D., Presumption of Law in Matrimonial Procedure, XI-111 pp., 1935.

95. MOEDER, REV. JOHN M., J.C.D., The Proper Bishop for Ordination and Dimissorial Letters, VII-135 pp., 1935.

96. O'MARA, REV. WILLIAM A., A.B., J.C.D., Canonical Causes for Matrimonial Dispensations, IX-155 pp., 1935.

97. REILLY, REV. PETER, J.C.D., Residence of Pastors, IX-81 pp., 1935.

98. SMITH, REV. MARINER T., O.P., S.T.Lr., J.C.D., The Penal Law for Religious, VII-169 pp., 1935.

99. WHALEN, REV. DONALD W., A.M., J.C.D., The Value of Testimonial Evidence in Matrimonial Procedure, XIII-297 pp., 1935.

100. CLEARY, REV. JOSEPH F., J.C.D., Canonical Limitations on the Alienation of Church Property, VIII-141 pp., 1936.

101. GLYNN, REV. JOHN C., J.C.D., The Promoter of Justice, XX-337 pp., 1936.

102. BRENNAN, REV. JAMES H., S.S., M.A., S.T.B., J.C.D., The Simple Convalidation of Marriage, VI-135 pp., 1937.

103 BRUNINI, REV. JOSEPH BERNARD, J.C.D., The Clerical Obligations of Canons 139 and 142, X-121 pp., 1937.

104. CONNOR, REV. MAURICE, A.B., J.C.D., The Administrative Removal of Pastors, VIII-159 pp., 1937.

105. GUILFOYLE, REV. MERLIN JOSEPH, J.C.D., Custom, XI-144 pp., 1937.

106. HUGHES, REV. JAMES AUSTIN, A.B., A.M., J.C.D., Witnesses in Criminal Trials of Clerics, IX-140 pp., 1937.

107. JANSEN, REV. RAYMOND J., A.B., S.T.L., J.C.D., Canonical Provisions for Catechetical Instruction, VII-153 pp., 1937.

108. KEALY, REV. JOHN JAMES, A.B., J.C.D., The Introductory Libellus in Church Court Procedure, XI-121 pp., 1937.

109. MCMANUS, REV. JAMES EDWARD, C.SS.R., J.C.D., The Administration of Temporal Goods in Religious Institutes, XVI-196 pp., 1937.

110. MORIARTY, REV. EUGENE JAMES, J.C.D., Oaths in Ecclesiastical Courts, X-115 pp., 1937.

111. RAINER, REV. ELIGIUS GEORGE, C.SS.R., J.C.D., Suspension of Clerics, XVII-249 pp., 1937.

112. Reilly, Rev. Thomas F., C.SS.R., J.C.D., Visitation of Religious, VI-195 pp., 1938.
113. Moriarity, Rev. Francis E., C.SS.R., J.C.D., The Extraordinary Absolution from Censures, XV-334 pp., 1938.
114. Connolly, Rev. Nicholas P., J.C.D., The Canonical Erection of Parishes, X-132 pp., 1938.
115. Donovan, Rev. James Joseph, J.C.D., The Pastor's Obligation in Prenuptial Investigation, XII-322 pp., 1938.
116. Harrigan, Rev. Robert J., M.A., S.T.B., J.C.D., The Radical Sanation of Invalid Marriages, VIII-208 pp., 1938.
117. Boffa, Rev. Conrad Humbert, J.C.D., Canonical Provisions for Catholic Schools, VII-211 pp., 1939.
118. Parsons, Rev. Anscar John, O.M.Cap., J.C.D., Canonical Elections, XII-236 pp., 1939.
119. Reilly, Rev. Edward Michael, A.B., J.C.D., The General Norms of Dispensation, XII-156 pp., 1939.
120. Ryan, Rev. Gerald Aloysius, A.B., J.C.D., Principles of Episcopal Jurisdiction, XII-172 pp., 1939.
121. Burton, Rev. Francis James, C.S.C., A.B., J.C.L., A Commentary on Canon 1125.
122. Miaskiewicz, Rev. Francis Sigismund, J.C.L., Supplied Jurisdiction According to Canon 209.
123. Rice, Rev. Patrick William, A.B., J.C.L., Proof of Death in Pre-Nuptial Investigation.

www.ingramcontent.com/pod-product-compliance
Lightning Source LLC
LaVergne TN
LVHW050243080826
844660LV00012B/589

* 9 7 8 0 8 1 3 2 2 3 1 0 0 *